The
TurnAround
ToolKit

The *TurnAround* ToolKit

Managing Rapid,
Sustainable School
Improvement

Lynn Winters ★ Joan Herman

Foreword by Carl A. Cohn

CORWIN
A SAGE Company

For information:

Corwin
A SAGE Company
2455 Teller Road
Thousand Oaks, California 91320
(800) 233-9936
Fax: (800) 417-2466
www.corwin.com

SAGE Ltd.
1 Oliver's Yard
55 City Road
London EC1Y 1SP
United Kingdom

SAGE India Pvt. Ltd.
B 1/I 1 Mohan Cooperative
    Industrial Area
Mathura Road, New Delhi 110 044
India

SAGE Asia-Pacific Pte. Ltd.
33 Pekin Street #02-01
Far East Square
Singapore 048763

Printed in the United States of America

Library of Congress Cataloging-in-Publication Data

Winters, Lynn.
The turnaround toolkit: managing rapid, sustainable school improvement/Lynn Winters and Joan Herman; foreword by Carl A. Cohn.
        p. cm.
Includes bibliographical references and index.
ISBN 978-1-4129-7501-8 (pbk.)

    1. School improvement programs. 2. School support teams. 3. Educational leadership. I. Herman, Joan L. II. Title.

LB2822.8.W56 2011
371.2'07—dc22   2010037395

This book is printed on acid-free paper.

10   11   12   13   14   10   9   8   7   6   5   4   3   2   1

Acquisitions Editor:	Debra Stollenwerk
Associate Editor:	Desirée Bartlett
Editorial Assistant:	Kimberly Greenberg
Permissions Editor:	Adele Hutchinson
Production Editor:	Jane Haenel
Copy Editor:	Cate Huisman
Typesetter:	C&M Digitals (P) Ltd.
Proofreader:	Cheryl Rivard
Cover Designer:	Rose Storey

Contents

Tools supporting the action steps in Chapters 1–8 can be found
on the companion website for *The TurnAround ToolKit* at
http://www.corwin.com/turnaroundtoolkit.

Foreword

In a recent *Washington Post* opinion piece, John Goodlad, a prominent education reformer who was dean of the Graduate School of Education at UCLA when Joan Herman, Lynn Winters, and I were promising doctoral students there in the 1970s, said, "Significant change in most organizations, corporations included, comes from inside."

In this practical insider's guide to turning around schools and districts, Herman and Winters—two assessment and evaluation scholars with deep roots in practice—have demystified much of what it takes to get schools and districts to initiate continuous improvement, employing a language and format that is, first and foremost, user friendly. Unlike so many of today's reformers, they fully understand the importance of Dean Goodlad's admonition about the starting point for real change—a healthy appreciation for fostering positive relations inside an organization and building on them.

In today's school improvement marketplace, real help for real people in schools is often hard to come by. But these two scholar-practitioners provide it, having honed their skills not only at UCLA's National Center for Research on Evaluation, Standards, & Student Testing (CRESST) but also in struggling schools and districts populated by teachers, principals, and district leaders who are trying mightily to rescue yet another generation of youngsters.

Back in 1994, as superintendent of the Long Beach (California) Unified School District, I was one such district leader who was trying to move a district toward continuous improvement with the help of the Program for Student Achievement at the Edna McConnell Clark Foundation of New York. Ours was a district and community that had been battered by the departure of the U.S. Navy, the collapse of McDonnell-Douglas, a decline in tourism, horrific gang violence, and declining student test scores. Hayes Mizell, the foundation's remarkable program officer and critical friend to our district, suggested that I might need to hire a genuine expert in assessment and evaluation if I really wanted to help our teachers enable our students to make coherent progress toward meeting state standards.

While Lynn Winters was far and away the best candidate in the applicant pool for the research position we created, I had no real idea at the time of what I was getting or of how Winters's work and that of her colleagues at CRESST, like Joan Herman and Eva Baker, would permanently move our school system forward on the path to continuous improvement—a path recognized in a forthcoming report from McKinsey on improving school systems worldwide.[1] What did she do that was so important, and what lessons did we learn that can be shared with struggling reformers in schools and districts across the country? They include working with funders as critical friends, building collaborative teams, recognizing the importance of leadership and communication in raising student achievement, adapting processes to the local context, and building on the inherent strengths of classroom teachers as evaluators. These are the big takeaways from this helpful toolkit to guide turnaround efforts for teachers, principals, district leaders, and all those who care about students and their betterment in an increasingly challenged world.

Carl A. Cohn

Clinical Professor of Urban School Leadership
Claremont Graduate University
Former Superintendent of Long Beach Schools
Long Beach, California

Publisher's Acknowledgments

Corwin would like to thank the following individuals for their editorial insight and guidance:

Dr. Kimberley Chandler
Curriculum Director
Center for Gifted Education
The College of William and Mary
Williamsburg, VA

Ginnie Drouin
Administrator
Regional School Unit #57
Alfred, ME

Dr. Cathy Galland
Director
Southern Regional Professional Development Center
Webb City, MO

Jim Lentz
Superintendent
Unified School District 402
Augusta Public Schools
Augusta, KS

Pamela H. Scott
Assistant Professor/Graduate Program Coordinator School Leadership
East Tennessee State University
Johnson City, TN

Leslie Standerfer
Principal
Estrella Foothills High School
Goodyear, AZ

Dana Salles Trevethan
Principal
Turlock High School
Turlock, CA

Shelley Joan Weiss
Educational Administration
Waunakee Community Middle School
Waunakee, WI

About the Authors

Lynn Winters was the assistant superintendent for research at Long Beach Unified School District. Her work there implementing systems for data-guided decision making was recognized by President Bush and won the 2004 Broad Prize for Urban Education. She currently consults for Urban School Imagineers, an education consulting group in Long Beach, California, training urban school data teams like those described in this book and evaluating an urban school leadership training program. Her prior positions include lecturer in social research methods at the UCLA Graduate School of Education, high school teacher (history, Spanish, and special education), county education office assessment consultant, director of research for Palos Verdes Unified School District, and project director for three grants at the UCLA National Center for Research on Evaluation, Standards, & Student Testing (CRESST). She has coauthored two books with Joan Herman of CRESST, *A Practical Guide to Alternative Assessment* (Association for Supervision and Curriculum Development, 1992) and *Tracking Your School's Success: A Guide to Sensible School-Based Evaluation* (Corwin, 1992) and is a reviewer for *Practical Assessment, Research &Evaluation; Educational Evaluation and Policy Analysis;* and *Educational Assessment.* In addition, she has over a dozen published journal articles and regularly presents at the American Educational Research Association's annual meeting.

Joan Herman is director of the National Center for Research on Evaluation, Standards, & Student Testing (CRESST) at UCLA. Her research has explored the effects of accountability and assessment on schools and teachers and the design of assessment systems to support school planning and instructional improvement. Her recent work has focused on the quality and consequences of teachers' formative assessment practices. She also has wide experience as an evaluator of school reform efforts. Dr. Herman is noted for bridging research and practice, particularly in applications serving English language learners and at-risk students. Among her books are *Tracking Your School's Success: A Guide to Sensible School-Based Evaluation* (Corwin, 1992) and *A Practical Guide to Alternative Assessment* (Association for Supervision and Curriculum

Development, 1992), both of which have been popular resources for schools across the country. A former teacher and school board member, Dr. Herman is an elected fellow of the American Educational Research Association, has published extensively in research journals, and has frequently advised prominent national and state research and development initiatives, including repeated service to the National Academy of Education. She is past president of the California Educational Research Association, and she has held a variety of leadership positions in the American Educational Research Association, the National Organization of Research Centers, and the Knowledge Alliance. She chairs the board of the Para Los Niños Charter School in Los Angeles and is current editor of the research journal *Educational Assessment*.

Introduction

The best place to turn around is a dead end street.

—Naomi Judd

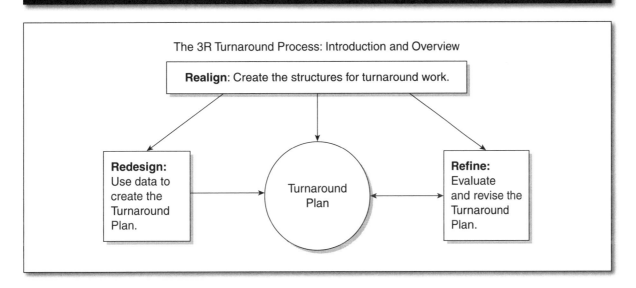

The 3R Turnaround Process: Introduction and Overview

Realign: Create the structures for turnaround work.

Redesign:
Use data to create the Turnaround Plan.

Turnaround Plan

Refine:
Evaluate and revise the Turnaround Plan.

POCKET SUMMARY

Introductory Information	Major Ideas
A definition of turnaround work	• Our shared work • Why use the term *turnaround* to characterize the continuous improvement of teaching and learning?
The 3R turnaround process	• Graphic organizer for the process and the book • How it incorporates the techniques of formative evaluation • How it builds upon your current school decision-making process • How it maps onto other continuous improvement models
How to use this book	• Book structure • Chapter structure • Special features

OUR SHARED WORK

If you are reading this book, we're pretty sure you are not on a warm beach in an upbeat mood thinking only about how to while away your time. Nope! We think you are faced with the same challenges we face daily. How can we do a better job with the staff, budget, and time available? How can we move all students in our school from struggling to stellar? How can we meet our accountability targets and avoid the dreadful sanctions associated with being labeled a "failing school"? How can we compete with other schools in the district, charters, and private schools?

You might be a principal, a consultant hired to assist a particular school or district, a lead teacher, an aspiring administrator, a central office administrator, a supervisor of principals, or a member of a state or county education agency. You might be an educational foundation officer seeking to find an efficient way to monitor your agency's investments in school change. Regardless of your title or assigned role, your job is both urgent and focused: You must

- halt downward achievement trends or enhance achievement at your school,
- meet both short- and long-term accountability or strategic plan targets, and
- institutionalize processes and systems to ensure your school's success when you are no longer there.

We, along with you, are committed to making schools great. For us, and we suspect for you as well, a great school is synonymous with tangible student achievement outcomes:

- Enabling all students to reach their potential
- Elimination of the achievement gap
- Preparation of more students for college
- Elimination of the need for remediation when students leave school
- Acceleration of the acquisition of English for English learners
- Preparation of special education students to meet the same standards as all students
- Elimination of high school dropouts
- Preparation of all students for college or the world of work

We, and you, recognize that making achievement gains and maintaining a reputation for excellence depend upon creating safe, family-friendly, community-connected schools.

We, and we suspect you too, believe in using a data-driven continuous improvement (CI) process, characterized by collaboration and rigorous reflection. We have been committed to school-level CI for a very long time. We wrote a book more than 18 years ago to help school principals use formative evaluation as a tool for managing school reform. The book was *Tracking Your School's Success* (Corwin, 1992), and at that time, if you can believe it, we dedicated a good portion of the book to convincing principals why a CI process would pay off for their schools. How times have changed! School leaders no longer need to be sold on the need to set improvement goals, collect data to measure progress, and revise programs based on their data. Nearly every school leader today is familiar with one or more approaches to CI. You might be currently using a state-created model such as those of Texas, Nebraska, Colorado, or Louisiana; a business model such as the Baldrige model, Total Quality Management, or Six Sigma; or a more generalized approach that might be labeled "data-driven decision making," "action research," or "strategic planning." No, convincing teachers and principals that CI should be part of their practice isn't necessary in the 21st century.

What we do need today is support for implementing or fine-tuning these CI systems so that they produce rapid results and are sustainable in the face of budget cuts, changing staff, and revised strategic goals. Since formative evaluation is the generic inquiry process underlying all CI models, we think it's time to revisit the original framework to help you fine-tune your school's current CI systems. And we would like to share some of the strategies, tools, and insights we have acquired in our own formative evaluation work to save you time and scaffold your school's improvement processes.

WHY INTRODUCE THE CONCEPT OF *TURNAROUND* TO CHARACTERIZE THE CONTINUOUS IMPROVEMENT OF TEACHING AND LEARNING?

The term *turnaround* comes from the field of business, where it has been used to describe the work of halting a downward trend in a firm's performance and creating a dramatic improvement in a short period of time. An essential part of the definition of turnaround in education is "a dramatic change that produces significant achievement gains in a short period (within two years) followed by a longer period of sustained improvement."[1]

We think the rapid results component of turnaround work is essential to CI. And we're not alone in our beliefs. Mike Schmoker argues convincingly that rapid results are in fact the foundation of school improvement.[2] Schmoker calls rapid results a breakthrough strategy, a strategy focused on obtaining goal-oriented, measurable results in one year. In his book, *Results* (ASCD, 1999), Schmoker demonstrates how quick wins create momentum, provide feedback for revising the tactical path to strategic goals, promote optimism, and focus staff on outcomes rather than activities.

Turnaround work as traditionally formulated focuses on reforming low-performing schools. It requires you to use strategies that will yield results quickly, on a much shorter timeline than schools are used to following. But why restrict these strategies to "failing" schools? We need to recognize that all schools face the same urgency to improve student achievement. The current educational context is one of competition for students. Schools compete with charter organizations, private schools, and even school choice options within their own districts. Schools that the public perceives as being successful attract students and remain open. Schools that the press or local real estate agents condemn as "ineffectual" struggle to attract students or suffer from poor community relations. Budget shortfalls in education and tight finances may make it essential for schools to replace successful but costly programs with lower cost options—but without sacrificing the current student cohort. The urgency to achieve significant academic results is the same when a successful program is cut as it is when students are uniformly unsuccessful and an effective program must be found. And last, federal Title I requirements for attaining accountability goals drive schools to examine their programs and to make changes on a short timeline that will quickly increase learning— at least as judged by test performance.

Because *turnaround* is used to express urgency and systemic change, we feel a turnaround attitude is central to any of the following tasks:

- Reducing the achievement gap among differently performing groups
- Providing unique and effective programs to enhance the achievement of the highest-performing students
- Providing interventions and a monitoring system to reduce the number of students referred to special education
- Enhancing the school's reputation in the community and with real estate agents
- Avoiding state and federal sanctions under their particular accountability requirements
- Creating distributed instructional leadership and enhancing teacher expertise

We also think that the research on turning around low-performing schools (i.e., turnaround work) applies to *all* schools. The tools in this *Turnaround Toolkit* can be used to manage any systemic change at the school level aimed at rapid improvements in student achievement *regardless of whether the school is "failing," "slowly improving," or clearly successful.* In Table I.1, we identify possible turnaround areas for struggling schools (on the brink of state takeover), "good enough" schools (parents are happy but students could do much better), and outstanding schools (recognized distinguished schools). Struggling schools do need to make a U-turn in the achievement trajectories of nearly all students. Good enough schools need to create areas of excellence and raise expectations and performance for all students. While the needs of outstanding schools may not seem as glaring as the needs of schools on the brink of state takeover, there are individual students and groups of students in as much need of a trajectory change as those in obviously low-achieving schools. Such schools are often accused of overlooking and underserving the "middle majority." These are students for whom college (or a prestigious college) is not a goal, or who have no particular academic deficits but who also have no particular areas of academic, social, athletic, or artistic strength. Parents of the middle majority often feel that their students get mediocre teaching, are unknown and overlooked, and are not pushed out of their comfort zones. Clearly, *turnaround*, with its emphasis on rapid change and sharp focus on students' achievement, is a concept that should not be limited to obviously struggling schools.

Table I.1 Potential Turnaround Areas for Different Types of Schools

Possible School Improvement Initiative Area	Struggling Schools	Good Enough Schools	Outstanding Schools
Student Achievement	Raise achievement levels of all students on accountability indicators	Monitor and raise achievement of any low-performing subgroups	Monitor and raise achievement of low-performing individuals whose needs differ from those of the majority of students
Curriculum and Instruction	Ensure curriculum is implemented as intended and learning time is maximized	Ensure curriculum provides enrichment and acceleration for students meeting standards	Ensure curriculum challenges high-performing students and is rigorous for students meeting grade-level standards
Parent and Community	Implement programs for community and parent involvement to support students outside of school	Implement programs for community and parent involvement to raise expectations for students	Implement programs for community and parent involvement to meet needs of students struggling to keep up with the reputation of the school or whose interests and talents aren't served by traditional academic programs
Safety	Ensure school is safe and secure, including emotionally, in classrooms, on the campus, and adjacent to campus	Ensure school is safe and secure, including emotionally, in classrooms, on the campus, and adjacent to campus	Ensure school is safe and secure, including emotionally, in classrooms, on the campus, and adjacent to campus, especially for students not meeting high academic standards or without academic interests
Staff Development	Improve teachers' ability to accelerate learning of students performing below grade level, model high expectations, and deliver a rigorous program for all students	Improve teachers' ability to create high expectations and deliver a rigorous program	Improve teachers' ability to differentiate instruction, enrich and expand the curriculum, and ensure student engagement
Reputation and Accomplishments	Retain or recapture neighborhood students; become recognized as a school that beats the odds	Retain or recapture students currently attending private or charter schools; become recognized for extending rigorous or college prep coursework to "middle majority" students; develop a recognized specialty program (arts, vocational, International Baccalaureate, etc.)	Become the preferred school of parents inclined to send students to private schools; increase the percentage of students attending college; develop a regional or national reputation for outstanding programs through competitions, school recognition programs, and faculty involvement in national staff development efforts

THE 3 R's OF TURNAROUND WORK: REALIGN, REDESIGN, REFINE

The term *turnaround* is shorthand for a rapid program improvement that enables students to realize significant academic gains. Embedded in this work are three major tasks:

> **REALIGN** your systems of leadership, team collaboration, outside support from experts, and central office or professional networks so that all resources are focused on implementing turnaround goals.

> **REDESIGN** your curriculum, instruction, and school context (climate, student behavior, and parent/community involvement) to address priority needs based on available accountability, assessment, and other available data, and create a plan to achieve your turnaround goals.

> **REFINE** and revise your program based on plan implementation and outcome data.

GRAPHIC ORGANIZERS FOR THE 3 R's OF TURNAROUND WORK

Language is a linear medium. Recursive processes—especially those conducted simultaneously with other activities in a school, such as program development and implementation, staff development, curriculum development, and deployment of specialized academic interventions to targeted groups of students—can be difficult to grasp when described in a linear fashion. Figure I.1 presents a graphic organizer to capture the major components of the 3R turnaround process. We use the graphic to help you locate yourself both in this book and in the process. The graphic organizer will guide you through the description of the 3R turnaround process, which is the subject of the first part of this book. We also use graphics to link the work of the process to tools that are available at the book's companion website in the online Toolkit. Whenever we provide a tool to support your turnaround efforts, you will find a graphic in the text to enable you to place that tool in context.

Below is the legend for the symbols used in the graphic organizers for Part I, The 3 R's of Turnaround Work.

- The large boxes are used to identify the three sections in Part I that correspond to the three sections of the turnaround process: Realign, Redesign, Refine.
- The smaller boxes within each large box correspond to individual chapters.
- The oval shapes within each large box have different meanings, each corresponding to the work core of the section. In the Realign box, the oval represents the prep work teachers and other school staff must do to become familiar with each other, with school programs, and with assessment data and data systems to get ready for turnaround. In the Redesign box, the oval represents the data analysis in which school teams will engage to create their Turnaround Plan. In the Refine box, the oval represents the turnaround work that is systematically monitored and refined through the use of formative evaluation strategies.

Figure I.1 Graphic Organizer for the Turnaround Toolkit

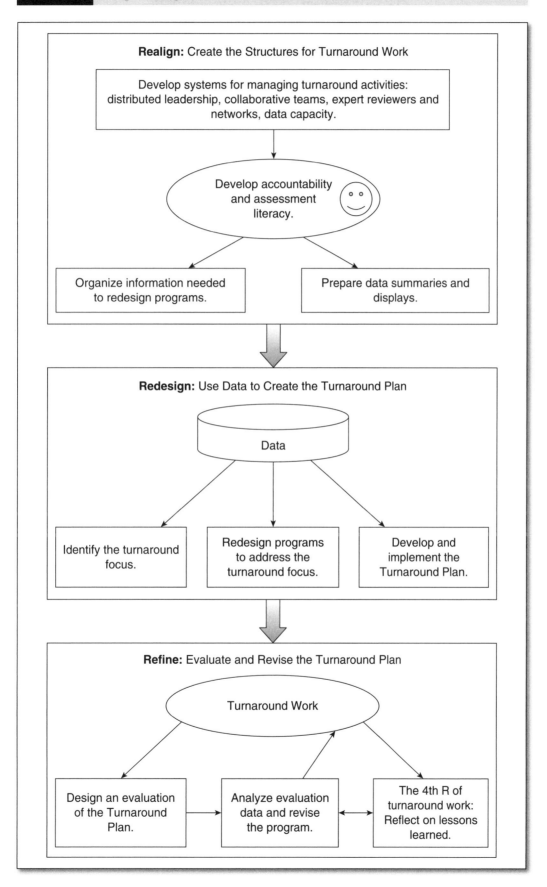

- The thin arrows indicate connections among turnaround tasks and suggest the dynamism and recursiveness of the process.
- The fat arrows show the way from one section to the next.

Each section begins with a reproduction of the entire graphic organizer, in which the large box relevant to that section is highlighted. Within the sections, each chapter begins with a reproduction of the section-relevant large box, and the small chapter box is highlighted.

We hope that you find the graphic organizer useful for both orientation and recapitulation.

THE 3R TURNAROUND PROCESS INCORPORATES THE TECHNIQUES OF FORMATIVE EVALUATION

A Realign-Redesign-Refine process captures the three purposes of data-driven decision making:

1. To use data to identify problems in teaching and learning

2. To use data to monitor student progress toward school goals and/or to monitor adequacy of program implementation

3. To use data to judge the effectiveness of changes in curriculum, instruction, and school context interventions in promoting student achievement or other important student outcomes

The process of gathering data for the purpose of program improvement is called *formative evaluation*. The formative evaluation process constitutes the Redesign-Refine stage of the turnaround cycle. Formative evaluation is something your staff already engages in, though perhaps not consciously. However, whenever educators collect data for the purpose of improving some aspect of curriculum, instruction, or school context for the purpose of improving student outcomes, they are engaging in formative evaluation.

Currently, school staff often use informal data-gathering strategies to make decisions about the adequacy of teaching and learning. A few of the examples cited below illustrate how the techniques of data-driven decision making and the dispositions of turnaround work may already exist at your school:

- Principals determine staffing and course assignments based on enrollment projections, inquiries from parents new to the neighborhood, and informal reports from teachers.
- Departments and administrators plan staff development sessions after determining needs through classroom observations, listening to teacher concerns at meetings or in the lounge, reading professional literature, and attending conferences.
- All staff review accountability assessment data to determine whether the school is meeting state and federal goals and whether particular subgroups of students are falling behind or need more challenging work.

- High school counselors and administrators monitor dropouts, graduates, college acceptance, and freshman GPAs to judge the success of their programs.
- School staff identifies similar schools and compare test results to determine if they are doing as well as they could with "similar" students.

Teachers are especially adept evaluators. They routinely and often informally gather data about students' attitudes and preferences, written and oral capabilities, and performance on curriculum-related quizzes and tests to make a range of instructional decisions:

- Which lessons are most appropriate for which groups of students?
- Which skills need reteaching, to whom, and how should the skills be presented the second time?
- How should students be grouped for instruction? How often should groups change?
- Why is a particular student struggling? What would help? How can I challenge the high flyer? What will interest the disengaged student?
- How are my students doing compared with those in similar classes? Compared with last year's group? Compared to the state standards and proficiency requirements?
- How can I do a better job? Why did today's lesson bomb? What kinds of feedback will help students improve their writing? What kinds of explanations and practice will make key concepts clearer to students?

It's a simple transition to move from classroom-level to school-level evaluation. Substitute the word *program* for *classroom* and *school* for *students*, and you will have identified the central questions in formative evaluation.

THE 3R TURNAROUND PROCESS INCORPORATES CONTINUOUS IMPROVEMENT PROCESSES YOU MAY ALREADY USE

You may have incorporated a continuous improvement (CI) process at your site already. Several current models have been introduced as part of the school improvement movement; these approaches have the same purpose as turnaround work and go through most of the same steps. There are two differences between these commonly applied CI models and the turnaround approach we advocate in this book. Table I.2 compares the steps in the 3R turnaround process with those in three other popular CI models. The Deming-Shewhart-Baldrige plan-do-study-act (PDSA) model has been the most widely adopted CI model across the country. Entire states, including Florida and Texas, have incorporated the PDSA process into their statewide school improvement plans.

Table I.2	How the 3R Turnaround Process Compares With Popular Continuous Improvement Models

The 3R Turnaround Process	Pivot Learning Cycle of Inquiry (COI)	Deming-Shewhart-Baldrige PDSA	Annenberg Self Study Cycle
Realign personnel and resources to distribute responsibility for turnaround work.			
Redesign: Use accountability and assessment data to identify improvement needs.	Identify problems.		1. Identify desired student outcomes.
Redesign: Use program data to redesign programs. Create a program description; identify the theory of action; identify the guiding questions.	Ask questions. Design a plan. Set goals.	PLAN: Plan ahead for change. Analyze and predict the results.	2. Develop essential questions.
Redesign: Develop and implement the Turnaround Plan.	Take action.	DO: Execute the plan, taking small steps in controlled circumstances.	5. Choose and implement actions.
Refine (formative evaluation): Collect data to identify what is needed (tools) to improve program outcomes. Identify evidence needed to determine how well the program is producing desired outcomes. Use multiple data sources as evidence. Set standards for determining program effectiveness.		STUDY: Check; study the results.	3. Identify, collect, and organize relevant data.
Refine: Analyze data to determine program strengths and weaknesses. (Evaluate impact according to specific criteria.)	Analyze outcomes.		4. Analyze data.
Refine and Redesign: Revise program to optimize strengths and eliminate weaknesses.	Repeat.	ACT: Take action to standardize or improve the process.	6. Evaluate impact on practice and outcomes.

As described earlier in this chapter, the CI or redesign-refine activities of the 3R turnaround process are really formative evaluation, a research-based approach to program development and improvement. The Redesign and Refine stages are simply an applied research process and do not belong to any company, group, or other organization. You will notice that when comparing the four CI strategies, the 3R turnaround process built on formative evaluation is more clearly specified and has clearer guidelines about what is to be done at each stage of the process. The major difference between the 3R process and formative evaluation is that, in the latter, evaluators focus on the redesign-refine activities but do not engage in setting up schoolwide systems for doing improvement work. Table I.3 shows how the steps commonly employed in formative evaluation are incorporated into the 3R Process.

Table I.3   Steps in Formative Evaluation

3R Process	Formative Evaluation Process
Realign: Create systems and develop skills for managing and carrying out turnaround work; improve staff understanding of accountability, assessment, teaching, learning, and curriculum if needed.	Realignment is not part of formative evaluation.
Redesign: Use data to identify areas needing improvement; create a Turnaround Plan for improvement.	Needs assessment is comparable to the Redesign stage.
Refine: Implement and evaluate the Turnaround Plan. Program development and formative evaluation occur simultaneously as part of a continuous improvement feedback loop operating in real time.	Program development is done in concert with evaluation but considered a distinct activity.
Evaluation of the Turnaround Plan includes the steps in formative evaluation.	Identify a theory of action or a logic model linking actions to outcomes. Create formative evaluation questions. Identify measures to collect data. Manage development or purchase of an evaluation instrument; administer evaluation; collect, store, and organize data. Summarize and analyze data.
Refine and revise the plan.	Interpret formative data to identify and implement needed revisions.
Communicate findings and planned revisions to stakeholders.	Communicate findings and planned revisions to stakeholders.

The other CI models incorporate many of the requirements of formative evaluation and may seem simpler than the 3R turnaround process. But in wide communication, the models may give short shrift to essential aspects of school reform. PDSA (plan-do-study-act, the Deming CI model), for example, was designed to help factory workers improve the production of widgets, much as formative evaluation initially was developed to improve programmed instruction. But the simplicity of the "targets" (improved production of widgets, improved performance on behavioral objectives) meant the model didn't need to specify program components, theories of action, multiple measures of implementation and outcomes, or the multiple functions of data analysis and discussion in evaluating and improving the effectiveness of educational programs.

If you are currently using one of these popular CI models, adopting the more elaborate but completely compatible formative evaluation strategies discussed in this book will be relatively simple (though it will require more time and thought). If you learn how to conduct formative evaluation, you will bring a more nuanced understanding of what the steps in each of the other models really require and will be able to adopt a more rigorous approach to your school's CI process.

HOW TO USE THIS BOOK

Book Structure

Now that you have a better understanding of the 3R turnaround process to address your school's most pressing issues, we are ready to begin this urgent work. We have divided the book into two parts. Part I is a how-to guide to turnaround work at the school level, focusing on improving student achievement. Part II presents Leader's Guides for each chapter that highlight the management tasks, decisions, and resources needed for doing the turnaround activities of that chapter.

The how-to of turnaround work, Part I, is organized into three sections, each corresponding to one of the three R's: Realign, Redesign, and Refine. Section I, Realign, contains three chapters focused on preparing for turnaround work. Section II, Redesign, includes three chapters describing how to identify the turnaround focus and then create and implement the Turnaround Plan. Finally, Section III focuses on Refine, which is the engine of turnaround work; it contains two chapters dealing with how to use embedded implementation and monitoring data to make both midyear corrections and yearly program revisions to your turnaround work. The final chapter in Part I is a call to reflect annually on your efforts, identifying lessons learned and looming challenges. Table I.4 summarizes the contents of Part I.

Part II contains the Leader's Guides for each of the action steps described in Chapters 1–8. The guides include key concepts from the chapter, a list of management decisions that must be made with each step, a Pocket Summary of the chapter (reproduced from the chapter introduction), a list of key challenges encountered in each step, and some useful

| Table I.4 | Book Structure for Part I: The 3 R's of Turnaround Work | |

Section	Major Content	Products
Section I. Realign—Create the Structures for Turnaround Work • Chapter 1. Develop Systems for Managing Turnaround Activities: Distributed Leadership, Collaborative Teams, Expert Reviewers and Networks, Data Capacity • Chapter 2. Organize Information Needed to Redesign Programs • Chapter 3. Prepare Data Summaries and Displays	This section describes the school-level systems as well as professional learning that should occur to ready your school for turnaround work.	• New organizational structures • New staff responsibilities • Expanded professional networks • Tables and graphs of school-level accountability data • Tables and graphs for school-level, district-level, or other common assessments • Tables and graphs of other useful data: parent, student, and teacher surveys; archival data (grades, attendance, discipline); demographic data
Section II. Redesign—Use Data to Create the Turnaround Plan • Chapter 4. Identify the Turnaround Focus • Chapter 5. Redesign Programs to Address the Turnaround Focus • Chapter 6. Develop and Implement the Turnaround Plan	This section describes how to use accountability and assessment data to identify student achievement goals and areas where curriculum and instruction need improvement. This includes developing a graphic organizer to present your cause-and-effect hypothesis about what should change and why—your theory of action—and developing data-driven turnaround activities. The result of this section is your Turnaround Plan.	• Graphic organizer to capture the logic or theory behind program changes • Focused learning goals • Multiple academic assessments • Revised curriculum • Revised instructional strategies • New procedures for staff development • Measures of student opportunity to learn, program quality, and parent involvement • New policies and practices to ensure school climate; student behavior and parent involvement to support turnaround goals

(Continued)

Table I.4 (Continued)

Section	Major Content	Products
Section III. Refine— Evaluate and Revise the Turnaround Plan • Chapter 7. Design an Evaluation of the Turnaround Plan • Chapter 8. Analyze Evaluation Data and Revise the Program • Chapter 9. The 4th R of Turnaround Work: Reflect on Lessons Learned	This section focuses on the formative evaluation of the Turnaround Plan, both implementation and outcomes. The emphasis is on identifying measures that will provide data to inform evaluation questions, analyzing data, and using the data to revise the plan.	• A list of aspects of your Turnaround Plan that need monitoring, which forms the basis of your formative evaluation activities • Questions to guide plan improvement • A management plan for instrument development and data collection • Methods for summarizing data that are easily used • Reflections that institutionalize your efforts and to share with colleagues in turnaround work

resources. The Leader's Guides also contain thumbnail images of the Tools referred to in the chapters; you may access these tools on the companion website for this book at www.corwin.com/turnaroundtoolkit. We will describe the companion website in more detail in the section below on special features.

Chapter Structure

Chapters 1–9 have a shared structure designed to make the how-to information central to turnaround work more accessible. Chapters open with a reproduction of the particular section of the graphic organizer for the 3 R's of turnaround work that will be the subject of that chapter. The chapter graphic is followed by a Pocket Summary, which provides a succinct guide to the major tasks for each turnaround task. The Pocket Summaries for the Introduction and Chapter 9, The 4th R of Turnaround Work: Reflect on Lessons Learned, highlight major ideas but do not deal with specific activities in the 3R turnaround process.

SPECIAL FEATURES

Chapter-Embedded Tips

Most chapters have two kinds of tips for readers. Tech Tips are notes about when or how to use technology to make a task more efficient. Expert Help notifications identify tasks that require expertise not ordinarily found at school sites, for which you might want to enlist a short-term consultant for expert help. The Tech Tips and Expert Help notes are indicated within each chapter by icons for easy identification.

Companion Website

The website offers both tools and research articles to help you in your school improvement efforts. This website is available at www.corwin.com/turnaroundtoolkit. The tools support each stage of the turnaround process described in this book. We have located the tools on the book's companion website so that you can access them even if the dog eats your book. Because they are electronic tools, you can easily modify templates and reproduce charts or tutorials without struggling with a temperamental, overheated, and often unavailable photocopier. A thumbnail of each tool is in the Leader's Guide for each chapter. The thumbnail references in the Guides help you connect tools to related turnaround activities. We have also listed the chapter's tools, and the website address, at the end of each chapter to provide an easily accessible table of contents for each chapter's Toolkit.

A chapter Toolkit may contain one or more of the following items:

- A template for a data display
- A useful chart summarizing tips for conducting an activity
- Protocols to guide discussion
- Toolkit tutorials: brief instructional readings designed to provide important knowledge of important technical information that may be unfamiliar but is needed to interpret data, select assessments, or do other kinds of specialized work in the turnaround process

In addition to the tools, this website also offers journal articles, research, or related readings to illustrate or expand upon major points in the book.

LET'S GET STARTED!

Introductions are complete, and it's time now to work together to make a difference for struggling students, overmanaged and pressured teachers, and administrators being pulled in too many different directions. We have presented a continuous improvement process based on data use, rapid-fire experimentation, and responsive revision that should be compatible with your current efforts to ensure all students meet grade-level standards in all subjects. Turnaround work contains no surprising tasks. The distinguishing features of the process are the sense of urgency for the work, its data-defined focus, and the demand that data-informed change occur more frequently that most of us familiar with a pretest-posttest model of evaluating our efforts are used to. The book organizes the steps in the turnaround process, and chapters are designed to provide an at-a-glance understanding of how the content is organized and what procedures are featured. We hope the book and chapter organization succeed in making the 3R turnaround process clearer and its application to your local setting easier than would be the case with a more conventional format. We also hope that your experience with *The TurnAround ToolKit* makes your work more efficient and provides you with support to meet your most daunting goals. Let the turnaround begin!

PART I

The 3 R's of Turnaround Work

Realign, Redesign, Refine

Section I

Realign

Create the Structures for Turnaround Work

You have to stand outside the box to see how the box can be re-designed.

—Charles Handy

The first step in turnaround work is to create systems and collaborative structures at your school that engage staff, community/parents, district leadership, and your expert networks in either participating in or supporting your turnaround efforts. We call this phase Realign, because we are focusing on a new way of doing business at your school. We are asking teachers to take leadership roles in redesigning and refining curriculum and instruction, to visit each other's classrooms and other schools, and to develop expertise in learning, instruction, and/or data analysis that may not have been part of their preparation or prior experience. We are asking all participants in the turnaround process to incorporate inquiry and formative evaluation into their practice, to eschew ideology and use results as the test of what constitutes a "good" solution, and to trust their colleagues and their supervisors enough that they try new strategies and ask questions throughout the process.

This first section has three chapters, each focused on a task that prepares the school to engage in turnaround work.

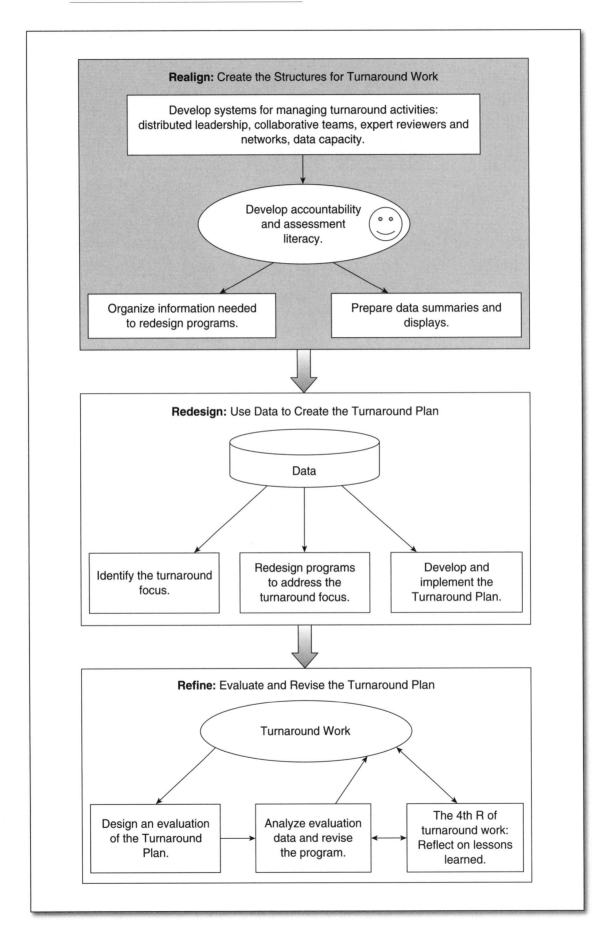

CHAPTER 1 ■

DEVELOP SYSTEMS FOR MANAGING TURNAROUND ACTIVITIES: DISTRIBUTED LEADERSHIP, COLLABORATIVE TEAMS, EXPERT REVIEWERS AND NETWORKS, DATA CAPACITY

Once you have created shared leadership systems for doing turnaround work, you will need to ensure that participants possess the knowledge of assessment and accountability needed to use data for instructional and school-level decision making. One of the first tasks of your school-level professional learning communities will be to develop or review knowledge of the key concepts in assessment and accountability needed to interpret data, create a Turnaround Plan, and revise that plan. Developing a capacity for data collection and use is part of this effort. We do not devote a separate chapter to "knowledge development." However, we have included instructional tools in the Toolkits for Chapters 2 and 3 that you can use to introduce or refresh your memory of key concepts needed for data interpretation and use.

CHAPTER 2 ■

ORGANIZE INFORMATION NEEDED TO REDESIGN PROGRAMS

Prior to reviewing your data to identify student needs and considering how to refocus programs to meet those needs, you will need to document what programs you have in place as well as those programs' goals, activities, and strategies. You will need to gather measures of program quality: How rigorous are your assignments? What is the quality of student work? Are programs being implemented as intended? You also need to catalog the kinds of data you have access to that can be used to guide instructional decisions or to evaluate the progress of your school. These inventories help you identify missing pieces in your curriculum and in the data set you need to make important decisions.

CHAPTER 3 ■

PREPARE DATA SUMMARIES AND DISPLAYS

A second aspect of the preparation for assessing student needs is to summarize available data in ways that enable staff to interpret findings easily and to identify actionable information quickly. The key to organizing and displaying data are the questions that will be used to review data summaries. The question is the key that unlocks interpretations buried in numbers. Data presentation is an art as well as a science. You will discover that some of the cleverest graphs and comprehensive tables are difficult to interpret and yield few generalizations. You may also discover that some of the simplest displays and leanest of tables highlight actionable information very well.

1

Develop Systems for Managing Turnaround Activities

Distributed Leadership, Collaborative Teams, Expert Reviewers and Networks, Data Capacity

People will support that which they help to create.

—Mary Kay Ash

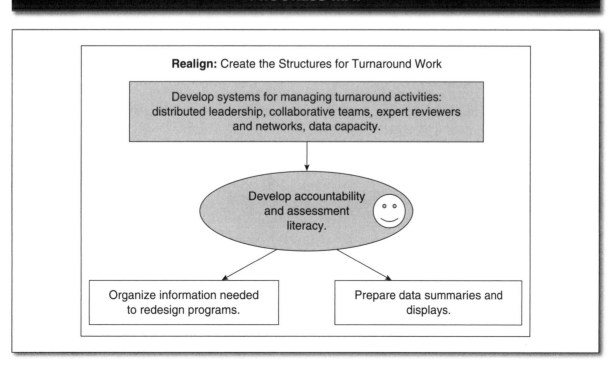

POCKET SUMMARY

Task	Major Activities	Purpose
System 1. Establish a system of shared leadership.	• Create a new vision of school leadership. • Identify leaders for turnaround work. • Work with de facto leaders to establish collaborative groups or professional learning communities. • Conduct leadership development with collaborative group leaders. • Establish a system for school positional leaders to participate in, monitor, and support work.	• Build capacity to institutionalize the work. • Create staff and stakeholder support. • Develop skills and knowledge.
System 2. Develop a collaborative work process.	• Provide time for collaboration. • Develop guidelines for "safe" and productive participation of all members. **Tool 1.1 Collaborative Considerations Protocol** **Tool 1.2 Focused-Discussion Guidelines Protocol** • Spend time team building. **Tool 1.3 My Posse Protocol**	• Shift initiative from independent contractor to collaborative colleagues.
System 3. Create expert review groups or networks to leverage learning.	• Recruit an expert group. • Identify benchmark sites at which you can observe best practices. • Establish connections with stakeholder groups.	• Ensure your efforts will be informed by the best available information and expertise. • Support change by identifying benchmark schools.
System 4. Develop capacity for data collection, integration, and reporting.	**Tool 1.4 Guidelines for Selecting Software for Data-Guided Decision Making** • Train a data team to manage data collection, summarization, and reporting. • Develop accountability and assessment literacy. • Realign available systems. **Tool 1.5 Toolkit Tutorial: Key Accountability Concepts** **Tool 1.6 Toolkit Tutorial: Key Assessment Concepts** **Tool 1.7 Toolkit Tutorial: Test Score Interpretation and Reliability**	• Automate reporting for time-efficient meetings and data-informed decision making. • Develop local expertise in data use.

ESTABLISH A SYSTEM OF SHARED LEADERSHIP

The most important systems in a school involve people. How can they best organize to do their work? How can they improve their skills and knowledge and stay current professionally? How can you distribute leadership responsibilities both to share the work and to institutionalize successful practices? The classroom teacher has the biggest direct influence on student learning, school climate, and the quality of curriculum and instruction. How can these classroom skills be leveraged for school turnaround?

Turnaround begins with realignment of traditional ways of doing business so that a more focused, efficient, and self-correcting system can replace school practices that are not improving student achievement. One approach to marshalling the person-power needed for this important work is to share leadership responsibilities among school staff. We refer to *shared* instead of *distributed* leadership, because distributed leadership is a complex concept, one that describes a particular perspective on leadership and specific kinds of interactions in a school. You may or may not be building distributed leadership systems, but you can start with the simpler task of involving more staff in planning, program monitoring, analyzing data for decision making, and staff development responsibilities than you have in the past.

The management tasks and challenges in realignment are summarized in the **Leader's Guide for Chapter 1**. The Guide reproduces the Pocket Summary above to use as you realign the four systems discussed in this chapter. The Guide also suggests readings to deepen your understanding of the kinds of leadership structures required to change the trajectory of student achievement.

Create a New Vision of School Leadership

Schools have natural organizational structures that need remodeling when learning and instruction require improvement. Research on leadership provides strong examples of how low-performing schools improve when staff and administrators share leadership, specifically through collaborative, professional groups—sometimes known as professional learning communities. Shirley Hord[1] of the Southeast Regional Educational Laboratory reviewed leadership practices linked to student achievement and found that effective teacher collaboration or professional learning communities have the following characteristics:

- Involve school principals in a facilitative and collegial role that invites staff input, decision making, and action on school issues
- Maintain an unwavering focus on improved student learning
- Develop shared vision and values
- Facilitate staff learning and application of new knowledge to address problems underlying low student achievement

In short, shared leadership is another way to view leadership of school turnaround. In contrast to positional leadership, which directs the work of school improvement to the principal, shared leadership is collective and yields multiple sources of expertise and vision. Teachers develop expertise by working collaboratively. Still, the hierarchical or formal leaders are essential in such a view of school leadership. Positional leaders are the glue of the organization. They hold organizational structures together and join people in productive relationships. In the words of Alma Harris, the central task of the titular leader is to create a "common culture of expectations around the use of individual skills and abilities."[2] Table 1.1 compares organizations led hierarchically to those with shared leadership.

Table 1.1   Creating a New Vision of School Leadership

Leadership Roles	Hierarchical Leadership	Shared Leadership
Who creates the vision?	District office, principal	Grade-level lead teachers, department heads, "champions," de facto leaders
Who leads the work?	Principal	Grade-level lead teachers, department heads, "champions," de facto leaders
Who selects and provides relevant resources (training, technology, funding, time)?	District office or principal	Selects—Principal in conjunction with other site leaders and district (if necessary) Provides—District, principal, community, parents, teachers
Who monitors the work?	District office or principal	Collaborative groups
Who evaluates the work?	District office or principal	Collaborative groups
Who revises the vision/plan and begins next steps?	District office or principal	Collaborative groups

Putting into place the structures and processes for shared leadership is one essential step in turnaround. Instilling the processes for reflective practice is a second ingredient for success. Reflective practice recognizes the power of continuous improvement and uses formative evaluation to accomplish it. The major tasks of formative evaluation—gathering data to assess student needs, using data to create program changes, gathering new data to check on implementation of program changes and resulting student progress, and revision of program changes based on new data—occur in collaborative groups (professional learning communities). Research conducted by Harris and Portin[3] has linked improvements in student achievement to the implementation of a continuous improvement process. Thus, prior to beginning turnaround work, you will need to put structures in place to establish the interpersonal relationships needed for collaboration and the capacity to use data for instructional improvement.

Identify Leaders for Turnaround Work

Leaders are the people who exercise discretion and influence over the direction of schools. All schools have individuals who, regardless of their title or job description, influence school climate, culture, and vision. These de facto leaders can be found helping colleagues identify issues that interfere with student learning, creating a more participatory environment, and bringing resources to bear toward meaningful change and reform. Schools also have de facto leaders who sabotage change, perhaps by invoking the union contract, by encouraging others to refrain from unpaid work, by defending the status quo, or by criticizing data (such as those gathered by the state or district testing system) that identify their schools as low performing. When inviting staff to lead your school's collaborative groups, you should be aware that change agents and resistors live in all organizations (and sometimes in the same person!). You will want to create collaborative relationships with your leadership team to create consensus about goals and processes for collaborative work and to address barriers that arise along the way. When identifying members for your leadership team, you will initially think of positional leaders, department heads, assistant principals, and district office specialists. However, search for those de facto leaders who exert influence and personal power at your site; these are essential members of your leadership team.

Work With De Facto Leaders to Establish Collaborative Work Groups or Professional Learning Communities

Given the nature of the work ahead, what kinds of teams are needed? Our first instinct is to think of the naturally occurring groups in our school, such as staff in particular grade levels, departments, or special programs such as special education, art, music, physical education, or education for English learners. However, in bringing about change, you want to create as many opportunities as possible for creative thinking and action. An art teacher or a special education teacher can provide valuable insights on student learning styles and cracking stubborn learning challenges. An English-learner specialist benefits greatly by understanding the mainstream curriculum, and her expertise with English learners will benefit teachers who need to adapt instruction for English learners. Teams with teachers from different grade levels enhance articulation between grades and develop a deeper understanding of grade-level standards. Collaboration among teachers of different grades on formative evaluation might also lead teachers to develop more flexible instructional groupings that involve sending students to different grade-level classrooms. As you work with your leadership team (your de facto leaders and administrative staff) to create working groups, consider the following questions:

- Will we establish a few groups to do the work and report to the rest of the staff, or will we engage everyone at some point in the formative evaluation process? (Think about your resource situation—for example, do you have adequate release time to free teachers from classroom duties for this process? Are there natural leaders for multiple groups?)

- Do we need specialized "functional" teams for our work, such as a data team, a logic model team, or a learning strategies team?
- Which staff represent important stakeholders (including student groups)?
- Which staff might have useful and different takes on instructional issues?
- Who are natural leaders who inspire confidence or are bridge builders in difficult situations?
- How large should our collaborative groups be?
- Will groups remain together for a long period of time (which increases efficiency) or be rearranged periodically (which increases the opportunity to establish relationships among a larger group)?

Composing effective collaborative groups requires difficult trade-offs and careful consideration. But don't get too bogged down, and remember the real tasks here: Involve others, and create working groups that will be able to quickly address student learning problems at your school and yield rapid increases in student achievement.

Conduct Leadership Development With Collaborative Group Leaders

Staff you have identified as being natural or de facto leaders will play an important role in turnaround work. They will facilitate collaborative group meetings, they might initiate research on their own to inform their group's work, and their interactions with team members will determine whether participants feel valued, are developing skills, and have results to show for their efforts. Given the importance of de facto leaders, you will want to spend some time in leadership development. You will want to model the leadership behavior you expect from your leadership team, mentor and monitor them, and then have them reflect on their growth. One resource you could use in leadership development is *Leading Every Day* by Joyce Kaser, Susan Mundry, Katherine E. Stiles, and Susan Loucks-Horsely.[4] This reference contains 124 actions and reflections for leaders. An entire section of 31 activities is dedicated to leading effective groups. There are 4 activities dedicated to formative evaluation. One of our favorite activities to use with leadership groups is Capitalizing on Resistance, which identifies sources of resistance and asks participants to think of "antidotes." This activity is especially useful in helping leaders look beyond negative stances from team members to see important underlying reasons for resistance. It can shift the leader's attitude from exasperation to proactive identification of a teachable moment.

Your leadership development approach will match your staff's talent and working style. However, the leadership team should have some understanding of and ability to demonstrate the following skills:

- Listening
- Facilitating

- Dealing with, capitalizing on, and resolving conflict, resistance, and the actions of disruptive people
- Questioning, giving feedback, summarizing, and moving the group forward to the next steps

Establish a System for School Positional Leaders to Participate in, Monitor, and Support Work

The school leader or the consultant leading turnaround work would ideally attend all meetings of the collaborative groups, but this is often impossible. Instead, collaborative group members could file online minutes for review and comment. You could arrange for a weekly briefing and response session, or you could engage staff in informal conversations about their improvement work as a way to keep all up to date.

The goal here is to enable collaborative group members to hold themselves accountable for their work, individually and collectively. How do the principal and community provide needed resources and support? How does staff stay on task, complete their work, and report efforts? Again, involving staff in generating solutions to the communication/ support issues will reveal viable solutions.

DEVELOP A COLLABORATIVE WORK PROCESS

Teaching is a lonely activity. It shouldn't be. The synergy created by professional collaboration keeps teachers energized, leverages knowledge and skills in your staff, and provides emotional support through tough times. However, collaboration doesn't always come naturally. It is a skill. It can be learned, and it's essential if you wish to maximize your chances for improving student outcomes. Collaborative work requires that you set aside time for teachers to work together.

Provide Time for Collaboration

Principals often have little time to visit classrooms or lead instruction, but they are masters at creating schedules. Meetings have opportunity costs and sometimes also direct "costs." You may have a union contract that requires you to pay teachers for after-school, weekend, or evening meetings. You may need to hire substitutes so that teacher teams can meet. And when staff members meet to collaborate, their individual work is not getting done.

Your leadership team should consider the cost issues associated with collaborative group meeting schedules. Table 1.2 presents some typical approaches to paying the costs of collaborative work, both direct and opportunity. Your site might have different cost categories and a different proportion of direct to opportunity costs, but increasing staff time for collaboration does have costs. A fair economic analysis also considers the benefits associated with changes in costs. Since research finds that professional collaboration increases student achievement, morale, and teacher capacity, the return on investment must be considered.

| Table 1.2 | Offsetting Meeting Costs |

Approaches to Direct Costs (salaries)	Approaches to Opportunity Costs (to offset what is not done in class while meetings occur)
Education foundation pays for substitutes.	District or community content specialists provide special activities for students.
School "banks" instructional time to have occasional shortened student days so teachers can meet.	Students do homework after school instead of in class.
Title I, Title II, or special teacher professional development funds can pay for meetings.	Supplemental service providers provide additional instruction for struggling students.
Collaborative groups meet on staggered schedules, so that colleagues can cover classes or combine classes for instruction.	Students meet in peer tutoring groups.

When resources are scarce but curriculum demands remain high, finding time to meet can seem impossible. You might want to consider how you can use technology to leverage meeting time. Online conferencing or chat rooms (of the instructional kind) might create additional collaboration opportunities. As your work progresses and benefits individual teachers, you might find that some of the barriers to collaboration will be less daunting.

Develop Guidelines for "Safe" and Productive Participation of All Members

Making the shift from a principal-directed (top down) workplace to a collaborative workplace will take some time. It begins with relationships: How will we talk with one another about our work and what will help us understand each other better? The first meeting, or even the first few meetings, of the collaborative groups should focus on developing norms for group participation and helping people develop productive working relationships.

A helpful strategy for team building is to engage your staff in developing guidelines for their work and in a few activities that will reveal similarities and differences in their work styles and beliefs. You've heard of protocols. In the world of computers, protocols describe how computers communicate with each other. In research, we develop protocols to guide data collection; for researchers, a protocol is a set of directions and a list of questions that governs and standardizes personal interviews with informants. In the world of education, we use the term *protocols* to describe the rules by which we teachers will communicate about an educational issue or a topic of professional practice. Specifically, we use protocols to manage group discussions. Protocols used to run collaborative sessions resemble a formal lesson plan. They are built around questions the group will be tackling but have guidelines to govern all aspects of the discussion. Some protocols contain a stated purpose for the discussion, a set of resources needed during the discussion (chart paper, an overhead projector, a time allotment), and finally, the steps that will occur during the discussion and the order in which they will occur.

While using protocols for teacher collaboration at first appears overly formal and artificial, consider why they have become a tool associated with effective collaborative groups. First, protocols provide necessary focus so that the teacher's most precious resource, time, is used effectively. Less-structured discussions may lead to staff venting or wandering off topic, excessive time spent on one or two topics, and perhaps hurt feelings. Protocols keep staff both on track and on time. Even a collegial and experienced staff appreciates how emotionally safe and productive meetings run with protocols can be.

We have developed protocols specific to turnaround work focused on formative evaluation. These protocols are evaluation-specific adaptations of two popular norm-setting protocols you may already be familiar with, the Fears and Hopes protocol[5] and the Setting Norms protocol developed by the Center for Collaborative Education in Boston.[6] The Fears and Hopes protocol is used to develop group ownership for each participant's expectations and concerns. We have shifted its focus slightly to reveal group versus individual working style preferences. Our **Tool 1.1, Collaborative Considerations Protocol,** asks participants to consider in which setting they are most comfortable tackling problems where they initially may not have much experience. Common examples include understanding data, diagnosing learning problems in an unfamiliar curricular area, and identifying strategies for effective parent involvement.

Tool 1.1

The Setting Norms protocol creates the rules for civil discourse guiding collaborative group work. It was designed to guide the discussion that sets the rules of engagement for collaborative meetings. Participants set norms for such areas as logistics, timelines, courtesy, decision-making process (hint: try to avoid a 2/3 majority norm), workload, and setting and enforcement of priorities. Our formative evaluation–themed protocol for norm setting is **Tool 1.2, Focused-Discussion Guidelines Protocol.** The protocol requires participants to generate participation norms for very goal-oriented discussions that have the potential to reveal staff insecurities and differences in styles and beliefs.

Tool 1.2

Table 1.3 summarizes the two turnaround-specific protocols for revealing participant reservations about group work and norm setting. Should you wish to use the more general Fears and Hopes or Setting Norms protocol, citations appear in the tables below, and full reference information may be found in the Reference section at the end of this book.

Table 1.3	A Comparison of the Collaborative Considerations and Focused-Discussions Guidelines Protocols for Identifying Group Concerns to be Addressed in Norm Setting

	Tool 1.1, Collaborative Considerations Protocol	Tool 1.2, Focused-Discussion Guidelines Protocol
Purpose	To help group members identify their own preferences during group work and to develop group respect for different styles	To engage participants in developing behavioral guidelines for their group work
Time	15–25 minutes	25–35 minutes
Resources Needed	Writing materials, chart paper and markers, handout with list of four questions about group work preferences, handout with formative evaluation questions	Chart paper, handout with list of six norms areas, handout with formative evaluation questions
Steps	Facilitator tells group they will be working on difficult issues of school improvement and asks them to consider four questions about working individually and in groups. Participants summarize group responses on charts. Facilitator asks for a gallery walk.	Participants work in groups of five to seven to develop guidelines for each of six areas: • Scheduling • Expectations • Consensus process • Responsibilities • Accommodating diverse styles • Group accountability Groups record suggested guidelines on six blank charts posted in the room.
Debriefing	Facilitator asks for advantages and disadvantages of individual versus group preference in style and focuses on how these can be accommodated in the group discussion guidelines.	Guidelines are consolidated and refined by the group and each approved before being accepted for group work.
Evaluating the Session: Formative Evaluation Questions	1. Did this activity remove any hesitations you might have about collaborative work? If so, can you pinpoint what caused this change? If not, what further concerns do you have?	1. Do you think the group-generated guidelines established conditions for quality group work? If not, what further concerns do you have? 2. Which guidelines might you challenge or find difficult to uphold?

	Tool 1.1, Collaborative Considerations Protocol	Tool 1.2, Focused-Discussion Guidelines Protocol
	2. What did you learn about your colleagues that you didn't already know? 3. Is this an activity you might use in your classroom? 4. Would you rate the activity a success or something less than useful? What suggestions do you have for improving it?	3. Which guidelines do you feel will be most valuable in creating focused, productive, respectful discussions? 4. Is this an activity you might use in your classroom? 5. Would you rate the activity a success or something less than useful? What suggestions do you have for improving it?

Sources: Tool 1.1 is adapted from Fears and Hopes protocol (McDonald, Mohr, Dichter, & McDonald, 2007, p. 24); Tool 1.2 is adapted from "Setting Norms for Collaborative Work," Center for Collaborative Education (n.d.).

Spend Time Team Building

Even faculties who have worked together for a long time may be unaware of professional perspectives or work styles that could surface during collaborative group work. We endorse allocating time for staff to get to know each other better when it comes to thinking and problem-solving styles.

We have developed three activities that introduce three different work-related perspectives of teachers (and others) as they relate to issues of teaching and learning. These activities help participants explore their diverse views of important components of teaching and learning, problem-solving styles, and preferred research methods.

The first activity, **Tool 1.3, My Posse Protocol,** asks teachers to explore their similarities and differences on issues of student learning and to consider how their stances impact their work. My Posse is adapted from the Diversity Rounds protocol.[7] My Posse asks participants to physically join others who are alike in their attitudes in three professional categories: educational outcomes, at-risk students, and favorite subject to teach. Participants define what constitutes membership in each category and physically sort themselves into groups. Groups then discuss how their selection affects their teaching. My Posse provides a general framework for organizing this sort-select process and can be adapted to any situation, focusing on cultural, experience, and other background factors that affect professional practice.

Problem-solving style activities are built upon theories of personality, such as those represented by the Myers-Briggs Type Indicator, by the Keirsey Temperament Sorter, or by creativity and problem-solving research grounded in cognitive psychology. Because these are theory-based approaches, we recommend you review our recommendations and others and select one that best fits with your team-building goals. In Table 1.4, we have provided references for activities to reveal problem-solving styles that you can use with your staff.

One style assessment we like is called simply Problem-Solving Styles Test. It has been used in inservice sessions with the Canadian Literacy

Tool 1.3

Project and has been published as a problem-solving guide by Linda K. Hite-Mills in *The Art and Science of Problem Solving*.[8] Another is the Problem-Solving Style Identifier, a short inventory of five categories followed by four statements that participants rank in order of preference. Based on their responses, participants are identified as preferring one of four styles: Diplomat, Professor, Detective, or Champion. The Diplomat is the mediator and consensus builder, the Professor is information driven, the Detective seeks causes and relevant explanations, and the Champion is results focused but often a lone wolf. Our description does not do justice to the complexity of each style, which is explained well in the activity. The approaches have advantages and disadvantages, and no individual prefers purely one style. However, teachers benefit from awareness of their own preferred problem-solving style as well as of those of others. This awareness can increase tolerance for team differences.

A third problem-solving style activity is inspired by Myers-Briggs classifications, which identifies problem-solving style more as a personality disposition than as a cognitive approach. The well-known Compass protocol exists in many versions. We reference two of these versions in Table 1.4; they share a classification strategy but have different debriefing questions. The short-debrief version appears on the National School Reform Faculty website www.nsrfharmony.org. The version with a more extensive set of debriefing questions was developed by the Center for Collaborative Learning in Boston and appears on www.turningpts.org. The Compass Points protocol asks participants to physically place themselves in one of four directions—North, South, East, and West—each of which represents a personal style in a *group* setting. The four styles are Acting, Speculating, Caring, and Paying Attention to Detail. Once sorted and in physically different parts of the room, groups answer a series of questions designed to assess their strengths and weaknesses and to explain themselves to other groups with different styles. When we've used this protocol, some participants asked to create compass points between the four major directions. People sometimes resist being classified broadly, so allowing groups to choose points such as Northeast or Southwest to describe themselves resulted in more detailed revelations about working style and better buy-in from the group.

The final activity you could consider is directly related to the collaborative work the staff will be doing. The Paradigms Exposed activity[9] asks teachers to choose the one statement from each of 15 pairs that best describes their beliefs. It was developed by the evaluation theorist Robert Stake at the University of Illinois to serve as a discussion protocol rather than to identify real differences in style or preference. His brief survey covering beliefs about inquiry asks respondents to consider their stances on such topics as conducting observations, interpreting results, relationships between variables, the meaning of facts, trajectories of change, which data are most useful, and other aspects of research. Respondents receive a profile that identifies the extent to which their worldviews are positivistic or naturalistic. They are asked to consider how their inquiry worldview might affect their work in evaluating programs. Identifying inquiry orientation helps team members understand that underlying worldviews diverge and can influence what kinds of questions people ask and what kinds of data they value. We hope this knowledge causes participants to value and solicit input from others with different beliefs about inquiry.

We have presented a small sample of the kinds of team-building activities you might use to prepare your staff for school turnaround work. Table 1.4 summarizes their purposes and shows where you can find the protocols or assessments to use with your staff.

Table 1.4   Team-Building Resource Summary

Purpose	Useful Protocols
To identify diversity affecting teaching	Tool 1.3, My Posse Protocol Diversity Rounds (McDonald, Mohr, Dichter, & McDonald, 2007, p. 25)
To allow team members to learn more about personal cognitive styles that influence how they approach tasks	Compass Points www.turningpts.org (long version) www.nsrfharmony.org (short version)
To have participants learn more about their own preferences for naturalistic or positivistic inquiry and be aware of these as they react to how formative evaluations are designed	Paradigms Exposed (Preskill & Russ-Eft, 2005, pp. 150–153)

CREATE EXPERT REVIEW GROUPS OR NETWORKS TO LEVERAGE LEARNING

As you work with the collaborative groups at your site, you will soon identify areas where "inside" knowledge is not enough to address the problems you wish to solve. After all, if you knew how to hit your accountability targets every year, or reduce the achievement gap, or increase the percentage of graduates going to college, you would have done it! People with other experiences and perspectives can support your staff at each step of the formative evaluation process. The support might be informal, such as sitting in meetings or reviewing agendas, survey items, and plans; or it might be more formal, such as providing written critiques of the strengths and weaknesses of your written documents.

Recruit an Expert Group

One of the most efficient ways to access expertise outside your school is to establish an advisory board or expert panel, different members of which may review your work or participate in your collaborative group meetings at crucial times. Expert groups leverage your work by bringing ideas and knowledge and by offering opportunities to join other professional networks that enhance skills and knowledge at your site. Your group could consist of experts only, but it could also include other people whose perspectives will improve your work and provide information you wouldn't find at your site. For example, perhaps you are focused on improving mathematics for African American males. Your expert group might have some math teaching experts and some experts on African American educational issues, but it also might have a math teacher from another school or district who has been successful with your target group.

Who qualifies as an expert? Experts are people identified by others as being especially thoughtful and knowledgeable. Experts have reputations, but not the kind that get them into trouble! Look for referrals from positional leaders such as your district curriculum director. District and state curriculum or accountability staff can also direct you to commercial programs, such as Safe and Civil Schools or the University of Chicago School Mathematics Project, that have staff with experience and success in addressing instructional issues and that might have consultants willing to help (for a fee).

You can identify an expert by finding out who is writing about the problems you wish to solve and whether other people are citing their work. The What Works Clearinghouse (http://ies.ed.gov/ncee/wwc/aboutus/investigators.asp#pi03), a website of the U.S. Department of Education's Institute for Education Sciences (IES), lists principal investigators who can refer you to experts in your region who may have worked on important IES studies. The websites of subject-matter professional organizations, such as the National Council for Mathematics Education or the International Reading Association, can also help you find people who are writing about or doing the work of reforming curriculum. Check the publications from leadership organizations such as the Association for Supervision and Curriculum Development (www.ascd.org) or American Association of School Administrators to find articles related to your school's problems. Who wrote them? Do you like what they said? Would that person act as a reviewer for your work?

You can define an expert as someone who has special experience or success with the problem you are tackling. The math teacher in the example above qualifies as an expert. A social worker or psychologist who provides support to dropout programs would be an expert. You might even consider your local education reporter as an expert in identifying what is wrong with the schools and one who holds high standards for certifying school success.

You can recruit your advisors and experts from many sources. Most will be quite willing to participate if you limit their time commitment and structure their input so that it is easy for them to support your collaborative group work. When you invite them to provide feedback about your work, you will want to be specific about

- the amount of time they will have to spend;
- when you will be asking them to respond;
- which topics they are to review;
- what you expect in the response—insightful suggestions, a critique, affirmation, or all of these; and
- whether you will be paying them a stipend for their work.

You will also need to tell them whether they are to be reviewing and responding to documents or to be observing your work and making comments. This group can be quite helpful in the early stages of your work as well. You might ask them to act as an advisory board for your planning meetings. Table 1.5 suggests sources of expertise and what perspectives you gain by including people from these sources.

Table 1.5   The Expert Field Guide

Where to Find Critical Friends	Type of Expertise
Central Office Staff	Curriculum Staff—Program description information; standards for correct program implementation; logic models underlying programs for reading, math, science, and so forth
	Testing Staff—How to understand what is tested; interpreting scores; appropriate test preparation; customized test reports to address school-specific needs
	Research Staff—Training in formative evaluation; development of logic models; data analysis, display, and interpretation
	Directors of Gifted Students, Special Education, and English Learner Programs—Instructional strategies; learning issues; testable solutions to learning problems
	Psychologists and Social Workers—Identification of student variables affecting learning; identification of programs to address behavioral issues and other special challenges
Local University	Research-based curriculum, instructional strategies, methods for including special needs populations, knowledge of standards students must meet to be college ready
	Connections to other experts nationally who could help
Community Experts: Activists, Journalists	Knowledge of student needs and resources outside of school to address health, psychological, and vocational issues
	Commitment to certain issues or groups of students that could translate into a better understanding of group needs
	Criteria for judging your school and a vision of what the school should be like
Parent Advocates	Ideas about how best to solicit parent input and communicate findings
	Ideas for improving parent involvement in new initiatives
Student Activists	Assistance in surveying students and summarizing results
	Student perspectives on innovations and current problems
	Review of measures, surveys, and communication for clear, understandable language

Identify Benchmark Sites at
Which You Can Observe Best Practices

A central aspect of turnaround work is helping staff at struggling schools see what success with a comparable student population looks like. Educators often give more credibility to practitioner experience than policy mandates or research findings. Practitioners are creative and great at adapting ideas, practices, and curriculums to their local context. Comparable schools provide models for improvement and collegial networks that can support your team during planning and implementation. A second reason to identify and create a relationship with one or more benchmark schools is that benchmarking is simply good practice. Your visits to benchmark schools will provide staff with strategies to consider when creating an improvement plan, and you may find that colleagues in the benchmark schools wish to become part of your advisory board or expert group.

What is benchmarking? The term comes to education from business and was first used by Rank Xerox. Benchmarking is a Total Quality Management (TQM) tool. TQM is a continuous improvement process, and benchmarking is the step in the process during which leaders in the field are studied to identify their best practices. Benchmarking methodology can have many goals and many steps, but a short version can easily be incorporated into your turnaround work:

1. *Conduct a needs assessment* to identify priority areas for improvement and to determine what kind of program you wish to learn from.

2. *Identify similar or comparable schools* using demographic, achievement, and other key data that define your school.

3. *Identify the outstanding schools* among the comparable schools. Criteria should include outstanding results in your priority areas for improvement but could also include climate, parent involvement, safety, community service, and other valued outcomes.

4. *Obtain initial information* about how your comparable benchmark school has obtained outstanding results. You could send an advance team to interview key leaders, read about the school in published case studies, or examine public data available on the Internet. The purpose of this preliminary study is to identify questions to ask about how they did it when you visit.

5. *Visit the comparable school* to identify practices they say caused their success.

6. *Implement best practices:* Get needed training, try the strategies, and . . .

7. *Evaluate them!*

Establish Connections With Stakeholder Groups

Finally, your external review system could include representatives of important, supportive, and creative people from your student body (if they are old enough), parent groups, foundations, community organizations, and perhaps even activist groups. For example, if your school is located near Washington, D.C., and is working to close the achievement gap, you might want to include someone from the Education Trust on your advisory board. You might have a local chapter of the National Conference for Community and Justice who can provide skilled observers for your collaborative groups and assess human relations at your site. Your local education foundation or a large national foundation might have expertise to help you view your work creatively.

DEVELOP CAPACITY FOR DATA COLLECTION, INTEGRATION, AND REPORTING

We conclude our overview of the major systems and processes you need with a discussion of the technological support and technical capacity essential to any data-guided continuous improvement system: These include hardware and software for data collection, integration, analysis, and reporting and staff able to summarize, analyze, and interpret data.

Up to this point, we have focused on the "people" issues associated with school turnaround work. And for us, it's always "people first." However, the people engaged in solving instructional problems need useful information and tools to easily access and analyze data. The important issues to consider in creating systems at your site for data collection, integration, analysis, and reporting are as follows:

- What kinds of data and what kinds of reports will we need?
- What kinds of data are available already in electronic form?
- What other, potentially important data are already available or could be easily collected?
- How can data collected locally or already available in nonelectronic form—such as student portfolios, behavioral information, lesson plans, and other nonstandardized test information—be entered into an electronic storage system?
- How will data from different sources—such as attendance records, individual course-taking, test scores, survey responses, grades, and demographic data—be assembled for analysis and reporting?
- Who will create data summaries—the central office, a school team, or individual teachers? What technology will they use?

The good news is that there are many vendors of add-on data systems (added to your district's data warehouse or student information system) designed to provide individual schools or teachers with the ability to create custom reports. Most of the add-on systems created for mining school district data have test-generation capabilities, and some even link test results to curriculum or individual student remediation work. These products "sit atop" your district's student information system and integrate data on student demographics, course-taking, and test scores stored in the central system or individual classrooms into a single system, so teachers can create custom reports whenever they need to. The bad news is that creating a system that will enable principals or teachers to create their own reports may require additional purchases your school cannot afford. Many systems have a per-pupil per-year pricing plan and house the data with the vendor. These requirements are difficult for districts, because their budgets are generally built one year at a time, and student confidentiality laws often make offsite storage unfeasible. But you can often negotiate with vendors to run the system in-house with district staff and pay a yearly licensing fee, which can both reduce the per-pupil cost and reduce fears about violating student and teacher confidentiality.

Your district's information systems (IS) department could have "business intelligence" tools that can generate reports for your school. Perhaps you could create a list of useful reports you will be requesting each quarter, semester, and year, and have your IS department program the report templates so that you can access them when needed. Generally, creating reports using business intelligence tools requires some programming experience and is not a task teachers can perform from their desktops. However, after you have been through a few cycles of formative evaluation to help you identify the kind of data you need and in what format, centrally designed reports can provide a cost-effective reporting solution.

Tool 1.4, Guidelines for Selecting Software for Data-Guided Decision Making, highlights some major decisions in selecting a data integration and reporting system for teacher use. The answers to these questions can be quite technical and require working closely with central office IS staff. In fact, setting up systems for data collection, integration, and reporting could be the focus of one of your collaborative groups. Your data collaborative group could use this tool (which appears in the Toolkit) to interview vendors or to have an intelligent conversation with the district IS department.

Train a Data Team to Manage Data Collection, Analysis, Summarization, and Reporting

Much of your systems realignment will be focused on creating capacity to do turnaround work, specifically to collect, analyze, and use relevant data to identify needed program changes, to monitor those changes, and to use the monitoring data for program revision. Continuous improvement and review of data requires that data be collected, analyzed, and summarized frequently and in a timely fashion. Traditional reporting periods, such as the yearly release of state and federal accountability reports, do not provide information quickly enough for schools to revise programs and make needed changes. Accountability data certainly are of little use for diagnosing classroom or individual problems of teaching and learning.

The most efficient approach to assuring more frequent data collection throughout the year is to create a school-level data team to be responsible for the regular collection, summarization, and interpretation of data. Data team members need not have formal training in statistics, but they should have some training in research methods, especially in identifying threats to internal and external validity of "experiments," in asking questions about data, in graphic conventions, and in interpreting descriptive statistics (including regression), as well as practice in communicating numerical information to others.

We conducted a focus group with school administrators who supervise principals and work as advisors to underperforming schools to identify the kinds of skills and knowledge a data team would need. Their responses are summarized in Table 1.6, Data Team Competencies.

Table 1.6 Data Team Competencies

Knowledge/Dispositions	Skills
Understand the details and calculations behind state and federal accountability system reports for the school	Organizing data
Understand key concepts in measurement, data analysis, and interpretation: reliability, validity, standard error, item difficulty, score distributions, correlation, scale score, raw score, percentile	Data analysis Graphing data
Understand what assessment results really "say," what they don't say, and what threats there might be to validity of results (alternate interpretations)	Leading discussions about data to get beyond superficial findings
Understand how assessments are tied to purpose and use and are developed to address specific questions	Asking probing questions about how students acquire content knowledge
Able to develop theories of action that explain the relationship between teaching events and what students learn (outcomes)	Ability to "unpack" or operationalize standards
Understand the importance of formative assessments and using the results in the classroom to immediately revise instruction	Extracting data from the district's information system and creating reports

Ideally, you will have three to five teachers and/or administrators interested in developing expertise in this area and willing to do the tedious work of collecting, organizing, summarizing, and presenting data and even reviewing classroom or district assessments. If you are graced with such courageous staff members, you can arrange to have them do a book study group led by one of your expert reviewers or a local university professor of research methods, or arrange to have the district office or local service provider, such as a county education office, organize training for the data team. In addition to the knowledge and skills noted above, data-team training could include the following topics:

- Using protocols for team building and collaboration
- Understanding the details of the state and federal accountability systems, including special rules, and the technical manual for the state assessment
- Understanding how to align to standards assessments created by the district or individual teachers
- Identifying student learning problems and teaching issues related to these problems
- Developing theories of action or logic models to link changes in curriculum or instruction to student outcomes

- Creating management plans for the administration of accountability, district, and common assessments in the school, and creating timelines for data collection and data sharing

While data team training may seem highly technical, we have found that when it is anchored to a book study group and supported by direct practice of the needed skills and some targeted technical information, 30 hours can prepare teachers interested in data to lead your school's data use efforts. Advisors can also be used to fill in any gaps in your data team's knowledge and skills.

Develop Accountability and Assessment Literacy

The data team will need a thorough understanding of the state and federal accountability systems and the technical characteristics of the assessments used in each. You might also decide that accountability and assessment literacy would help all of the teaching staff to use data better. Knowing how tests are developed, what their technical strengths and weaknesses are, and how the school's accountability standing is calculated, although these issues seem incomprehensible on the surface, tends to empower educators. Accountability and assessment results are used to vilify and praise schools, to select promising and lagging students, and to measure the impact of teaching. Once teachers see what is under the hood of these vehicles, they tend to be less defensive about results and more creative about how they can augment test results with other information to make more accurate decisions. They are also able to communicate student and school results more clearly to parents and help them to put into perspective the hyperbole about school performance that often accompanies the public reporting of scores.

We have included in the Toolkit for Chapter 1 three key tutorials that can serve as a primer for accountability and assessment literacy:

Tool 1.5, Toolkit Tutorial: Key Accountability Concepts

Tool 1.6, Toolkit Tutorial: Key Assessment Concepts

Tool 1.7, Toolkit Tutorial: Test Score Interpretation and Reliability

The literacy tutorials provide an introduction to the concepts needed for interpreting tests and are easy to understand. We hope the tutorials entice some staff to develop more in-depth understanding of the educational policies and assessments that are driving teaching practice today. It's time to take the clothes off the emperor (and perhaps buy him a whole new wardrobe!).

Realign Available Systems

This chapter focused on realigning people and practices in the school prior to designing the turnaround plan. It was lengthy, because changing behavior, attitudes, roles, and responsibilities takes both time and patience. The focus in our first realignment task is on processes, attitudes, and developing knowledge. It involves helping people responsible for turning around student achievement—teachers and other staff, parents, and community—buy into the mission and develop a passion for getting better results. Once structures for turnaround work are in place, we can begin realigning our available information to make it more useful and accessible for program redesign. Specifically, in the next chapter we will catalog programs already in place and inventory data to identify student needs.

CHAPTER 1 TOOLKIT

DEVELOP SYSTEMS FOR MANAGING TURNAROUND ACTIVITIES

Distributed Leadership, Collaborative Teams, Expert Reviewers and Networks, Data Capacity

The Tools for Chapter 1 can be found on the companion website for *The TurnAround ToolKit* at http://www.corwin.com/turnaroundtoolkit.

Tool 1.1   Collaborative Considerations Protocol

Tool 1.2   Focused-Discussion Guidelines Protocol

Tool 1.3   My Posse Protocol

Tool 1.4   Guidelines for Selecting Software for Data-Guided Decision Making

Tool 1.5   Toolkit Tutorial: Key Accountability Concepts

Tool 1.6   Toolkit Tutorial: Key Assessment Concepts

Tool 1.7   Toolkit Tutorial: Test Score Interpretation and Reliability

2

Organize Information Needed to Redesign Programs

Give me six hours to chop down a tree and I will spend the first four sharpening the axe.

—Abraham Lincoln

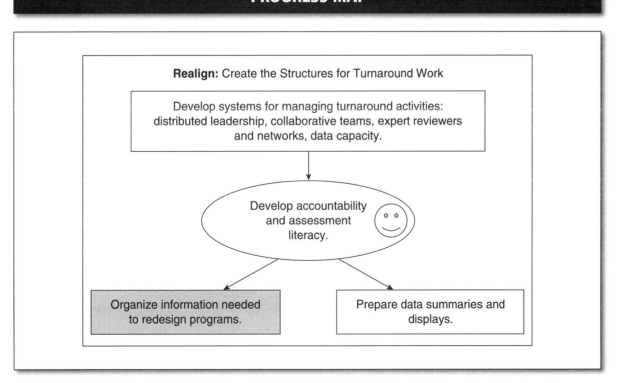

45

POCKET SUMMARY

Task	Major Activities	Purpose
Organize resources for needs assessment.	• Identify key sources of information about your instructional programs and available data on current quality.	• Analyze program-related data to identify areas needing improvement.
Create program descriptions to use in turnaround redesign.	• Catalog your programs. • Create brief program descriptions. **Tool 2.1 Program Catalog Template** **Tool 2.2 Brief Program Description Template**	• Understand the big picture to inform decision making. • Help teachers develop a shared understanding about the current instructional program.
Develop or select program quality measures.	• Create assignment review guidelines. **Tool 2. 3 Program Quality: Assignment Rigor** • Gather protocols for looking at student work (LASW). **Tool 2.4 Program Quality: Protocols for Looking at Student Work** • Develop/select classroom walk-through guidelines. **Tool 2.5 Program Quality: Classroom Walk-Through Guidelines**	• Provide a small sampling of current practice. • Encourage discussion about what changes may be needed.
Align assessments with standards-based outcomes.	• Review school and district assessments against standards to check alignment with instructional goals. **Tool 2.6 Toolkit Tutorial: Aligning Assessment to Instruction**	• Clarify teaching targets. • Communicate what is expected to both teachers and students.
Organize data needed to develop a Turnaround Plan.	• Create a data inventory. **Tool 2.7 Data Inventory Template** • Review the quality of available data. **Tool 2.8 Data Quality Evaluation Guidelines: Assessment Reliability** **Tool 2.9 Data Quality Evaluation Guidelines: Archival and Self-Report Data** **Tool 2.10 Data Quality Evaluation Guidelines: A Rubric for Evaluating Data Quality**	• Explore multiple data sources. • Inventory available student data. • Determine areas where additional data are needed. • Capture judgments about potential usefulness of available data.

ORGANIZE RESOURCES FOR NEEDS ASSESSMENT

Once your "people systems" are in place, your next step is to assemble and organize the resources you'll need to analyze the strengths and weaknesses of your current program. Before you can fix what is not working, you need to look under the hood, examine all of the engine parts, and run some diagnostic tests to better understand what in your current program is working and what's not, for whom, and why. Your analysis—or needs assessment—is the essential underpinning of your Turnaround Plan, a plan for redesigning instructional programs to better meet students' learning needs. Although educators also use the term *program* to refer to a specific set of instructional materials along with required strategies, teaching guides, and assessments (the example of Open Court comes to mind), in this book, we use the term *program* as shorthand for all the special interventions, curriculum materials, teaching strategies, student activities, assignments, and assessments that together address specific learning goals (based on standards) and produce specific outcomes (defined by tests and student performances). These are the instruments of change for your Redesign.

This second preparatory step focuses on documenting major aspects of your program as well as gathering available data to diagnose areas of strength and weakness. Here, we take an expanded view of the term *data*. Most schools see data as scores from student achievement, accountability, state assessment, district assessment, and even common grade-level or department assessments. Some even have parent and student satisfaction survey data. However, schools generally don't think of information about how well their programs are implemented as *data*. Program implementation data, or program quality data as we call them, are an important part of the data picture. Without data about program quality, you are missing a crucial part of the landscape and are blind to an important source of information about where to begin your redesign efforts. Results don't change until programs (and the people implementing them) change! Program descriptions, measures of program quality, and an inventory of all available data provide your turnaround teams with a fuller picture of the landscape.

Granted, it takes substantial time to pull together all this information. But by spending time now, you can accelerate your redesign process and avoid momentum-draining delays down the line. Turnaround work is designed to make a *quick* change in the trajectory of student achievement, from downward or flat to upward. It is resource intensive in terms of time, requires enormous emotional effort, and is stressful to participants, who must make changes in their perspectives and practice. Advance organization and availability of resources can help avert one unnecessary source of stress.

The **Chapter 2 Leader's Guide** summarizes what information needs to be collected and prepared for the next steps of your redesign work.

CREATE PROGRAM DESCRIPTIONS TO USE IN TURNAROUND REDESIGN

An important aspect of preparation for turnaround work is documentation of both the kinds and quality of curriculum and instruction currently in place at your school. The easiest way to begin is to create brief, but explicit and focused, descriptions of programs now in place. Again, we use the term *program* to refer to all of the expected activities in a particular subject and grade level. Thus, the third-grade reading program would include required textbooks, pacing charts, expected instructional strategies, time allocations, staff development related to the reading program, and, most important, the instructional goals and assessments—in short, any aspect of what teachers are expected to deliver that can be observed and perhaps revised to improve learning and achievement. If you are planning on redesigning your program, you need to know what components it contains and to identify some weak areas that could be shored up.

Catalog Your Programs

The first step in developing a deep understanding of your current program is to simply get a bird's-eye view (an eagle, not a vulture!) of your school offerings. This big-picture overview can be done relatively quickly. You will need to do a program round-up, much like the one you will need to do with your data sources. A program catalog would include all school instructional programs addressing the achievement challenges in your school. For most schools, the drama program and physical education would not be cataloged. However, for high-achieving schools with involved parents, these two programs might require attention and need "turnaround." Programs most likely to be reviewed, in addition to core courses, include the following:

- Programs for special students, such as those with disabilities
- Programs for English learners
- Behavioral intervention programs
- Short-term, targeted, remedial, catch-up, or intervention programs for students at risk of dropping out or being retained
- Programs related to school climate and safety
- Programs for family involvement or student behavior designed to support academic achievement

Tech Tip

If you can enter your program catalog into Access or Excel, you will be able to sort and group your programs by grade level, subject matter, and type. This grouping process makes it easier to identify grade-level disparities in service and other curriculum gaps or emphases.

Your program catalog allows you to put your hands on information about school curriculum and special programs quickly and provides a big-picture view of what your school offers students.

Table 2.1 shows a sample program catalog for a typical middle school. The sample catalog is limited to English language arts and mathematics. A complete catalog would include all core subjects, such as science and social studies, and might include elective programs if those areas are a focus of your data analysis and instructional improvement efforts. Once you have a listing of your major instructional programs, you are ready to create very brief program descriptions.

Table 2.1 Sample Program Inventory for English and Mathematics at a Middle School

Program Name	Grade Levels	Target Population	Subject	Text and Materials	Years in Use at Our School
Reading-Writing Remediation	6–8	Students reading below grade level; intervention during school day	Reading, writing	*Language!* Jane Fell Green Sopris West	5
Core English Language Arts	6–8	Core curriculum, grade level, all students	Reading, writing	*Language of Literature* McDougal-Littell	3
Reading Development	6–8	After-school intervention for students reading below grade level	Reading development	*Fast Track Reading* Wright Group/McGraw-Hill	3
English Language Development Levels 1–3	6–8	English learners not yet reclassified	English language development	*High Point* Alfredo Schifini Hampton Brown	4
Response to Intervention	6–8	Special education and potential special education students	All	Teacher training and school management system	Less than 1 year
Prealgebra Math	6	All students in Grade 6, students performing below grade level in Grade 7	Math	*Everyday Mathematics* University of Chicago Mathematics Project Wright Group, CTB-McGraw-Hill	2
Grade 7 Math	7	All Grade 7 students performing at grade level	Math	*California Mathematics & Algebra I: Concepts, Skills, & Problem Solving* Jack Price et al. Glencoe	3
Algebra	8	Grade 8 and accelerated students in Grades 6 and 7	Math	*Algebra* University of Chicago Mathematics Project Scott Foresman–Addison-Wesley	2
Safe and Civil Schools	6–8	All students, Grades 6–8	Behavior, safety	ParaPro, CHAMPS, Start on Time! Randy Sprick	3
Family Friendly Schools	6–8	All parents	Schoolwide	*Family Friendly Schools* Steve Constantino Inscape Publishing	3

Create Brief Program Descriptions

Why create program descriptions? Why not rely on teachers or curriculum specialists to provide oral descriptions of programs and interventions you may wish to adopt, modify, or even eliminate? In the subsequent redesign steps, you will be working with collaborative teams or the entire staff to focus your formative evaluation efforts. The focus will be, of course, on a strategy, program, intervention, or modification your school will be making to raise student achievement. Brief program descriptions serve several purposes:

- Program descriptions make it easier for staff to have a shared understanding of what a "program" entails.
- The program description specifies key outcomes, and the actions designed to reach those outcomes, so that you understand how the program is related to student results. (This is often called a *theory of action* and will be discussed more fully in Chapter 5.)
- Brief, clear descriptions make it easier to compare program costs, implementation requirements, activities, and potential outcomes.

By clarifying what teachers and students are expected to do to attain desired outcomes, a program description makes it possible to more clearly identify what exactly you expect to *cause* the improvement you seek. Conversely, if, after implementing a program or strategy, you don't have good results, your understanding of the cause-and-effect relationship between what is supposed to happen in a program and student outcomes will help you identify program weaknesses or areas to revise. Your brief descriptions might include other information, such as relative emphases of activities; for example, writing is 30% of this program, or math problem solving is 50% of this program. The complexity and length of your descriptions will depend upon the resources you have available to develop descriptions and your staff's need for explicit information in order to discuss program strengths and weaknesses knowledgably. Detail about program goals can help you understand the match between them and available assessments.

Table 2.2 displays a very brief program description containing salient information for a group wishing to understand what might have contributed to student performance on high-stakes accountability tests. It would not be enough detail to understand why students were struggling with particular skills in a particular part of the curriculum. Similar unit-level descriptions could be made by teachers to support their discussions on improving classroom instruction in specific skill areas.

**Tools
2.1 & 2.2**

Basic templates for the program catalog, **Tool 2.1, Program Catalog Template,** and the program descriptions, **Tool 2.2, Brief Program Description Template,** appear in the Toolkit for this chapter. You can customize each to fit your local turnaround efforts.

Table 2.2 Sample Brief Program Description for English Language Arts

Literature to Go	Grades 6–8 Core Program
Purpose/Goals	Develop reading strategies and comprehension and analysis skills, motivate student interest
Required Materials/Resources	Pacing guides, district benchmark assessments, embedded assessments (4)
Delivery Method	Teacher-directed, 50-minute classroom period, 5 days a week
Required Training	30 hours inservice prior to implementation, coaching for struggling teachers (modeling, mentoring, peer observation)
Major Activities	Vocabulary development, nonfiction text analysis, literary analysis, persuasive and analytic essays, grammar
Implementation Issues	Text too difficult at times for grade-level readers with little background knowledge and poor vocabulary, pacing guides move too quickly, too much material to cover in a year, embedded tests poorly constructed and not diagnostic
Data Supporting Effectiveness	State assessments indicate students read and comprehend literature adequately, write short essays well, but struggle with multiple-choice grammar items and comprehension of nonfiction

DEVELOP OR SELECT PROGRAM QUALITY MEASURES

You will need methods for evaluating the quality of instruction to help you pinpoint needed program improvements that will increase student learning and achievement. In the realignment phase of turnaround work, you will want to create or gather instruments that you can use to measure program quality. For every learning issue, there is a teaching need. Thus, you will want to be prepared to collect data about teaching as well as learning.

Look for aspects of program quality that research shows are related to student learning. Among the most important are the following:

- How well is instruction aligned to grade-level standards?
- What is the rigor of assignments?
- What is the quality of student work?
- Do students understand their learning goals? Are they engaged in learning and getting adequate feedback to meet goals?
- Are we implementing the program as intended?
- What kinds of staff development do teachers need to improve instruction?

The answers to these questions provide specific guidance for your turnaround efforts and belong in your Turnaround Plan.

Let's look at the kinds of measures that can address these questions. There are three widely used strategies that do so and provide a window into the classroom:

1. Assessing the rigor of student *assignments* (and by implication, their alignment with grade-level standards)

2. Assessing the quality of *student work*

3. Focused classroom *walk-throughs*

Create Assignment Review Guidelines

One simple strategy to determine if classroom instruction both addresses grade-level standards and demands grade-level rigor is to have teachers review their assignments against the grade-level standards. There are many possible review strategies, some holistic, some more precise, but an assignment review (like all of Gaul) has three parts:

1. Review of assignment content, topics, and task requirements

2. Determination of the kinds of student skills needed to complete the assignment satisfactorily

3. Determination of whether both the task as described and the student skills required to complete it match at least the minimum grade-level knowledge and skills specified in your grade-level state standards

Assignment review can be conducted in grade-level or department meetings. Teachers bring common assignments to review (less threatening) or assignments they feel are key indicators of grade-level standards. The group then can discuss the assignment directions, topic, stimulus materials (reading passages, assigned chapters, math problems), and scoring criteria to determine whether these match grade-level standards. Next, teachers can complete the assignment and list the kinds of skills, or even background knowledge and prerequisites, a student needs to complete the assignment acceptably. Again, a determination is made as to whether the assignment meets grade-level standards. Finally, taking both the assignment prompt and the required response, the group determines the rigor of the assignment; that is, at what grade level are the required skills and the actual topics and prompts and expected student responses? When you have teachers classify the skill and knowledge required by their assignments, you may find that students are being asked to do work below grade level, sometimes far below grade level. This is true of many textbook assignments as well as teacher-developed assignments. One of the easiest places to begin your redesign work is the revision of what teachers ask and expect of students.

Expert Help

Nearly all intermediate educational agencies—such as county offices, state departments of education, and certainly private educational consultants—have developed procedures, protocols, and checklists for evaluating the rigor and alignment of student assignments to standards. You might consider inviting an expert to lead your first review session or to conduct a "trainer of trainers" session with staff leadership. You might ask the expert to work with you on all aspects of reviewing curriculum quality— assignments, student responses, and classroom observations, as these three activities are closely related.

Perhaps the most important part of reviewing classroom assignments is creating a list of suggestions for improving their quality. Three aspects of quality are especially important:

1. The assignment should provide students with practice of important skills and knowledge (as opposed to busy work) related to mastering grade-level standards.

2. The scoring guides or grading strategies should provide students with specific feedback about how to improve their performance (no more smiley faces or letter grades without comments).

3. The scoring guides should help teachers understand the kinds of content and skills students struggle with, so that reteaching can be strategic.

A general guideline for developing assignment review sessions appears in the Toolkit: **Tool 2.3, Program Quality: Assignment Rigor.**

Tool
2.3

Gather Protocols for Looking at Student Work

Looking at student work is a practice that emerged from the school reform efforts of the National Writing Project, Coalition of Essential Schools, Annenberg Challenge, National School Reform Faculty, and myriad subject-matter professional organizations during the past 20 years. The Carnegie Report, *A Nation at Risk* (1983), set the educational world on its heels and focused national attention on addressing the problem of making schools more challenging while improving the skills of an increasing number of underprepared students. The national school reform movement of the 1990s was the incubator for the standards movement of the new millennium. Thus, many of the strategies developed during the past two decades have continued to be used to this day. Looking at Student Work (abbreviated as LASW) is a commonly employed term for the practice of teachers discussing the kinds of learning problems that surface in assignments or assessments that require a student-constructed response.

Before you select a collaborative LASW protocol, consider the following questions, each of which will help you more clearly define why you are looking at student work and what you expect teachers to learn from the process.

1. What is the purpose of the particular LASW session I am planning? What kinds of review questions do I want teachers to address? Select a strategy, set of questions, or formal protocol based on the purpose of the session. **Tool 2.4, Program Quality: Protocols for Looking at Student Work,** provides a selection of protocols designed for different purposes.

Tool
2.4

2. Do we want a course- or subject-specific review strategy, or a generic strategy that can apply to any assignment type or subject matter?

3. If we need to identify student learning problems that are specific to a particular subject, might we find LASW protocols on websites specializing in that subject (e.g., history, science, mathematics, art, etc.)? If not,

should we hire a subject-matter expert to help us create a review strategy that will reveal subject-matter-specific learning issues?

4. What kinds of training or familiarization should teachers have before scoring and discussing student work? Do they need an explanation of the scoring guide or rating criteria? Do they need sample papers for all score points?

5. What kinds of student work samples should be reviewed? Examples that are "typical" of a class or grade level? Examples of poor performance, stellar examples, a range of examples?

The steps in LASW resemble those in reviewing the rigor of teacher assignments, but the focus is not on the task but on the student response and what it says about learning needs and improving teaching practice. Student work protocols include the following steps:

- Understand the assignment—Read the assignment and scoring guide and discuss what skills and knowledge students need to meet standards (as defined by the scoring criteria). Sometimes teachers actually do the assignment, much as they did in reviewing assignment rigor, and score their own papers to better understand the student performance expectations.
- Understand the range of student responses—Read student responses representing a range of performance from abysmal to stellar, perhaps applying the scoring guide to rate the work.
- Catalog the learning issues surfacing in the work—Discuss what makes a poor response fall short, an adequate response acceptable, and an exemplary response grab the reader's attention. List the kinds of skills that need to be developed from the examples of the low performers and how average and even above-average papers could be improved.
- Brainstorm teaching strategies to address the learning issues surfacing in the student work.

Time spent reviewing student work has several payoffs for developing Turnaround Plans. First, teachers find the process less threatening than having the rigor of their assignments reviewed. Second, examples of student performance provide teachers with concrete evidence of learning difficulties and serve as a springboard for discussing how to improve or change teaching practice. Finally, the practice of LASW helps teachers to become comfortable with sharing their practice, asking for advice, and understanding that they are part of a larger community of professionals all dedicated to helping each other and their students get better results.

We move from one of the least threatening reviews of program quality, student work review, to one of the most focused classroom visitations or the classroom walk-through.

Develop/Select Classroom Walk-Through Guidelines

The classroom walk-through has been used extensively in conjunction with professional learning communities' work and in school reform implementation, and as a way to collect information about what aspects of teaching need better support. Walk-throughs have different purposes; however, in turnaround work, the purpose is to identify areas of program implementation that need fine-tuning or revision. This narrow focus on gathering formative data means that your turnaround teams will not be using the walk-through process for teacher evaluation, principal or department chair supervision, or summative judgments about school quality. The walk-through should not set off alarm bells with union representatives. Done well, it is collegial and nonthreatening, and it provides concrete information for deciding how well program implementation is proceeding and what midcourse corrections could be made.

So what is a walk-through? It's a brief, focused classroom visit by a small team of teachers, of teachers and administrators, or perhaps of members of your expert review group and teachers, for the purpose of observing how particular program activities "look." Classroom walk-throughs are used to determine whether essential elements of a program are occurring and/or whether a program change—perhaps a change in the percentage of time spent in student engagement or lesson delivery—is taking hold or being implemented as planned, or even how teachers have adapted the element or change to better fit their particular student populations.

Walk-throughs share a structure similar to that of all collaborative program quality measures. The walk-through plan has four major parts:

Expert Help

We recommend that unless your turnaround team includes staff experienced in leading classroom walk-throughs, you involve a central office, local service agency, or experienced consultant to help you plan and conduct your first two or three reviews. An expert can help you navigate the most difficult aspects of visiting classrooms: setting a clear focus, debriefing with objective (not judgmental) language, and creating next steps.

1. A preparation time to familiarize participants with the process and to establish the instructional focus

2. A pre–walk-through meeting on walk-through day to brief participants on focus, observation ground rules, visit time, and debriefing time

3. Brief, 10- to 20-minute classroom visits

4. A final debrief where the information gathered is listed and implications for program practice discussed

We provide more specific information about each walk-through step in **Tool 2.5, Program Quality: Classroom Walk-Through Guidelines.** However, as you determine when and for what purposes you will schedule classroom visits, you may need to consider the following kinds of strategy and policy questions that address major issues related to opening up the classroom to other professionals:

Tool
2.5

1. Should we conduct walk-throughs on our current program to use in our redesign planning?

2. Which aspects of the redesigned program are best monitored through classroom visits?

3. How much training does staff need, and who is best to lead it?

4. How will we know that we have a safe enough environment to have collegial observations?

5. What is the best way to deal with teacher concerns related to classroom observations and discussion of practice?

Align Assessments With Standards-Based Outcomes

We finally come to student assessment data, the central information used in determining what needs redesign. When most educators hear the word *data*, they think immediately of test scores. However, we ask that you develop a deeper understanding about what assessment data does and does *not* tell you.

There are numerous kinds and levels of assessments. Schools governed by federal accountability laws have the results of accountability assessments created by the state; these are high-stakes tests, scored offsite, that have standard reporting formats for all schools and students. Many districts have created required "benchmark," "periodic," "quarterly," or end-of-semester exams that all schools are required to administer as a way of monitoring student progress on state standards, identifying students in need of intervention and support, and even evaluating their programs. Some schools have developed "common assessments"—assessments that all teachers in a subject or grade level administer at prespecified times to monitor student progress toward meeting grade-level standards or students' readiness for the state or district assessments, as well as for diagnosing student needs and revising instruction. Finally, individual teachers select or create classroom assessments to use in grading and grouping and to provide formative feedback for both students and instruction.

The problem with all of the kinds of assessments teachers may be required or choose to use is that the results don't always give us a clear understanding of what exactly we can say about student mastery of standards. Of course, the score may tell us the student is "proficient." But exactly what does "proficient" mean in a subject that may encompass 27 different vaguely worded standards? The state assessments operationalize the grade-level standards. The kind of content selected, the number of items allocated to each different skill, and even the item formats define what it means when we say, "The student is proficient in Grade 7 Mathematics." If we were to administer a different test with different content emphases, different item formats, and item formats requiring different skills, the student might or might not be shown to be "proficient."

Here's an example from a middle school math standard: Students should be able to find the area of a triangle. We have a lot of latitude in how we operationalize the standard. Figure 2.1 presents four strategies for assessing student understanding of the geometric concept of area, each with a different item type and context. Decide which best defines the expected learning in the standard.

The best assessment, item format, or strategy, of course, is the one that best matches grade-level instruction and related mathematics standards. Any of the four item types could be used, but depending upon which is used, you will have a different interpretation of what your students know

Figure 2.1	Four Approaches to Assessing the Standard: Understanding Area of a Triangle

---

STANDARD: AREA OF A TRIANGLE

Item Type 1. Multiple Choice

Find the area of a triangle with a base of 6 and a height of 5.

- A. 11
- B. 30
- C. 15
- D. Cannot be determined from the information given

Item Type 2. Explain Your Thinking

Find the area of a triangle with a base of 10 feet and a height of 20 feet. Show your work, and explain your reasoning at each step of the way.

Item Type 3. Complex Relationships

What is the area of an equilateral triangle inscribed in a circle with a radius of 6?

Item Type 4. Problem Embedded in a Real-Life Situation

Sam has a rectangular garden. The north and south boundaries each measure 10 feet. The east and west boundaries each measure 6 feet. Sam decides to plant half the garden, so he stakes out a diagonal border bisecting the rectangle. What is the area left for planting?

---

and are able to do with the concept of "area of a triangle." While this example may be a bit extreme, it makes the point that until you know something about item formats, the difficulty of the test language and other "distractor" information, and the test content sampling of the standard, you really can't interpret the student scores in a way that informs instruction.

You may have access to sample items and a test sampling plan (blueprint) for your state assessment. This is a good place to begin understanding what student scores on the accountability assessment mean. However, it is quite likely that there is no descriptive information about how your district, school, or even textbook-related tests were developed. You really don't know if item format issues, test language, and even content sampling were considered when the tests were developed. We recommend that your data team, or perhaps district content specialists, develop operational definitions of the content standard that can guide test item selection for classroom assessments or test development for your school or district. These descriptions are called either *test specifications* or *domain descriptions* and are intended to make clear to teachers exactly what each standard means in terms of specific grade-level content and skill. We have included a brief tutorial on the creation and use of domain descriptions in **Tool 2.6, Toolkit Tutorial: Aligning Assessment to Instruction.**

Once you have an understanding of how grade-level standards are operationalized in your accountability, district, school, and classroom assessments, you can work on the alignment issue. Alignment is simply a

Tool
2.6

term that means "lined up," "in line with," or "having a shared view-point." How closely should your district, school, and classroom tests mirror the accountability assessment? Each other? The standards? These are alignment decisions you will need to make about the tests you currently use and new ones you may develop or purchase.

First, as you can see from our mathematics example, one standard can be defined in multiple ways. How your teachers interpret the standard when preparing classroom assessments may differ greatly from how the corporation that publishes your state test defines the standard (especially if the corporation must publish psychometric data, such as reliability and validity studies, that require a nearly normal distribution of scores to be technically adequate). You need to rely on the descriptive information provided by your state to get a better understanding of what each standard "means" for accountability purposes. However, you should also consider that alignment to standards means more than simply having your assessments look like the state test. There is much that cannot be assessed on a paper-and-pencil assessment. Some of the most important interpretations of the grade-level standards require writing, demonstrations, projects, affective measures, and other assessment approaches. Your task in aligning the assessments you must use for instructional decisions is simply to determine what kind of decision you need and whether you have the descriptive information necessary to make an informed use of the test results. Table 2.3 provides some guidelines for determining the alignment method needed for your assessments.

Your goal in reviewing how well the assessments you use are aligned to state standards is to understand curricular emphases, the match of the language used on the test to that used during instruction, and why perhaps your students are successful on classroom and school-level assessments but fall short on the accountability test. An example of the kinds of alignment issues you could encounter include the following problems that your colleagues have actually encountered:

- The reading items on the state accountability test ask students to read excerpts from two different genres, such as a diary and a fictional account, or a newspaper article and a firsthand biography, and then answer questions comparing viewpoints from the two passages. But most classroom teachers do not ask students to analyze two or more genres on the same topic.
- Items reported as measuring "literary response and analysis" are often linked to informational text passages. But in class, teachers use samples from fiction when asking questions about theme, language use, and the like, which are more commonly associated with analysis of fiction.
- Mathematics "word problems" use formal language from the mathematics text or an unusual amount of narration, which students must deconstruct in order to set up a problem to solve. In class, students have practiced multiple types of math word problems but not the formal language of the discipline.
- Items said to test "writing strategies" are in fact multiple-choice items asking students to choose grammatically or stylistically correct ways to complete a sentence. But in class, teachers have asked students to write, rather than to analyze, written sentences for whether they adhere to the rules of Strunk and White (1999).

Table 2.3 Alignment Activities for Different Kinds of Assessments

Test Type/Alignment Activity	Test mirrors state test item formats and content sampling plan	Test emphasizes important content not tested at state level	Test correlates highly with (predicts) state test results or predicts student performance from one grade to the next	Test includes prerequisite skills for diagnosis and interventions
State Accountability Test			x	
District End-of-Semester or Course Test	x		x	
District/School End-of-Unit or Quarterly Tests		x		
School Common Assessments		x		x
Classroom Assessments / Formative Assessments		x		x

Don't be ambushed. Understand what your accountability tests measure, how items are posed, and how these can differ from how the material is taught.

You *do not* want your entire assessment system to be practice for or to replicate the accountability tests. However, you do want to understand the link between your instruction, local assessments, and the "public definition" of the standard embodied in the state system. You can and will choose to assess content and skills not emphasized by the state. You certainly will use different item formats. However, if you have no link between the kinds of assessments your students take regularly and the kinds they encounter yearly (or must pass to graduate), you will want to revise and align some of your local assessments as part of your turnaround work.

ORGANIZE DATA NEEDED TO DEVELOP A TURNAROUND PLAN

After you have your program descriptions and program quality measures and have considered (and hopefully improved) the alignment of your tests to important standards, you can turn to completing your data inventory with some understanding of what the data do and do not tell you about student mastery of grade-level standards.

By this point, you have probably noted that we consider a variety of information sources, not just assessment results, to be useful data for turnaround work: program descriptions, assignments, student work samples, classroom observations. Any information about your student outcomes—academic, behavioral, or attitudinal; school climate; parent preferences; and satisfaction—parent, student, and teacher—are also important indicators of what is working well and what needs changing. So before we begin to "summarize data," we ask you to think broadly about the kinds of information you may have available (and by extension, what you don't have and would like to obtain) to summarize during your redesign activities. We ask you to go on a data hunt and to list your found data on a data inventory. The data inventory speeds up your data review, because you have at your fingertips a guide to all the information you can summarize, to the information you do not have but may need, and as a bonus a note about the quality of the information so that you can shore up weak data sources with additional information.

Tech Tip

We recommend that you document your data sources and store the documentation electronically for future evaluation work. We like Access or Excel, or a similar spreadsheet-database application, because these programs allow you to sort information on selected columns (variables). You can quickly organize your data sources by important variables of interest such as grade level, subject, or date.

Create a Data Inventory

Err on the side of inclusion. What information do you have about your students, programs, and correlates of student achievement (last year's results, ethnicity, program type, years in school, etc.)? Where is this information stored? How can you get it? What is the quality of available data? Some of the information you have will be useful; some less so. However, at this point it is too early to know exactly what you can ignore.

We provide a sample data inventory containing only formal assessments in Table 2.4. A complete data inventory template appears in the Toolkit: **Tool 2.7, Data Inventory Template.**

Tool
2.7

Review the Quality of Available Data

You will notice that in addition to listing which data you have available to address which questions and where it is located, we have asked you to indicate the quality of the available data (see the shaded column in Table 2.4). Data quality directly affects the usefulness of your information. Your notes about data quality also will indicate areas where you will want to collect better information, collect missing information, or use additional information to help you make better decisions.

Expert Help

An expert from your review panel could help assess the strengths and weaknesses of each data source available to you. As you prepare your data inventory, you might consider including someone from your panel to educate your data team on the best use of available data as well as its limitations. An expert can also help you improve tests and surveys created at the school (or district) level.

High-quality data are data that result in accurate decisions. Since you won't know if your data-guided decisions are correct until you have observed the results of your work, the best you can do to ensure accuracy is to examine what you know about the information at hand, note the areas were you have evidence that your data are credible, and note the areas where you may be uncertain about their accuracy.

Table 2.4 Sample Data Inventory for Formal Assessments

Data Source	Quality	Purpose	Subject(s)	Grade Level(s)	Respondents	Date Administered	Where Kept
State Accountability Test	High	Identify failing schools	Reading Math Science History	3–8, once in high school	Students in Grades 3–8	Testing window	District student information system, online reporting system
State Content Assessment	High	Monitor mastery of state standards	Reading Math Science History	K–12	All students in all grades, every year	May–June	District student information system
High School Graduation Test	High	Certify students for high school graduation	English Math	9–12	All students in Grade 9; repeaters in Grades 10–12	December, March, May	District student information system
ACT Plan	High	Identify skills students need to be ready for college	English Math		All middle school students		
PSAT	Moderate Not match our population	Identify AP potential	English Math	9 or 10	Volunteers not in honors classes	November	District student information system
District Benchmarks	Unknown	Let teachers know if students are on track to meet state standards	Which subjects?	Which grades?	Which students must take these tests? Voluntary or required? Special education students? English learners?	Testing window	District student information system, online reporting system
Department/ Grade Common Assessment	Poor but able to collect information from teachers so scores never used alone	To provide diagnostic information and monitor progress toward meeting state standards	Which subjects?	Which grades?	Which students must take these tests? Voluntary or required? Special education students? English learners?	Testing window	District student information system, online reporting system Hard copy at sites? Individual classrooms?

In technical terms, you are examining the reliability, validity, and utility of your available information.

Data Reliability

Reliability is an indication of how consistently an assessment measures its intended target and of the extent to which scores are relatively free of error. If a measure is reliable, the items composing it cohere around something stable, and you get essentially the same result regardless of when or where it is given or who does the scoring. Depending upon the kind of data you will use and how you plan to use it, you will need to look for different kinds of reliability information. **Tool 2.8, Data Quality Evaluation Guidelines: Assessment Reliability,** provides guidelines for selecting the appropriate kind of reliability information for specific decisions. Why is reliability important? If your school climate survey is reliable, you would get pretty much the same school ratings next month as you did this month. Otherwise, the results may be as much a function of when the survey is administered as of how respondents feel about school climate. If your test scores are reliable, students would score just about the same regardless of whether they were tested in the morning or the afternoon, this week or next (without intervening instruction, of course), and regardless of who scores the data. If your suspension and expulsion data are reliable, you would make the same decisions about "bad" student behavior in a month as you did when those kids were suspended. And different administrators would decide that suspension is appropriate were they to judge the noted offenses. If your dropout data are reliable, you are consistent in how you count students who have dropped out of school, and the data don't contain duplicate ID numbers or other errors. If your data are not reliable, you have no confidence that your test or survey results provide accurate or useful information.

Tool
2.8

Data Validity

Valid assessments are those that do in fact measure what they claim to measure and provide sound information for decision making. If your parent surveys about school climate are valid, then the results give you an accurate picture of important aspects of school climate as parents perceive them. The meaning is unambiguous. Questions allow for honest answers (are not leading, don't telegraph the socially desirable response). If your dropout data are valid, the missing students have indeed dropped out of school; they haven't moved away and enrolled in another school. If your test scores are valid for determining proficiency, the test actually addresses the standards expected for proficiency, and students who did well on the test really have mastered the standards and are ready to move on, while those who do poorly are not. If your test scores are valid for diagnosing the skills students need to attain the standard, the test must not only address the standards but also provide reliable diagnostic information about the strengths and weaknesses of students' skill development. You get the idea! The key validity concern is the match between the information provided by a measure and what we want to know.

Validity depends on the purpose for which you want to use a test. You could purchase a test that provides "validity coefficients" correlating student scores to some desired criterion, such as success in algebra. However, just because the student sample upon which this coefficient was calculated yielded high correlations (at least .80 or above), it doesn't mean that the test addresses the important prerequisite skills for success in *your* algebra course or that your students who score high on this algebra predictor test will do well in algebra. You should always look at what the test is supposed to measure, its alignment with your curriculum and learning goals, and collect data on student performances you wish to use for prediction purposes, and then calculate your own correlation coefficients. This is a simple operation with Excel. A student can do it! Your local results might be different. If you find that locally the algebra success prediction is higher than the one given in the test manual, that's useful information. If you find that the correlation is low and rather unpredictable from year to year, you know the algebra predictor test is not a predictor for your school! The information contained in test manuals is always based on the sample taking the trial edition of the test. It will be different for your students. If it's wildly different, the test (or your school programs) may need to be replaced.

Data Utility

The third dimension of data quality is the utility of the data. Just how useful is this information? If parents give consistently high ratings to everything in your school program, you aren't getting much information from a parent survey. It's good public relations and feels great, but you don't have much to act on in your quest for improving your school. You might have to design a different kind of survey or solicit feedback via interviews, where you can ask probing questions. If the state test scores, which are reliable and valid for determining student standards mastery, don't provide you with diagnostic information, they aren't useful at the classroom level. You will need additional information for instructional planning. Again, there is no one piece of data that will tell you all you need to know for multiple purposes (despite the claims of the test publisher). Your experience using the data will augment test scores and make individual data sources more useful.

Never abandon the quest for corroboration and elaboration when it comes to information. There are two important test characteristics that increase score utility for classroom decisions: First, the test is aligned to grade-level standards, and second, teachers have clear descriptions of the content, skills, and item types (because specific item types require skills apart from mastery of particular content) so that they can make decisions about mastery of specific skills. The more specific the skill descriptions and student reports, the more useful the data become for reteaching, grouping, and intervention decisions.

We feel the use of brief test specifications improves the usefulness of test scores. A brief specification is a document used to guide the development of test items and would include the following:

- A description of the content areas or topics being tested
- A description of the skills students will be asked to apply or demonstrate

- A sample item or two to provide insight into item format
- Guidelines for writing multiple-choice items and distractors

Table 2.5 presents one small section of the test specifications created by one district for the development of their high school end-of-course English tests in Grade 9. Notice how the specification clarifies the teaching target, provides multiple strategies for assessing the target, and presents sample items from the state assessment so that teachers understand item formats, kinds of text used, and the complexity of the language used on state items.

Table 2.5	Sample Test Specification for a High School English Standard: Structural Features of Informational Material

Substrand	Explanation	Example Items
Structural Features of Informational Material **Standard 2.1** Analyze the structure and format of functional workplace documents, including the graphics and headers, and explain how authors use the features to achieve their purposes.	*Literal Comprehension.* Students identify and use the structural features of functional texts (employee handbooks, forms, advertisements, technical directions, signs, order blanks, bulletins, labels, schedules) as aids to interpreting text. Students use explicit and implicit evidence to draw conclusions about the relationships between structural features and organization and the meaning that the author is attempting to convey. **Eligible Content and Assessment Objectives** Passages likely to be used are employee handbooks or other workplace documents (but may also include school reports, newsletters, instructional manuals, etc.). Students demonstrate proficiency by their ability to: • Identify and compare structural aspects (chapter headings, table of contents, title, byline, subheadings, graphic images, etc.) of different types of informational materials *(incl: placement of title[s]; line spacing, headers or footers [e.g., page number, etc.]; font size and type; table of contents; headings and subheadings; diagrams/charts; index)* • Identify and compare purposes (to persuade, entertain, inform, contradict, instruct, etc.) of different types of informational materials	1. The instructions from the owner's manual are clear because the writer used • Simplified language • Graphic images • Charts and graphs • A paragraph structure 2. What type of additional information should be included in the heading of Geno's report on wildflowers? • His teacher's name • His own name • The due date of the assignment • The name of the class 3. At what point in the process of assembling a piece of furniture would you be most likely to examine the picture? (Students select from various stages in the process of assembly.) 4. What is the major difference between the instructions for assembly and the warranty on the furniture? (Students identify types of information contained in each, e.g., they choose between responses that focus on procedures and responses that focus on quality of furniture.) 5. Which of the following is LEAST likely to be included in the "Problem Solving and Repairs" section of the owner's manual? (Students select from various topics that are more or less likely to be in that section.)

Substrand	Explanation	Example Items

	• Effectively using graphic organizers to locate, clarify, understand, or organize information (timelines, flowcharts, webs, illustrations, tables of contents, indexes, glossaries, headings, graphs, charts, diagrams, tables, etc.). For example:
	  ○ Use headings to locate where needed information is likely to be found.
	  ○ Use tables of contents and indexes to locate specific information.
	  ○ Use graphics to clarify information.
	• Explain or draw conclusions about the relationship between the structure and format of materials and the author's purpose.
		6. The advertisement convinces customers to buy the product by —— (e.g., using medical terms to lend legitimacy).
		
		High School Exit Released Item
		(12) [instructions for creating Internet password] The two boxes included at the end of the document illustrate information that is primarily found in which two paragraphs? (e.g., paragraphs 1 and 2, 3 and 4, etc.)
		
		High School Exit Released Item
		(26) [employee manual for video store] What is the order in which new movies are moved through the store? (Students choose from responses describing inventory control procedures.)

Sources: Content in left-hand and middle columns is from California Department of Education (2009). Content in right-hand column is from Long Beach Unified School District.

Imperfect Data

No data source can be perfectly reliable, valid, or useful. All data should be used in conjunction with other evidence to corroborate inferences about student achievement or programs. For example, when you examine student essay performance and see many grammatical errors, do you have data from multiple-choice grammar tests that might indicate whether students know the grammar rules but can't apply them? If you do, your instruction can work on applying the rules rather than begin with introduction of the grammar concepts themselves. You also know that student writing performance varies greatly by topic familiarity and genre. Before you decide "students can't write," you will want samples with multiple topics within a genre and across genres. Performance data are notoriously specific to topics and test occasions; they are imperfect, or as the psychometrician would say, "unreliable."

How can you rate data quality for your various data sources? Your data quality judgments are just that: judgments. You may be more confident about the quality of some information than other information. Being uncertain is fine. In fact, it means that you are developing the habits of a good researcher. If your data are of unknown or even poor quality, that doesn't mean they are useless. Data of unknown quality are data for which you have no evidence that students would obtain the same or similar results on a different occasion, and for which you have no evidence that they actually relate to something important (usually a correlation between that particular measure and another measure or observed performance). Again, these are data lacking formal reliability and validity information. You will simply keep in mind the limitations of the data and either not give much weight to them, find a better method of measuring the construct that currently is poorly measured, or collect additional information to support your inferences.

Tools
2.9 & 2.10

Self-report data, surveys, interviews, and some kinds of performance assessments fall into the "imperfect" category. You can use **Tool 2.9, Data Quality Evaluation Guidelines: Archival and Self-Report Data,** to help bolster confidence in some of your less formal data. **Tool 2.10, Data Quality Evaluation Guidelines: A Rubric for Evaluating Data Quality,** provides informal guidelines for judging data quality; you can use these to evaluate the quality of data in your data inventory.

Summary and One Last Realignment Task Ahead

We have now completed putting our documents in order, creating structures for collaborating on turnaround work, and herding our data into the data corral. Our last preparatory task is really *the first task in using data to make decisions about program redesign:* preparing data summaries and displays. By the time you have reached this stage in preparing for turnaround work, you have already accomplished crucial tasks to support program redesign: You've built the foundation for a formative evaluation and revision process and for changing how your school views teaching and learning. The investment in preparation is one that, once made, operates as a sort of perpetual motion machine (or continuous improvement process) to nudge you forward in improving student achievement.

CHAPTER 2 TOOLKIT

ORGANIZE INFORMATION NEEDED TO REDESIGN PROGRAMS

The Tools for Chapter 2 can be found on the companion website for *The TurnAround ToolKit* at http://www.corwin.com/turnaroundtoolkit.

Tool 2.1   Program Catalog Template

Tool 2.2   Brief Program Description Template

Tool 2.3   Program Quality: Assignment Rigor

Tool 2.4   Program Quality: Protocols for Looking at Student Work

Tool 2.5   Program Quality: Classroom Walk-Through Guidelines

Tool 2.6   Toolkit Tutorial: Aligning Assessment to Instruction

Tool 2.7   Data Inventory Template

Tool 2.8   Data Quality Evaluation Guidelines: Assessment Reliability

Tool 2.9   Data Quality Evaluation Guidelines: Archival and Self-Report Data

Tool 2.10   Data Quality Evaluation Guidelines: A Rubric for Evaluating Data Quality

3

Prepare Data Summaries and Displays

If you do not ask the right questions, you do not get the right answers. A question asked in the right way often points to its own answer. Asking questions is the A-B-C of diagnosis. Only the inquiring mind solves problems.

—Edward Hodnett, British Poet, 1871–1962

PROGRESS MAP

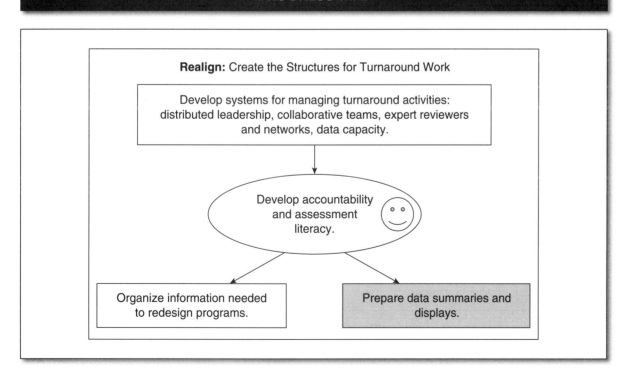

Realign: Create the Structures for Turnaround Work

Develop systems for managing turnaround activities: distributed leadership, collaborative teams, expert reviewers and networks, data capacity.

Develop accountability and assessment literacy.

Organize information needed to redesign programs.

Prepare data summaries and displays.

POCKET SUMMARY

Task	Major Activities	Purpose
Identify data review questions.	• Questions drive interpretation. • Begin with questions about student outcomes. **Tool 3.1 Data Review Questions for Identifying Instructional Focus Areas** • Consider a range of program questions to create your Turnaround Plan. **Tool 3.2 Needs Assessment Questions for Identifying the Turnaround Focus**	• Identify questions to guide data selection and interpretation.
Use data inventory to identify data needed to answer program redesign questions.	• Find data sources in your data inventory to address each question. • Keep a list of important questions for which you lack data to use in the formative evaluation of your Turnaround Plan.	• Develop a reference to help you find data when needed.
Prepare tables and graphs from published reports.	• Keep in mind the questions each table or graph will address. • Begin with published reports. • Break up published information into bite-sized summaries. • Prepare explanations for complex data tables. • Keep displays simple. **Tool 3.3 Table and Graph Considerations: Student Performance** **Tool 3.4 Table and Graph Considerations: Achievement Gap Analysis** **Tool 3.5 Table and Graph Considerations: Important Comparisons**	• Develop model reports for your own data by reviewing state reports. • Develop tables and displays that tell a story and are easy to interpret.
Summarize local data.	• Select an appropriate score to summarize local test data. • Summarize survey data to best answer your needs assessment questions.	• Avoid data distortions that can lead to faulty interpretation.

IDENTIFY DATA REVIEW QUESTIONS

Questions drive interpretation. Data can be like dead fish. They pile up and begin to perfume the air after a period of time. While data don't emit a pungent smell, they certainly can evoke a queasy, visceral response akin to the one we get strolling past the fish market. When we look at the ever-growing stacks and stacks of reports or data from parent surveys, student tests, and teacher grade reports piling up on our desks, in a closet, or in the file cabinet, we may begin to ruminate in a manner that resembles the following internal monologue:

> **Me to self:** Look at all that paper. Look at all those reports. And more coming in all the time. I know I should do something with them, but exactly what?
>
> Do I really understand what these reports are saying? Do I even agree with what they are saying? If the data are useful, then why don't they speak to me clearly? What story are the pages of mind-numbing tables attempting to tell? And how about those spiffy 3-D graphs? They look so appealing, but what do they indicate?
>
> Uh-oh, I just found the results of our school's department quarterly assessments. No one has summarized them, and I certainly don't have time. But if we don't do something with them, teachers will think the tests are a waste of time. And rightly so! But I have a real job to do, and it requires me to work with teachers and students, not sit in my office and be an accountant. Where should I begin?

It's a truism of psychology that people should trust their instincts, and many of us have an instinctual response to data that says, "I am not sure how useful this information is. There's a lot of it. It's nicely packaged and reported by experts, but my gut says I need to approach this stuff with caution."

Our mixed feelings about data are well founded. The data alone can be nearly useless, because data alone, like dead fish, have no life. They have meaning only in terms of the research *questions they may help us to address*. All data you receive were collected with a specific purpose in mind and to answer specific questions. Table 3.1 presents some of the common questions that can be answered by information administrators and teachers receive on a regular basis. When you receive the reports, however, the questions are often omitted, as is a discussion of how well the data answered the questions and what the limitations were on the findings. As you skim Table 3.1, start with the third column, "Type of Report," and ask yourself, is it clear how to use these results? Then look at the first column, "Question Guiding Data Collection." Did you have an "aha" moment? Do the reports seem less daunting, more focused, and more useful?

We hope our revelation that data are linked to questions and do not have a raison d'etre apart from the questions they can help to answer will help you see your daunting data depository in a new light. If you

Table 3.1	Typical Questions Implicit in the Collection of Commonly Reported School Data	

Question Guiding Data Collection	Data Source (Measure)	Type of Report
What percentage of students is meeting state standards?	State accountability test	Percentage of students scoring Proficient and above on test
What do we know about the students who are not meeting standards? Are there inequities in the performance of different racial, language, or socioeconomic groups? Are there program differences?	State accountability test	Percentage of students scoring Proficient and above sorted by ethnic, economic, gender, or program (English learner, special education) subgroup
Students may do well at this school, but are they actually competitive with their peers? How are our students doing compared to similar students in the state? Compared to those in schools serving similar students?	National norm-referenced test State accountability test	Percentile rank of our students in a national norm group or special norm group (high socioeconomic schools, Catholic schools, etc.) Similar schools' rank Percentage of students scoring Proficient and above at our school with comparable percentage at a demographically similar school
My students are struggling; what do they need to know before they can do grade-level work?	Locally developed or selected test designed to measure specific standards and having enough items per skill to provide diagnostic information	Percentage of students in my class answering each set of items related to a specific skill correctly
What can we do to increase parent involvement in this school?	Parent survey providing involvement opportunities and listing ways to overcome barriers to involvement (meetings scheduled after work, transportation provided, etc.)	Bar graphs showing percentage of parents marking agreement for each survey question

approach your existing reports and other data with a good sense of the questions that you need answered, you can quickly determine which of the data you have accumulated should be used and which should be bypassed. Arming yourself with data review questions allows you to cut through stacks of information and capture the true meaning of each report. What began with a question must be understood with a question. Keeping the secret of the underlying question in mind, we begin our work of preparing data summaries and displays by considering the set of questions we want those summaries and displays to address.[1]

The data summaries and displays you create as you read this chapter will be used by your school turnaround teams in Section II to create your Turnaround Plan. The first set of data summaries involves the analysis of student outcomes to identify a primary area of instructional focus for your Turnaround Plan; this is the focus of Chapter 4. Once you have identified this instructional focus, Chapter 5 will take you through the process of delving deeper into your data to diagnose current program strengths and weaknesses in the focal area. The program changes needed to address identified weaknesses will be the specific target of your Turnaround Plan. Remember, when we talk about "programs," we refer to all aspects of schooling—curriculum, instructional materials, instructional strategies, staff capacity, technology, school climate, parent support, and so forth—that contribute to student learning and the improvement of student performance.

By knowing in advance the questions you need to answer to identify the elements of your Turnaround Plan, you can create better and more useful summaries and displays. There's an additional incentive for spending quality time identifying data review questions and preparing data summaries. You will use these same procedures to summarize the data you collect while monitoring and revising your turnaround activities, which we describe in Section III.

Begin With Questions About Student Outcomes

Always begin data preparation with accountability and other high-stakes student achievement data before moving to local and other outcome data. Let's discover what is broken, generate hypotheses as to how we can fix it, and then move on to identifying program repairs for our Turnaround Plan. As we have noted, data summaries and displays are more useful if they are constructed to answer a few important questions. Table 3.2, which presents frequently asked questions about student outcomes, also is reproduced in **Tool 3.1, Data Review Questions for Identifying Instructional Focus Areas.**

Tool
3.1

You will notice that Table 3.2 organizes questions by assessment type first and then by the kind of question each assessment can address. You can use the table in two ways: (1) to generate questions that you may want to answer or (2) to identify what types of assessments can answer specific questions. For example, if we wish to identify achievement

Table 3.2   Data Review Questions for Identifying Instructional Focus Areas

Student Outcomes: Accountability and High-Stakes Assessments	
• **Trends:** In which areas have we improved over the last 3 to 5 years? Maintained? Declined? • **Content and Grade-Level Patterns:** Are there performance differences by content or grade level? • **Benchmark Comparisons:** How do we compare with our benchmark schools in achievement patterns, content and grade-level patterns, and subgroup patterns? • **Politically Important Targets:** How do we compare with target criteria such as the state standard, the highest-performing schools in the state, and schools serving similar students in terms of subject, grade-level, and subgroup patterns? • **Subgroup Patterns:** Within content for each grade level, are there performance differences by important subgroups: English learners, special education students, gifted students, significant ethnic groups, economically disadvantaged students, students new to the school, students from particular feeder schools?	

Student Outcomes—Local and School-Level Common Assessments	Student Outcomes—Other Valued Outcome Indicators
• **Pinpointing Specific Achievement Patterns:** Do results show differences by content, grade level, or subgroup, particularly for politically important targets? Are patterns similar to those in the accountability and high-stakes assessments? • **Identifying Areas of Weakness:** From areas identified as weak in accountability assessments, what specific content, skills, subgroups, or grades are causing us to miss targets or not improve?	• **Dropouts:** How do our *dropout rates* compare over time with those of benchmark schools, the state, and other politically important targets? • **Quality of Preparation:** How does our percentage of students graduating *prepared for college or the next level* (reading fluently, entering Grade 1 prepared, etc.) compare over time to those of benchmark schools and to target criteria? • **Achievement Gap:** Has there been a change in the size of our *achievement gap* between traditionally high-achieving groups and traditionally "left behind" groups? • **Title III Targets:** How are our *English-learner reclassification* rates trending over time, and how do they compare to those benchmark schools? To state targets?

patterns on specific skills, we likely would use a local assessment, because state assessments rarely provide reliable data on specific skill areas. We would then review data organized to address one or more of the following questions:

- What are the trends in content area performance on state or district assessments over time? Is performance in each area improving, remaining flat, or declining?
- Are there some content areas where performance is significantly above or below expectations?

- Are there some grade levels where performance is significantly above or below expectations? Or significantly above or below that of other grades?
- Do some subgroups perform significantly above or below the grade-level average?
- How well are students performing on politically important targets, that is, targets that are particularly important for our school, parents, and the community?

Use the table to identify or inspire the questions you will use in your data review.

Consider a Range of Program Questions to Create Your Turnaround Plan

Once you have used student outcome data to identify the instructional focus for your turnaround, you will need to examine all aspects of your school program that could contribute to improving student results in that area. Again, we use the term *instructional program* in its broadest sense: curriculum, instruction, staff, school climate, and parents and community. Your programs connect to all of these areas, and it's possible that your redesign work will result in a Turnaround Plan that addresses staff development, student behavior change, and parent participation, as well as specific strategies in your area of focus. When considering program redesign, it's important to take a broad view of what might be contributing to poor student outcomes before settling on a focused action plan.

In this second phase of needs assessment, the task is to find areas of weakness to fix, identify strengths to build upon, and add activities to address program omissions. It is at once detective work, trying to identify possible causes of student success and struggles, and research! You begin with a question, look at data, form hypotheses based on a theory of what is causing student outcomes—both good and poor—and then design an experiment (a program change) to test your theory. Turnaround is called "rapid-fire experimentation" because of these research or inquiry-based strategies.[2] And the inquiry discipline we (and others) use is formative evaluation: action research for the purpose of improving programs.

As with student outcomes, we start our data summarization work for programmatic needs with a consideration of the entire range of questions that could be considered to identify program strengths and weaknesses, as shown in Table 3.3, which also is reproduced in the Toolkit for easy reference and reproduction as **Tool 3.2, Needs Assessment Questions for Identifying the Turnaround Focus.** You could certainly add more categories to examine and specific questions to address; however, the questions shown here can start your thinking. You cannot address all of these questions, but as you consider your student and program needs, you might collect information, even informally, about most of these areas in search of what is sabotaging learning at your school.

You will notice that data review questions related to program needs proceed in two steps. First we consider curriculum and instruction, the

Tool 3.2

Table 3.3   Needs Assessment Questions for Identifying the Turnaround Focus

Curriculum and Instruction Needs Assessment Questions	
Curriculum	**Instruction**
• **Alignment:** Is our curriculum aligned with state standards? • **Operationalized Standards:** Do we have clear goal statements (knowledge, skills, core competencies) for each curriculum area? Do teachers have a shared understanding of these goals linked to standards? • **Common Assessments:** Do we have common classroom assessments for key curriculum standards? Are they aligned to state standards? • **Clear, Shared Goals:** Are course goals and expectations comparable for all subgroups? How do we know? • **Staff Development:** What kind of training and support do teachers get in implementing curriculum? • **Resources:** Do we have enough textbooks, computer access, lab opportunities, and so forth so that all students have access to the curriculum?	• **Differentiated Instruction:** Do teachers have support in differentiating instruction in their classes? • **Student Engagement:** Are students asked to practice skills? Do teachers engage their prior knowledge and ask for connections to current learning? • **Effective Lessons:** Does direct instruction show evidence of pedagogical content knowledge? Present content correctly? Identify student misconceptions and preconceptions and attempt to revise these? Provide correct and useful feedback and answers to student questions? Provide students with organizers for new content knowledge and ways to connect to other learning? • **Interventions:** Are interventions provided to students who cannot do grade-level work? • **Flexible Grouping:** Are students flexibly grouped and moved out of intervention groups when they meet grade-level requirements? • **Technology:** How is technology used to support student learning? • **Instructional challenges:** Are there student groups we feel our instructional strategies are not effective with? • **Collegial Work:** Do we have opportunities to observe colleagues, visit other sites, and keep informed of best practices? • **Evaluating Programs Regularly:** What impact has instruction delivered by supplementary service providers with our Title I money had on achievement? Have the providers reached their goals?

School Context Needs Assessment Questions		
School Climate	**Staff**	**Parents and Community**
• **Safe:** Do students, parents, and community members perceive the school as safe, orderly, and prepared for emergencies (civil, natural disasters, police action in the neighborhood, etc.)?	• **Hold High Expectations:** Do parents and students perceive staff as supporting high levels of achievement, holding high expectations, and delivering a rigorous curriculum?	• **Communication:** Does the school have a system for regular communication with parents about student progress (online access to assignments, progress reports, e-mail communication with teachers)? • **Involvement:** Does staff notify parents about student

School Climate	Staff	Parents and Community
• **Behavior:** Does the school have policies and programs to deal with important behavioral issues such as bullying, drug use, alcohol and tobacco use, and sexual harassment? • **Integrated Student Support Services:** Does the school have mental health referral services for students, staff, and parents? • **Positive Relationships:** Do teachers, students, parents, and administrators report they have positive working relationships and methods for dealing with disagreements? • **Risk Taking:** Does staff feel support for innovation and risk taking, and do they feel they are appreciated and recognized for their efforts? • **Pride:** Are students proud of their school? Do they attend regularly, participate in activities, and feel the school has a good reputation?	• **Support Learning:** Are staff seen as being available to provide help and clear feedback to students? • **Have Expertise:** Are staff assigned in their areas of expertise? Do all meet Highly Qualified Teacher criteria? Do some have National Board certification? • **Involved in Distributed Leadership:** Is staff involved in identifying and planning relevant professional development? Do they find it useful? • **Receive Professional Growth Support:** Are mentors, coaches, and/or curriculum experts available to support staff? • **Participate in Continuous Improvement Processes:** Are staff involved in collegial walk-throughs to observe curriculum implementation and discuss how to improve practice or capitalize on best practices?	progress and involve parents in supporting student work? • **Connected to School:** Do parents feel comfortable visiting the school to discuss concerns with teachers and administrators? Do parents know how to get information about student assignments and progress? • **Accommodate Parents:** Does the school provide involvement and volunteer opportunities for parents that take into account differences in work and child care obligations, language and educational backgrounds, and parent interests/expertise? • **Community Support:** Does the school have community and/or business partnerships supporting specific programs? Do those need to be increased? • **Community-Based Programs:** Does the school take advantage of community-based programs to leverage learning? Examples include library summer reading programs; human relations training offered by the National Conference for Community and Justice and other community organizations; university partnerships; YMCA-YWCA child care, fitness, and camping programs; volunteer teacher aides; and so forth.

areas having the most direct impact on learning and achievement. We next turn to school context factors—areas that support curriculum and instruction, and in some cases powerfully so. However, the specific school context variables and questions we address will depend upon what we identify as not working well in curriculum and instruction. Turnaround requires a tight focus. You cannot take care of all aspects of student achievement at once, but perhaps you can leverage work on curriculum and instruction to address other areas of need, such as student behavior, staff development, and parent involvement.

USE DATA INVENTORY TO IDENTIFY DATA NEEDED TO ANSWER PROGRAM REDESIGN QUESTIONS

Once you have your data review questions identified, you will gather available information for addressing each question.

- Select a few questions from each of the five program categories in Table 3.3: curriculum, instruction, school climate, staff, and parent/community.
- Refer to your data inventory to find and gather data related to each question.
- Use the questions and relevant data reports to prepare data summaries and displays.

You may well find that you do not have information available to address all of the student outcome or program questions you have identified. But their identification indicates that they are potentially important at your school. Keep a record of important questions you want to answer; you will need them to design the evaluation of your Turnaround Plan. The questions also can raise awareness among staff about the kinds of activities and outcomes that are important to improving achievement at your school.

Recall that your data inventory indicates the quality of each data source. Use these quality ratings to identify priorities for data reporting, as long as the data are important and valued at your school. While not all of your data will be of high quality or meet professional standards of technical quality, this does not mean that you should ignore lower-quality information. Pay attention to data if it is important to school stakeholders and addresses important data review questions. Data-supported decisions always include the decision purpose and context. If you are a politician and your decision purpose is to identify the "worst" schools in the state, but your context puts you far from an actual school building, you must use high-quality data. A decision with high stakes made out of context requires high-quality data. Mistaken decisions about "failing" schools cost money, anger communities, and can destroy a political career. However, when you are working in a school every day, you have enough other kinds of data—such as teacher experience, parent comments, and classroom observations—to use to make sense of data judged to be of less than high quality. Additionally, the kinds of decisions you will be making—program changes, staff development, and so on—are easily modified should you make an incorrect assessment. The technical quality notation in your data inventory is there to remind you that when your data are not of high quality, you will need additional data sources or should avoid making irrevocable decisions using that information.

PREPARE TABLES AND GRAPHS FROM PUBLISHED REPORTS

Keep in mind the needs assessment questions each table or graph will be used to address. Once you've gathered your reports and other information and organized them by needs assessment question, you should begin your first table or graph by writing the question the data summary is to answer. By putting the review question at the beginning of the data summary, you help both yourself and the group analyzing the data to focus on the relevant aspects of the information. Thus, your very first data summary might be titled, "How have students performed in Grade 7 Mathematics over the last three years?"

Your task is to use your data inventory to locate the Grade 7 Mathematics reports for the past three years. You will most likely find you have several kinds of assessment data that address your question: accountability, district-level, and even school-level test data. Where to begin? Should you use the "best" report, or all of them?

Tech Tip

You will need to use a spreadsheet to create your tables and graphs. For large data sets that need to be organized, you may need to have your district or county technology person extract data from the district's database and format it so that you can use it in Excel.

Begin With Published Reports

One reason we suggest you begin summarizing outcome data from your state accountability assessments (and perhaps also from professionally prepared reports from district-level assessments, if available) is that published test reports are often complex and contain technical information that needs explanation. We like the "it's all downhill from here" approach to data analysis. If you climb the steep hills of the published reports first, then you can move into the more comfortable territory of simpler data with the wind at your back.

A second reason we suggest you begin with professionally published data is that your needs assessment question may not be as straightforward to address as you think. Let's take our example in the preceding section: How have students performed in Grade 7 Mathematics over the last three years? As you rummage through three years of testing reports and find Grade 7 Mathematics scores, you find that *more than one score is reported*. In fact, professionally published reports often contain a variety of scores related to the same performance. Here are just a few:

- Percentage in each proficiency category
- Average scale or standard score
- State average scale score
- Percentage scoring proficient or above for a given grade level
- Raw score or percentage correct

Uh-oh! Another decision!

Recently, there are even more kinds of scores. States and districts more and more, for example, are reporting value-added scores. Value-added scores tell you how gains in student performance at your school compare to schools in a particular comparison group, such as the district or state. So these scores tell you about your relative performance, not about your absolute gains. Since these scores capture multiple measures and are created by complex statistical models and assumptions, you will want to get expert help in interpreting them for your particular student population.

At this point, you will need to stop and decide what score best represents student "performance" for purposes of identifying student needs. Local tests, in contrast to state tests, tend to be simpler: You may have only a raw score or average percentage correct. By reviewing the published reports first, you will get some ideas about how to summarize your local data to make it more useful.

Break Up Published Reports Into Bite-Sized Summaries

As we have mentioned, start your summaries with published accountability reports and other high-stakes test results. Unfortunately, state- and publisher-produced summary reports and data displays are created for the purpose of communicating a lot of information in an efficient manner to a variety of audiences. They often contain lots of information crammed into a small space. Your data team will have to create smaller subsets of tables and graphs from these documents so that the data are more understandable.

One strategy we use in preparing data is to cut and paste large documents (either digital documents from the Internet or paper documents scanned into a digital format) into a spreadsheet. Once we have an electronic version of results, we can create smaller tables targeted to a subject, grade level, or time period, so that we have separate tables for each of the questions we created from the five categories in Table 3.3.

For example, Table 3.4 shows a typical year-end report provided to our schools in California and also available on the California Department of Education's website for the press and public. The purpose of this report is to indicate whether a school has met the state's NCLB targets for Title I. Results are used to determine whether the school enters into Program Improvement, exits Program Improvement, or stays in Program Improvement another year and "advances" closer to Year 5, at which point school restructuring is required. Schools not receiving Title I funds receive this report but are not assigned to Program Improvement.

Although the California accountability report is clear and could be shared without modification, we will use it as an example to address two important data review questions:

- Have we met our state accountability targets?
- In which areas did we fail to meet our targets?

The California tables contain information on ten subgroups, but our sample school has only six subgroups. We could edit the smaller table we make for ourselves so it focuses only on our six subgroups. However, you will notice that one of those groups is "White." Since the White subgroup's achievement is an important political target (usually, the achievement gap is defined as the difference in performance between White or White Asian and other groups), we will include it in our table. However, we won't include Pacific Islanders or American Indians. You will also notice that the accountability results are summarized in two tables: one to report the participation rates, and the second to report the actual percentage of students who have scored Proficient or above. Since our sample school has met its participation target, that information would not need to be included on a separate table.

Table 3.4 California Annual NCLB Accountability Report

Needs Assessment Questions: Have we met our Title I accountability targets? In which areas did we not meet our targets?

NCLB Year End Report	English Language Arts: Target 95%					Mathematics: Target 95%			
Groups	Enrollment	Number Tested	Percent	Met AYP Criteria	Met 17 of 27 Targets	Enrollment	Number Tested	Percent	Met AYP Criteria
Schoolwide	948	943	99	Yes	Did not make AYP	948	938	99	Yes
African American	148	146	99	Yes		148	146	99	Yes
American Indian or Alaska Native	1	1	100	–		1	1	100	–
Asian	78	78	100	–		78	78	100	–
Filipino	11	11	100	–		11	11	100	–
Hispanic or Latino	591	589	100	Yes		591	585	99	Yes
Pacific Islander	13	13	100	–		13	13	100	–
White (not of Hispanic origin)	100	99	99	Yes		100	98	98	Yes
Socioeconomically Disadvantaged	773	769	99	Yes		773	764	99	Yes
English Learners	413	411	100	Yes		413	409	99	Yes
Students With Disabilities	119	118	99	Yes		119	117	98	Yes

(Continued)

Table 3.4 (Continued)

Groups	English Language Arts: Target 35.2% Did Not Meet Target					Mathematics: Target 37% Did Not Meet Target			
	Valid Scores	Number At or Above Proficient	Percent At or Above Proficient	Met 2008 AYP Criteria	Alternative Method	Valid Scores	Number At or Above Proficient	Percent At or Above Proficient	Met 2008 AYP Criteria
Schoolwide	907	327	36.1	Yes		904	225	24.9	No
African American	134	40	29.9	No		134	25	18.7	No
American Indian or Alaska Native	1	–	–	–		1	–	–	–
Asian	76	39	51.3	–		76	30	39.5	–
Filipino	8	–	–	–		8	–	–	–
Hispanic or Latino	577	186	32.2	No		574	133	23.2	No
Pacific Islander	13	7	53.8	–		13	3	23.1	–
White (not of Hispanic origin)	93	47	50.5	–		93	30	32.3	–
Socioeconomically Disadvantaged	752	248	33.0	Yes	Safe Harbor	748	179	23.9	No
English Learners	403	70	17.4	No		401	58	14.5	No
Students With Disabilities	106	5	4.7	No		106	4	3.8	No

Source: California State Department of Education (2008), Dataquest, http://data1.cde.ca.gov/dataquest.

Note: Safe Harbor refers to an alternate calculation of AYP results for schools that may fall short in one or more subgroups but that still show progress both in those subgroups and schoolwide.

Table 3.5 presents an abridged table we think will help staff better focus on the questions of where we did not meet accountability targets. Since we believe people need to process information to make sense of it, we also deleted the "Met AYP Criteria" column and will ask the staff to compare each subgroup's performance to the English language arts and math targets. This has the advantage of making staff familiar with the targets and having them actively consider differences among subgroups and each subgroup's distance from the goal.

Table 3.5   (Abridged from Table 3.4) Middle School Accountability Results

Groups	English Language Arts: Target 35.2%			Mathematics: Target 37%		
	Valid Scores	Number At or Above Proficient	Percent At or Above Proficient	Valid Scores	Number At or Above Proficient	Percent At or Above Proficient
Schoolwide	907	327	36.1	904	225	24.9
African American	134	40	29.9	134	25	18.7
Hispanic or Latino	577	186	32.2	574	133	23.2
White Asian (for comparison purposes)	93 76	47 39	50.5 51.3	93	30	32.3
Socioeconomically Disadvantaged	752	248	33.0 Safe Harbor Ok	748	179	23.9
English Learners	403	70	17.4	401	58	14.5
Students With Disabilities	106	5	4.7	106	4	3.8

Source: California State Department of Education (2008), Dataquest, http://data1.cde.ca.gov/dataquest.

Prepare Explanations for Complex Data Tables

Accountability reports are succinct compared to annual reports of test results. Once your school has identified the subjects and subgroups for which it has not met its accountability goals, you will need to turn to the detailed test results to examine possible "causes." Which subgroups by grade and subject? Unfortunately, the test results reports are not as easily read as the Adequate Yearly Progress accountability report. These reports often contain data for several grade levels, several subjects, and multiple proficiency levels. They will include numbers of students tested, percentage tested, average scale scores, and percentages of students in multiple proficiency categories. The test reports are dense!

Table 3.6 shows a typical California Standards Test (CST) school report. You can see that the CST report might be more useful if it were broken into several smaller reports, one for English language arts, another for

Table 3.6   California Standards Test Results

Needs Assessment Questions: Are there performance differences by content or grade level?							
California Standards Test: ALL STUDENTS	6	7	8		8		8
Reported Enrollment	327	304	317		317		317
CST English Language Arts				**CST History/ Social Science (Grade 8 Cumulative)**		**CST Science (Grade 5, Grade 8, and Grade 10 Life Science)**	
Students Tested	324	303	314	Students Tested	310	Students Tested	312
% of Enrollment	99.1%	99.7%	99.1%	% of Enrollment	97.8%	% of Enrollment	98.4%
Students With Scores	323	301	313	Students With Scores	310	Students With Scores	312
Mean Scale Score	327.2	337.2	322.1	Mean Scale Score	316.7	Mean Scale Score	305.3
% Advanced	7%	14%	11%	% Advanced	10%	% Advanced	12%
% Proficient	27%	27%	21%	% Proficient	15%	% Proficient	18%
% Basic	37%	30%	31%	% Basic	30%	% Basic	22%
% Below Basic	18%	19%	21%	% Below Basic	22%	% Below Basic	19%
% Far Below Basic	11%	11%	17%	% Far Below Basic	23%	% Far Below Basic	29%
CST Mathematics				**CST General Mathematics (Grades 6 and 7 Standards)**		**CST Algebra I**	
Students Tested	325	301		Students Tested	226	Students Tested	84
% of Enrollment	99.4%	99.0%		% of Enrollment	71.3%	% of Enrollment	26.5%
Students With Scores	322	298		Students With Scores	225	Students With Scores	84
Mean Scale Score	322.8	315.4		Mean Scale Score	296.7	Mean Scale Score	332.9
% Advanced	6%	4%		% Advanced	2%	% Advanced	4%
% Proficient	25%	20%		% Proficient	12%	% Proficient	26%
% Basic	30%	35%		% Basic	29%	% Basic	50%
% Below Basic	30%	27%		% Below Basic	34%	% Below Basic	19%
% Far Below Basic	8%	13%		% Far Below Basic	24%	% Far Below Basic	1%

Source: California State Department of Education (2008), Dataquest, http://data1.cde.ca.gov/dataquest.

mathematics, a third for science, and a fourth for social studies. Since middle schools are departmentalized, each department could examine reports for its subject, address questions of strength and weakness, and then share results with the larger group.

Test score reports, and sometimes accountability score reports as well, require some understanding of technical information underlying the scores. When preparing data tables for test scores, it is essential to refer to the test's technical manual (if one exists) to address inevitable questions about differences in performance within a grade level, between grade levels, and among different content areas. Some of the tougher questions that require some review of the technical manual when discussing test data include the following:

- What is a *mean scale score,* and what does it mean when it differs from grade to grade in the same subject?
- What are the cut points for the proficiency levels?
- Why are the cut points for the same scale score (in our case, a scale score of 350 is considered Proficient) different at different grade levels?
- Just how good is "proficient"? What does that mean in terms of how well a student has done on the test (regardless of test difficulty, which changes from grade to grade and year to year)?
- What does our value-added score mean? How was it computed? How accurate is it?

Organizing and summarizing data also raises many questions that require the data team to understand and share test information that can be found only in the test's technical manual or in reports with disaggregated data. Thus, you will want to have in your back pocket the information needed to understand more clearly what is presented in tables and graphs. Some of the most frequently needed ancillary information includes the following:

- Cut Point Scores for Proficiency Levels—For students who didn't score Proficient or above, just how close did they come to hitting the target?
- Standard Errors or Classification Consistency Data—What proportion of this group didn't make the Proficient cut by chance alone?
- Subgroup Disaggregations for All Proficiency Levels, Not Just Proficient and Above—Do the reports disaggregate the data enough to address questions of equity? For example, are subgroups such as Hispanic students, English learners, or special education students disproportionately represented in the Below Basic and Far Below Basic categories?
- Test Form and Item Difficulties—Is the difference in performance between grade levels due to differences in test difficulty?
- Correlations Between Test and Other Variables (other tests, future performance, grades, etc.)—Do students have to do well on this test to be successful in the next grade? Do our district tests assess the same content and have the same level of difficulty as the accountability tests? Would teaching reading in the content areas improve our reading test scores?

Expert Help

After you have prepared your data summaries, have one of the individuals from your expert panel or critical friends group work with you to find and explain the background information needed to interpret your scores. The expert can use the technical manual to find cut points, standard errors, form difficulties, and correlations between your test and other criterion variables that will tell you more precisely the limitations on your test score inferences.

Keep Displays Simple

Don't be a data diva! Spreadsheet programs such as Excel will allow you to do many things that you should not do!! Just because you can create a 3-D pyramid-pie-line chart doesn't mean that it makes any sense. In fact, there's a whole academic discipline dedicated to "data visualization."

Expert Help

You could have one of your expert panelists help you choose appropriate displays to answer your data questions.

For assistance in this task, you may wish to consult one of the many websites dedicated to data visualization. One we like was created by a political scientist and has some clear directions about how best to organize and display data. The website is called Just Plain Data Analysis and was created by Gary Klass, who has a book by the same title.[3] We have included complete access information in the References and Resources section at the end of the book. We have created a brief summary of some data display do's and don'ts in Table 3.7.

Table 3.7   Data Display Do's and Don'ts

	Use	**Misuse**
Pie Charts	Rarely. To show proportions of a whole; for example, percentages of the budget allotted to various programs, percentages of students in different ethnic groups, percentages of the school day allocated to various activities.	Do not use to compare. More than one pie chart is way too much pie! Do not use for items that conceptually don't represent a percentage of a whole.
Line Graphs	To show trends over time; to compare different groups or tests over time (using a different line for each entity).	The entity tracked—for example, tests or groups—must be comparable from year to year. Tracking cohorts over time isn't misleading; tracking tests that change in difficulty from year to year is wildly misleading.
Bar Charts	To show comparisons with a small number of subgroups or subjects.	Do not use for large numbers of groups and subjects. Sometimes difficult to track over time.
Stacked Bar Charts	Shows proportion of a bar; good to show proportion of students falling into different proficiency categories for one subject or one grade level.	Wildly difficult to use to compare more than one subject, grade level, or year. Hard to "read across" bars because there is no "baseline" to make comparisons.
3-D Charts, Pies, and Bars	NEVER.	These distort data and are difficult to read.

	Use	Misuse
Box and Whiskers	To show test distributions when test scores are converted to percentiles; good for comparing distributions.	You must convert scores to percentile ranks. It's hard to find conversion functions in Excel or nonspecialized graphing programs.
Scatterplots	To show bivariate distributions (when you have two scores for each data record); to show relationships leading to inferences about correlation. Both variables should be continuous, such as test scores on pretest and posttest.	Display needs some explanation; interpretation is not intuitive. You can't use these with categorical and continuous variables together (such as ethnicity and test score).

We have also included guidelines for summarizing data from accountability and published assessments in the Toolkit. The guidelines for tables and graphs are organized into three categories:

Tool 3.3, Table and Graph Considerations: Student Performance

Tool 3.4, Table and Graph Considerations: Achievement Gap Analysis

Tool 3.5, Table and Graph Considerations: Important Comparisons

Tools 3.3–3.5

SUMMARIZE LOCAL DATA

Once you have organized published test data by data review question, you have a good idea of how you can use your district and school data to support findings, raise new questions, or fill in missing information. Your local data will most likely be more extensive and richer than those provided by the state or even the district. While the discussion of data preparation to this point has focused on summarizing student outcome data, when we get to locally gathered information, we are more likely to have programmatic information that can help identify the specific strengths and weaknesses that will be the target of the Turnaround Plan. Most schools have the following kinds of results, and some have much, much more!

- District monitoring assessments for individual quarters, semesters, or years
- School-level common assessments by grade or department, quarterly or by unit
- Classroom assessments, frequent and often informal, with various formats
- Parent satisfaction surveys
- Drug, alcohol, and tobacco use surveys prepared by the state
- Physical fitness test results prepared by the state
- English-learner proficiency assessments
- Individualized Education Programs (IEPs) for special education students

The same strategies for aligning published assessments to specific data review questions before preparing summary tables and graphs apply to the results of locally developed tests and satisfaction surveys. The only difference in preparing data from locally developed measures is that you, rather than the state or test publisher, must calculate a test "score" to determine how survey responses are to be quantified and summarized. Once you have determined the method of capturing the information in a score, then table and graph development follows the same guidelines as those for data from published sources.

Select an Appropriate Score to Summarize Local Test Data

Begin preparing your local data summaries by identifying the question(s) the summaries will address, and then decide what kind of a "score" or data summary speaks to the question. Typically, for local tests, you'll be using a score based on percentage correct. But be aware that using percentage correct scores is not always as easy as it seems:

- Sometimes, the items measuring one skill are simply more complex or perhaps trickier in nature than those measuring another skill. So it's important to review the actual items in areas where students did poorly or particularly well.
- When comparing scores over time—for example pretest to posttest or this year to last—the test items need to be the same, or the tests should be statistically equated. Otherwise, you're comparing apples and oranges.

Sometimes you will want to compare how students do on local tests with their proficiency on state tests. Here, you will want teachers to define what score indicates that a student is proficient on skills measured by the local test. Typically, teachers will want to consider percentage correct scores. For example, they may define *proficient* as 70% correct. You can then compare whether students proficient on local tests are also proficient on state tests.

You will not be able to compare local and state performance if your state assessment reports percentiles or scale scores and you do not have these kinds of transformed scores on your local assessments. Sometimes, schools and districts purchase published tests for local use that have percentiles or scale scores. However, most often local tests are developed by a district or school. The psychometric properties, reliability and validity, of these assessments are unknown, and it would not make sense to calculate percentile ranks or scale scores on small samples of students for the purpose of comparing local and state performance.

Summarize Survey Data to Best Answer Needs Assessment Questions

It is likely you will have some survey data available about parent satisfaction, school climate, or even student reports of the kinds of practice provided in various classes. Survey data need to be summarized to answer school context and program quality questions. Avoid using the average score on a survey. Look closely at the rating system, then decide whether you will calculate percentage of respondents making positive choices or whether you are most interested in calculating the percentage of respondents who make negative choices. Perhaps you are interested in knowing if students feel safe at school. You may be more interested in the percentage of students who report they have been bullied in school (a negative choice) by grade level than the percentage who report no incidents.

Many surveys also include respondent comments and suggestions. You can review your surveys and note comments and suggestions that relate directly to your needs assessment question of interest.

PREPARATION IS COMPLETE: THE JOURNEY BEGINS

We have reached the end of realignment activities:

- Your school has collaborative groups or professional learning communities committed to examining their practice and using student data to improve both programs and practice.
- You may have a data team to handle data collection, storage, and reporting.
- You have collected measures of program quality and state and local assessment data, and you have cataloged what you have and its quality.
- You have on file brief program descriptions.
- You have prepared data to address several questions you will answer to identify your school's instructional focus and program revision needs.

The majority of the preparation work requires adopting new ways of doing business, new relationships among staff and administration, and new knowledge. The time spent realigning your school structures will most likely be longer than the time it will take to create, implement, and revise your Turnaround Plan. However, if you hadn't created the foundation for turnaround work in this first phase, you would lack the skills and attitudes needed to convert program improvement from a series of periodic, unconnected crisis management episodes to a continuous improvement cycle that supports your daily work.

CHAPTER 3 TOOLKIT

PREPARE DATA SUMMARIES AND DISPLAYS

The Tools for Chapter 3 can be found on the companion website for *The TurnAround ToolKit* at http://www.corwin.com/turnaroundtoolkit.

Tool 3.1   Data Review Questions for Identifying Instructional Focus Areas

Tool 3.2   Needs Assessment Questions for Identifying the Turnaround Focus

Tool 3.3   Table and Graph Considerations: Student Performance

Tool 3.4   Table and Graph Considerations: Achievement Gap Analysis

Tool 3.5   Table and Graph Considerations: Important Comparisons

Section II

Redesign

Use Data to Create the Turnaround Plan

Things alter for the worse spontaneously, if they be not altered for the better designedly.

—Francis Bacon

The second major step in turnaround work is to review data about student outcomes to identify your turnaround focus. In this phase you will use needs assessment data about curriculum, instruction, staff development, and school context to redesign your programs and support systems so that students meet both short- and long-term achievement goals. This second section has three chapters, each describing a separate aspect of the program redesign process: identification of student outcomes or the turnaround focus, program redesign and development, and implementation of a working document, a plan, to guide turnaround activities.

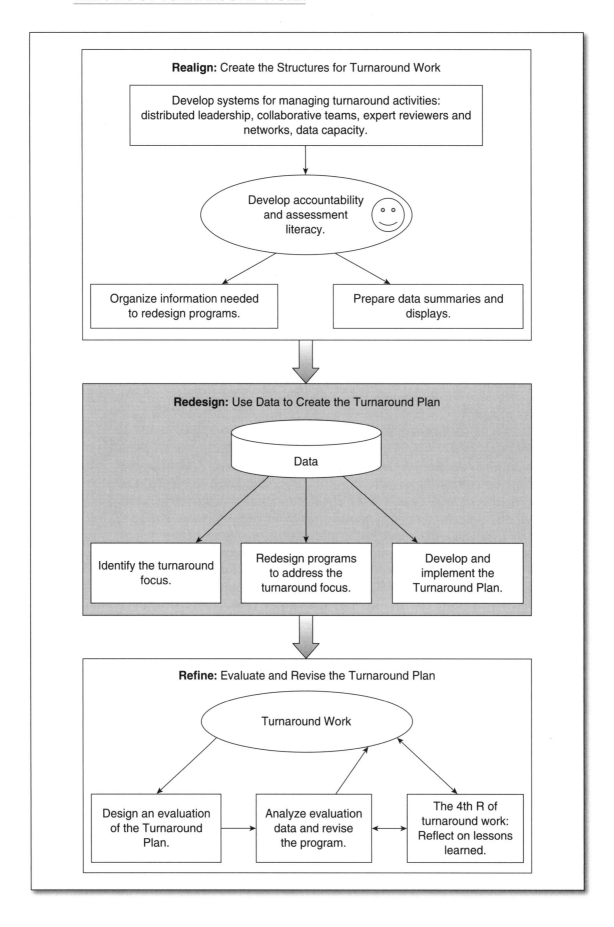

CHAPTER 4 ■

IDENTIFY THE TURNAROUND FOCUS

Chapter 4 is data intense. Schools are drowning in student outcome data. In Chapter 4, we tackle the task of turning the data into useful information. What do students know? What is the set of skills that students must learn en route from current performance to grade-level expectations? What do accountability, state standards tests, and local common assessments indicate about where our turnaround efforts need to focus? The result of reviewing student data will be a set of short-term grade-level or year-end outcomes and long-term accountability or life skills goals.

CHAPTER 5 ■

REDESIGN PROGRAMS TO ADDRESS THE TURNAROUND FOCUS

Program redesign specifies the activities of turnaround work. The turnaround focus identified in Chapter 4 is used to identify specific changes or activities needed in curriculum, instruction, staff development, and school context that will result in achieving the Chapter 4 outcomes. Those changes are documented in a diagram called the theory of action. Your theory of action makes explicit the relationships between your turnaround activities and desired outcomes and is used to develop a common understanding of your work among stakeholders as well as to develop the Turnaround Plan and formative evaluation of your efforts.

CHAPTER 6 ■

DEVELOP AND IMPLEMENT THE TURNAROUND PLAN

In this chapter, we build a Turnaround Plan, which is very different from a school improvement plan, required ESEA compliance plans, and strategic plans. Our plan is brief and mutable; for each activity, it assigns responsibility and embeds a monitoring activity to evaluate implementation quality and student progress. During implementation, we expect to change our work, make midcourse corrections, and document our successful strategies for future replication. Although formative evaluation will not be covered until Section III, our Turnaround Plan will incorporate program monitoring activities, and we will collect data and review it as part of our turnaround work. Once we have designed our formal evaluation of the year's turnaround work as described in Chapter 7, we will revise our plan and add activities for management, measurement development, and data collection to our program redesign turnaround work.

4

Identify the Turnaround Focus

If you are looking for a big opportunity, find a big problem.

—Anon

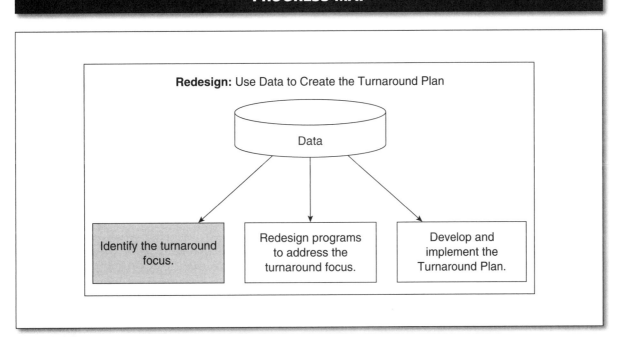

Redesign: Use Data to Create the Turnaround Plan

Data

Identify the turnaround focus.

Redesign programs to address the turnaround focus.

Develop and implement the Turnaround Plan.

POCKET SUMMARY

Task	Major Activities	Purpose
Select data for review, and set criteria for identifying strengths and weaknesses.	• Identify and sequence your prepared summaries and displays to address needs assessment questions. **Tool 3.2 (in Chapter 3 Toolkit), Needs Assessment Questions for Identifying the Turnaround Focus** • Set criteria for defining strengths and weaknesses. **Tool 4.1 Performance Criteria for Reviewing Student Outcome Data**	• Efficient data review. • Identify areas of weakness and strength.
Begin with the big picture: Analyze accountability data.	• Determine status relative to targets, and identify trends. **Tool 4.2 Understanding Your State Accountability System** • Examine important comparisons. **Tool 4.3 Data Discussion Summary Template**	• Enhance validity of decisions about areas of weakness.
Tighten your focus: Review state or local standards assessments.	• Examine achievement differences by grade level and content. • Start with mean score trends by content and grade level to identify patterns. • Examine differences in the proportion of high- and low-scoring students by grade level and content. • Examine trends for subgroups and compare with your benchmark school. • Summarize your review of state and local test data.	• Move from big picture to detail decisions. • Link inferences among different tests.
Clarify and corroborate instructional focus areas with local assessments.	**Tool 4.4 Discussion Protocol: Reviewing Sample Items or Released Tests** • Use local assessments for diagnosing specific learning needs.	• Fill in gaps in understanding of student needs.
Review other valued outcomes.	• Analyze dropout data. **Tool 4.5 Analyzing Dropout Rates to Determine Instructional Focus** • Examine progress on student preparation goals. **Tool 4.6 Suggestions for Reviewing Progress on Student Preparation Goals** • Consider English-learner reclassification rates.	• Include important outcomes other than test data, so you won't miss authentic and politically valued outcomes of schooling.
Choose the turnaround focus areas.	• Pinpoint the grade levels, content areas, and skills (if you have the data) that will serve as the focus for your Turnaround Plan.	• Specify the instructional focus to guide all turnaround work efforts.
Don't move on until you have identified your strengths.	• Use student achievement data to indicate skills and knowledge you can build upon to strengthen weak areas.	• Include areas of strength to leverage turnaround work.

Why Begin With Student Outcomes?

Your first turnaround step is to conduct a needs assessment with readily available student outcome data to identify priorities for action. The needs assessment involves school stakeholders in analyzing easily gathered information from your state, district, and even school-level assessments to address a first set of data review questions: How are students doing? Where are you making the grade, and where are you falling behind in student achievement? Because the purpose of turnaround work is to improve student achievement, we begin our initial work by describing school-level achievement patterns.

- Where are students falling short of accountability targets and other goals?
- What strengths can we build upon in our improvement efforts?
- What questions do the data raise that we want to address when we create our Turnaround Plan?

Our initial focus on student achievement data does not mean that information about other aspects of your school—for example, school climate and safety, curriculum, instruction, staff development, and parent and community involvement—are not important. Indeed, curriculum, instruction, student engagement, and school climate provide crucial supports for improving learning, and data about them are essential in creating a Turnaround Plan. However, from our perspective, your review of essential learning support variables should be focused on how these elements affect and can be better orchestrated to support student learning. How do they need to be improved? What strengths in these areas can we build upon to reach our achievement goals? Surely the data review of these school variables is essential for creating the Turnaround Plan, but not for identifying turnaround priorities or the primary indicators through which you will judge the effectiveness of your turnaround efforts.

Practically and politically, moreover, your initial needs assessment efforts logically focus on publicly important indicators of school effectiveness. Once your school learning needs are identified, you will have a chance to review data related to all of the learning support factors essential to address those needs and create a Turnaround Plan.

The **Leader's Guide for Chapter 4** provides an overview of the leadership issues connected with reviewing student outcome data to identify the instructional focus of your turnaround work.

Select Data for Review, and Set Criteria for Identifying Strengths and Weaknesses

To begin your needs assessment, you first must organize the process for reviewing the data. This involves identifying and sequencing the specific data you will be reviewing and establishing criteria for identifying school strengths and weaknesses. Establishing these criteria in advance provides a more independent and objective standard for deciding on school priorities.

Identify and Sequence Your Prepared Summaries and Displays to Address Needs Assessment Questions

You have spent considerable time preparing program descriptions, data inventories, program quality measures, and data summaries and displays for your turnaround needs assessment work (see Chapters 2 and 3). The data you will need to identify the instructional focus of your turnaround work, or the areas where student achievement needs improvement, will appear on your data inventory of student outcomes. We have reproduced the entire set of data review questions in **Tool 3.1, Data Review Questions for Identifying Instructional Focus Areas**, in the Chapter 3 Toolkit.

Begin with the big-picture accountability data to provide an overall picture of student performance. Look at both current status—are students meeting accountability targets? and trends—is performance improving, staying the same, declining? While accountability reports are notoriously general, providing a general thumbs-up or thumbs-down for the school as a whole and perhaps special subgroups, they can raise red flags and indicate subject areas that demand more detailed attention. For example, they can identify reading, mathematics, or science as a relative weakness for the school or specific subgroups that are not making progress. Then bring forward your state assessment data to answer more specific questions about the sources of the problem. State assessment results provide more specific information to detect patterns in how students are performing by grade level, content, and subgroup to target more specific areas of relative strength and weakness. Value-added results may tell you how relative gains at your school compare with other schools in a particular comparison group. Even so, these high-stakes tests often do not provide the diagnostic information you need to understand why performance is as it is or how to improve it, and thus you may need to turn to district or school-level assessments to get the detailed perspective you need to create your turnaround goals. If you are fortunate enough to receive reports listing specific skills, or if you have a district or school testing program designed to monitor student progress toward meeting state standards, you may be better able to come up with specific strategies for improving achievement.

Obviously, seriously reviewing all these data is a big job and could be overwhelming for a single data review session. Consider how to sequence the review over a number of sessions. And if you plan to develop Turnaround Plans for multiple areas—for example, for mathematics and English language arts, consider starting with an overall review of accountability data and then creating subcommittees to provide more detailed analysis of each subject area.

Set Criteria for Defining Strengths and Weaknesses

In addition to organizing data for your data review sessions, you will want to discuss with your staff or leadership team the criteria you will use to determine what constitutes a strength and what comprises a weakness in student achievement. This is not the no-brainer it might first appear to be. The federal government and your state have developed accountability targets for your school. Those expectations certainly will be part of your school's performance standards. However, these targets define only the broadest expectations for the majority of students. If you work with populations that perform at the extreme ends of the achievement distribution, comparing your performance only to the state and federal targets may not give you the information you need to establish priorities for turnaround. Here the issues are likely to be *relative* strengths and weaknesses. Staff at higher-performing schools will want to wrestle with the question, "How good is good enough for us to continue what we are doing?" Staff in schools at the opposite extreme will want to consider, "How low does performance have to be in an area for us to decide it should be the focus of turnaround?" In either and all cases, you will want to consider both the current status of student performance (Are we meeting targets? How far above or below?) as well as trends in performance over time (Is the school's performance improving, staying the same, or falling further behind?).

When considering these thorny questions, it is helpful to have data on benchmark schools. A benchmark school, as introduced in Chapter 3, is similar to yours demographically or in other ways, but its students are performing much better than yours in some areas. The benchmark shows you what is possible; it demonstrates a standard of excellence. A benchmark differs from a comparison school in that a comparison is a similar school, but not necessarily one that is doing well. Your goal is to set school expectations high while reassuring staff that the expectations are realistic. For high-achieving populations, a statewide accountability standard, while important, doesn't always capture the "what is possible" aspect of standard setting. It is possible to be an underachieving high-scoring school, just as it is to be a relatively high-achieving school with scores somewhat below the highest in the state.

In other words, you make sense of the data by looking objectively at them and comparing how you are doing relative to established targets and relative to others. To whom you compare is partially a matter of what constitutes a politically important comparison and what counts as credible evidence of your school's progress for your community. In some communities, a comparison to the district or state average is considered weak, because the school is considered "highly academic" or serves high-achieving students. In such communities, a comparison to the top-scoring schools in the state will be more credible than one to the state average. In other communities, the state average captures the performance expectation satisfactorily. In still other situations, especially in small communities serving students who are atypical of the state population, the state average is aspirational rather than a performance expectation, and a comparison with a demographically similar but higher-performing benchmark school would make more sense.

How do you find your benchmark school? The school should be similar to yours in the demographic characteristics of students that are most highly correlated with differences in student test scores and in school context. Research has shown the strongest correlates of student achievement are

Tech Tip

Since your data review will entail moving from big-picture questions to more detailed analyses of student achievement needs, using a computer and projector can enable you to toggle easily between data sets—from accountability measures, from state tests, from district assessments, and other data from your inventory—and will eliminate much shuffling of papers and searching for data as your discussion progresses.

Expert Help

A member of your expert advisory group with experience in large-scale assessment, data analysis, and psychometrics as well as issues of practical significance can help you set criteria for determining when your performance is out of the range of the normal annual fluctuation in test scores.

- prior year's performance,
- socioeconomic status,
- belonging to an ethnic group that has been considered "disadvantaged," and
- being an English learner (EL).

These variables are intercorrelated. It is the job of the school to "break" these correlations and help students perform better than the correlates of achievement would predict. Thus, your benchmark school should serve populations that "look" similar to yours, have about the same socioeconomic status, and are about the same size. Many states have websites that make it easy to find demographically similar schools and may even provide your school's performance relative to similar schools. Your job is to identify those similar schools and find those that are performing better than your school in various areas.

In summary, different schools will have different ways to identify their relative strengths and weaknesses and to establish priorities for turnaround. Most will consider the following:

- Performance relative to an important target (e.g., meeting or not adequate yearly progress goals, proportion of students scoring Proficient, number of students receiving advanced placement scores of 3 or above).
- Change in performance over time (either up or down). If students are not meeting an important target but performance is improving, the situation is quite different than if students are making no progress or their performance is declining. Even if they achieve performance targets, schools have reason for concern if performance trends are on a downward slope.
- Status or change in performance relative to an important comparison group. Areas where status or trends are different from those in a high-performing, demographically similar school provide important food for thought, particularly areas where your school's performance is also disappointing relative to important targets.
- Value-added scores for your school can be used to compare the growth in student test scores with that of a comparison group, such as other schools, the district, or the state. High-scoring schools may have relatively low value-added scores due to test ceiling effects. And schools showing growth in the middle of the distribution (PR 25–75) may look as though they are growing, but the actual improvement is not all that much. Thus you will want to look at absolute growth as well as the value added (predicted versus actual growth) when using the results of value-added analysis.

Table 4.1 summarizes data sources, analysis strategies, and possible comparisons for using student outcome data to identify turnaround priorities. In addition to student outcome data, the table also includes other data that may be available related to student outcomes—for example, data on dropouts or course completion. The table is reproduced in **Tool 4.1, Performance Criteria for Reviewing Student Outcome Data.**

Tool
4.1

Table 4.1	Performance Criteria for Reviewing Student Outcome Data

Data Source	Kind of Analysis	Performance Standards
Accountability or Published Tests Used Over Multiple Years	Status Relative to Established Targets	• AYP percentage Proficient status • District established yearly growth targets • State established yearly growth targets
	Trends	• Change over time compared with benchmark school, state, or highest-performing schools • Change larger or smaller than standard error
	Benchmark Comparisons	• Scores compared with those of demographically similar schools that are doing much better • Scores compared with those of schools we wish to emulate or compete with that are doing better
	Politically Important Comparisons	• District average • State average • Met accountability targets
	Content and Grade-Level Patterns	• Improvement over time • Increase in students meeting targets, such as AYP or score of 3 or better on AP tests • Comparison of performance between content areas • Comparison of performance between grade levels
	Subgroup Patterns	• Gap between percentage of subgroup scoring Proficient or better and percentage of all students scoring Proficient or better • Subgroup percentages scoring in lowest proficiency levels by various groups • Subgroup performance over time by grade and content
District- and School-Level Common Assessments	Skill Diagnosis	• Skill areas with highest and lowest average percentage correct • Comparison of above with skills emphasized on state accountability tests
	Classroom Comparisons	• Classrooms of similar students scoring highest and lowest • Classrooms doing well with struggling students
	Subgroup Patterns	• Average percentage correct for different subgroups • Subgroup performance over time on district tests
Archival Data	Dropout Rates	• Rates by subgroup • Rates by length of time in district or school • Rates related to credit accumulation, failing high school exit, Algebra completion, or other "discouraging" factors
	College Readiness	• Percentage by subgroup of students completing college readiness courses upon graduation • Trend in readiness completion over time
	Career Readiness	• Percentage subgroup of students completing career readiness courses upon graduation
	Factors Related to Poor Grades	• Credit accumulation correlated with dropout status • Algebra completion (by grade level) correlated with credit accumulation or dropout status • Attendance correlated with grades, state test scores, or high school exit status

Note: AYP = adequate yearly progress; AP = advanced placement.

BEGIN WITH THE BIG PICTURE: ANALYZE ACCOUNTABILITY DATA

Now that we have organized available data for our needs assessment and identified primary questions and analysis strategies, it's time to dig in and start the analysis.

Determine Status Relative to Targets and Identify Trends

We begin with the big picture, which is our accountability data. Accountability data provide the basis for high-stakes decisions, and outside audiences consider them an important measure of school quality. We will use an example—a set of real middle school data—to go through the process of identifying priorities for instructional focus. The sample middle school, as you will quickly discover, has work to do in several areas. For purposes of demonstration, we will do a thorough analysis of only one possible area of instructional focus, the area where student performance is falling short by the largest margin and is not improving over time. In your school, you may want to analyze several areas.

Let us begin with our two big-picture questions: Did we meet our state adequate yearly progress (AYP) target (based on this year's results)? And what are our achievement trends over time based on this year's and past years' results? Are we improving, declining, maintaining, or erratic?

Table 4.2 presents accountability data for addressing whether My Middle School reached its annual state targets, as well as its three-year trends for significant subgroups in English language arts and mathematics. You will note that this particular accountability report does not indicate which grades may be meeting targets and which might be below expectations. We will have to review the state assessment results to identify problems at particular grade levels.

Table 4.2 needs to be interpreted keeping in mind the nature of the accountability system. The accountability data in the table are an example of a status system. This system reports the percentage Proficient and compares the percentage to a yearly target. Targets increase each year. Schools either hit the target or do not. The system reports scores as percentage Proficient, but it aggregates the percentage across grade levels, so it's difficult to know if one grade is responsible for the trends or if the trends are schoolwide. The trend reported is for students who compose the student body in each year, not the same students across the three years. Changes in the composition of the student population or subgroups need to be considered when reviewing the results.

Students belong to at least two groups, the schoolwide group and one subgroup, and a student could belong to as many as five of the groups shown in the table. That is, a single student could simultaneously be in the English-learner, special education, and socioeconomically disadvantaged subgroups as well as the schoolwide group and an ethnic subgroup. Thus, some students "count" more than others toward school accountability results.

Finally, the data in the table are real, which is why they are so messy. It's difficult to make sweeping, unqualified statements with these data. You will encounter this issue with your school data as well. You can see that we have to have a detailed understanding of the rules of the state accountability

Table 4.2	My Middle School Accountability Results: Three-Year Trends for Subgroups in English Language Arts and Mathematics

Data Review Questions

1. Did we meet our state accountability targets this year?

2. What are our trends over time for significant subgroups in English language arts and mathematics?

Subgroup	Year 1 ELA Target 24.4%	Year 2 ELA Target 24.4%	Year 3 ELA Target 35.2%	Subgroup	Year 1 Math Target 26.5%	Year 2 Math Target 26.5%	Year 3 Math Target 37%
Schoolwide	32.6	31.6	36.1	Schoolwide	27.9	22.2	24.9
African American	22.7	28.6	29.9	African American	18.8	18.3	18.7
Asian	37.8	40.8	51.3	Asian	37.3	33.7	39.5
Hispanic or Latino	30.5	26.9	32.2	Hispanic or Latino	25.1	18.6	23.2
White (not of Hispanic origin)	44.6	50.0	50.5	White (not of Hispanic origin)	40.7	34.6	32.3
Socioeconomically Disadvantaged	28.2	26.7	33.0	Socioeconomically Disadvantaged	24.3	19.6	23.9
English Learners	17.9	14.7	17.4	English Learners	18.4	12.0	14.5
Students With Disabilities	3.9	5.8	4.7	Students With Disabilities	6.5	7.7	3.8

Observations

1. Met targets this year? The answer is yes for English language arts and no for mathematics.

2. Subgroup trends over time
   - English language arts: African American, Asian, and White subgroups show an increase over a three-year period. Hispanic and socioeconomically disadvantaged had a dip last year but made up the drop this year. Students with disabilities were improving but dipped this year.
   - Math: Most groups dipped in Year 2 and had a gain this year, but not enough to make up for the Year 2 dip, except Asian. The White subgroup had a steady decline over the three years, and students with disabilities had an increase in Year 2 but a significant loss this year.

Note: ELA = English language arts.

system to identify the limitations on data interpretation. For example, an English learner in our state is defined as a student who has not been reclassified to Fluent English Proficient status or a *reclassified student who has not scored Proficient in English language arts for three consecutive years.* Therefore, the English-learner subgroup includes both beginning English speakers and students who have exited the program but for as many as three years haven't yet scored fully Proficient in English language arts or mathematics (much like English-only speakers who are at a grade level but not scoring Proficient.) This little-known rule in the accountability system could help explain why English-learner students may as a group score higher than other subgroups in English language arts, which is a counterintuitive result until you know that many in the group are not "English learners" in the truest sense! **Tool 4.2, Understanding Your State Accountability System,** presents some questions you can use to gather information about your own accountability system that will help you better understand your accountability results.

Examine Important Comparisons

Although we answered our first two questions about school status and progress toward important targets rather quickly, we need more comparative information to interpret the results. Are the trends we see a reflection of our student performance or of changes in the state test? Maybe the test was harder in some years than others. And how strong or weak are our results? As we discussed above, there are two important questions in interpreting our performance: First, how do other schools like ours (benchmark schools) perform? Second, what is the state average (a politically important goal)?

Table 4.3 displays demographic data for My Middle School, for a comparable benchmark school, for all schools in the state, and for the highest-achieving middle school in the state. It allows us to see both what schools serving similar populations can do and what is possible at the grade level given well-prepared students.

Since My Middle School serves Grades 6–8, we would like our comparison schools to serve the same grade levels. We know that K–8 schools tend to outperform middle schools (often because the younger students outscore the older ones and raise the school scores). Therefore, we have selected for comparison only schools serving Grades 6–8. The highest-achieving school differs wildly from both the state and My Middle School in its percentage of English learners, socioeconomically disadvantaged students, and special education students. We see also that the majority of students at the highest-achieving school are Asian, while those at My Middle School and the benchmark school are majority Hispanic, with a large proportion of African American students. My Middle School has the largest proportion of special education students. These demographic and program factors are often associated with performance differences; however, the large difference between My Middle School and the benchmark school in mathematics cannot be explained by "favorable" demographics at the benchmark school. Both My Middle School and the benchmark school are above the state average in enrollment of students who receive a free or reduced-price lunch, who are socioeconomically disadvantaged, and who are of Hispanic and African American origin. Special education enrollment is close to the state average, and White enrollment is significantly lower than the state average. Our conclusion is that our benchmark school is well chosen. School size is similar, and demographics at the benchmark school are equally "challenging," and more so at both schools than the state average and at the highest-achieving school in the state. In short, we have a credible comparison school.

Table 4.3	Demographic Data for My Middle School, Benchmark School, Highest-Achieving School, and the State

Data Review Questions

1. How do we compare to our benchmark school?

2. How do we compare with the state average and the highest-achieving school in the state (politically important comparisons)?

Part I. Demographic Characteristics of Our Comparison Schools and the State				
	My Middle School	**Benchmark School**	**Highest-Achieving School**	**State (percentage)**
Student Enrollment	952	1027	1099	
Free/Reduced-Price School Lunch	86.1%	89.1%	3.3%	51
Socioeconomically Disadvantaged	81.5%	80.3%	3%	51
English Language Learners	21.2%	33.9%	3%	24
Students With Disabilities	12.5%	8.9%	4%	10
District Characterization	Large City	Urban Fringe	Midsize City	State
American Indian/Alaskan Native	0.00%	0.20%	0.10%	1
Asian	8.00%	2.50%	78.90%	9
Pacific Islander	1.40%	1.20%	0.40%	1
Filipino	1.10%	1.20%	0.90%	3
Hispanic/Latino	63.10%	65.90%	2.30%	49
African American	15.40%	25.30%	0.50%	8
White	10.50%	2.10%	14.00%	29

Part II. Benchmark and Politically Important Comparison Data								
	English Language Arts Percentage Proficient				Mathematics Percentage Proficient			
Year	**My Middle School**	**Comparable Benchmark**	**Highest-Achieving School**	**State**	**My Middle School**	**Comparable Benchmark**	**Highest-Achieving School**	**State**
3	36.1	39.2	92.6	48.2	24.9	51.6	92.0	51.0
2	31.6	37.2	90.4	45.5	22.2	43.8	86.8	48.5
1	32.6	35.3	91.6	44.8	27.9	45.6	90.7	48.0

Observations

1. There is a math dip in Year 2 at all comparison schools, even the highest in the state, but not at the state level. How is this possible? Could it be because our schools span Grades 6–8, but the state results are for Grades 2–11?

2. Our benchmark school has about 21% more students Proficient in mathematics than My Middle School but only 6% more in English. What a huge difference in mathematics. And they still do better than we do in English despite having 12% more English learners.

Once we have reviewed the accountability data tied to our key questions and noted our observations, we will summarize our discussion and indicate what other information we will need to address the issues raised in our review. Table 4.4 presents an example of a Data

| **Table 4.4** | Data Discussion Summary Table: Accountability Results for My Middle School |

Area	Data Used	Findings	Questions Raised	Other Data to Examine
Trends (Schoolwide)	Accountability reports for past three years: Percentage Proficient in English and math by school	• We met our English targets all three years, even though the targets increased. • We met our math target in Year 1 but failed to attain targets in the next two years. • We are improving in English. • We are erratic in mathematics and lower in math than we were three years ago.	• Was last year's test harder than earlier tests in math and English? • Did we have a cohort difference in 2007 that would explain the performance dip? • Were there curriculum changes in the math program? • Were there staffing changes in the math program?	• Technical manual for accountability test • Teacher observations • Data going back several years • Demographic data • Teacher reports • Principal reports
Content and Grade Level (Schoolwide)		• We have no grade-level information. • We are doing better in English than math. • Our English scores dipped in 2007 but are higher in 2008 than our baseline year. • Our math scores dipped in 2007 and climbed in 2008 but are still lower than our baseline year.	• Is the math weakness at all grade levels? • If it's a cohort effect, why didn't math increase past the baseline level like English did?	• State test results
Subgroups (Trends and Content)		• English: Asian is our highest-performing group, steadily increasing by a large amount. • English: White is our second-highest group; it started higher than the Asian group but has had a slower increase.	• Why would ELs do worse in math than English when they started higher in math three years ago?	• EL specialist report • Math teacher report • Demographics • Reclassification information

Area	Data Used	Findings	Questions Raised	Other Data to Examine
		• English: Lowest groups are special education students and ELs, with a dip from baseline and a lower current score than baseline score. • Math: Asian is our highest-scoring group, followed by White. Only Asian made the math target this year. • Math: White is second-highest group, but scores are steadily declining. • Math: African American students do almost as poorly as ELs. • English and math: Hispanic students compose the majority of students in the school, but they still score lower than the school average, which is helped by Asian and White students. Their performance is probably the best summary of school performance.	• What has changed about the EL cohort? • Why would African American students do so much worse in math than English? • Is our White population changing or declining?	
Benchmark Schools and Politically Important Comparisons	Great Schools.org and NCEA Just for the Kids websites to identify benchmark schools State accountability reports with state average scores	• We are well below our benchmark school and the state average in both English and math. • Statewide, students do better in math than English; we don't!	• Given our demographics, why are we below the state average? Weak programs? Mobile population? • Why is our math program below our English program?	• Benchmark school visits • Math specialist visit

Note: EL = English learners.

Discussion Summary Table. A template for this table is provided in **Tool 4.3, Data Discussion Summary Template.** We can see that even the most general data summaries generate many questions that require a variety of other data to answer.

Tool 4.3

TIGHTEN YOUR FOCUS: REVIEW STATE OR LOCAL STANDARDS ASSESSMENTS

Time to move on to the specifics of state and/or local school results. Here, you move in from an overall picture of student performance and use of variety of analyses to gain a more detailed portrait of school strengths and weaknesses by grade and content area.

Examine Achievement Differences by Grade Level and Content

Accountability reports are generally based on data aggregated across several grade levels. When you find a weakness in student performance, the accountability report may not indicate whether particular grade levels or subgroups of students disproportionately contributed to the low scores. An in-depth examination of student performance by subject, grade level, and subgroup requires that you have access not only to cross-sectional or cohort comparisons (the performance of students at a given grade level in one year compared to those in the same grade level in prior years) but to longitudinal analyses as well (the same students as they progress through the grade levels). State test results typically are reported for grade-level cohorts of students, but such comparisons make it difficult to disentangle whether changes in performance are the results of a change in who is being tested or of changes in the school program.

This is particularly problematic for small schools. For example, if this year's fifth graders perform better than last year's, is it because this year's fifth graders had greater ability to begin with, or because of a new fifth-grade program? By monitoring the same students over time, as they progress through school, you eliminate this problem. For a more fine-grained analysis of content strengths and weaknesses, such as which skills pose the most challenge to students, you will need to refer to the assessment blueprint or specification upon which the accountability system was based and/or dig out item analyses to gain perspective on the types of items on which students are performing relatively the best and the worst.

Expert Help

If you would like to make the most of your state and district test scores and be able to look at students both as cohort groups and longitudinally, you might want one of your expert panel to help you merge individual student results with other enrollment and demographic information from your student information system. Your expert can then produce custom reports for your school to address both cohort and longitudinal growth questions or even to address such important questions as, "How much turnover do we have as students progress through the grades?" and "Are our ninth-grade students still with us in Grades 10, 11, and 12?"

Start With Mean Score Trends by Content and Grade Level to Identify Patterns

State test reports usually include both scale scores and proficiency scores. A scale score is an algebraic or other type of mathematical transformation of a raw (number correct) score that allows you to compare a student's performance relative to that of others on the same test. Depending upon the method used to create the scale score, comparisons of student scores may be limited to a particular grade level and content, or the score can support comparisons between content areas and grade levels. You will need to check your state technical manual to determine exactly what kinds of comparisons are valid and which should not be made.

Regardless of the particular scaling technique used, each student's raw score on a test is converted by a mathematical formula to a common scale, so that students' scores in a subject area can be directly compared from one test form to the next and from year to year. Most scale scores describe where a student's score falls relative to a continuum of all students who took the test—a continuum that runs from the score of the lowest-scoring students to that of the highest-scoring students. Item response theory (IRT) scale scores, used in many states, also indicate the approximate difficulty level achieved by students. More precisely, an IRT score says that students with this score have a 50/50 chance of answering items at this difficulty level on a test. Of course, the higher the score, the more difficult the material that a student or group of students has mastered.

Scale scores are used to classify students by proficiency level; typically these levels have names like Below Basic, Basic, Proficient, and Advanced. For example, a student whose scale score is above 85 may be classified as Advanced, while a student whose scale score is between 50 and 64 may be considered Basic. You can see that the scale scores give you a more differentiated view of student performance, while proficiency levels separate students into gross categories. Because the two kinds of scores provide different perspectives on student performance, we suggest you start by analyzing (mean) scale scores, and then add an analysis of the percentage of students scoring at various levels of proficiency. You can use these scores to compare content patterns by grade level (or course) by graphing mean scores by content area for each grade level over a period of time. For example, you could graph what math performance in Grades 3–5 looks like over the last three years. Is performance improving, staying the same, or declining from year to year and from grade to grade? Does one grade level stand out as problematic or particularly outstanding? If courses have special entry or placement criteria, such as reading improvement, advanced placement, or specialized mathematics courses, it is helpful to track course enrollment data along with test scores to consider whether *selection bias* may be influencing test scores. For example, if Algebra I was previously offered only for high-ability eighth graders, and now all eighth graders take Algebra I, the difference in who is now taking the course may influence end-of-year Algebra test scores.

Figure 4.1 displays three-year trends for My Middle School in mathematics by grade level. We find, not unexpectedly, that the most selective course, Algebra, scores highest and the "tracked" course, Grade 8 General Mathematics, the lowest. The surprises are Grades 6 and 7 Mathematics. Students enter doing well, and then begin faltering in Grade 7. When we examine Grade 8 Mathematics courses, we see that more students are being diverted into the less-selective General Mathematics, which could explain the spike in Algebra scores Year 3. The biggest "diversion" of lower-scoring students to General Mathematics, however, occurred in Year 2, which also accounted for the largest drop in Algebra and the largest gain in General Mathematics scores. Could the placement policies be faulty?

Figure 4.1   Three-Year Mathematics Trends by Grade Level With Course Enrollment Information

Data Review Questions

1. Are mean (average) math scores improving over time?
2. What is the pattern?

State Mathematics Results: Three-Year Mean Scores

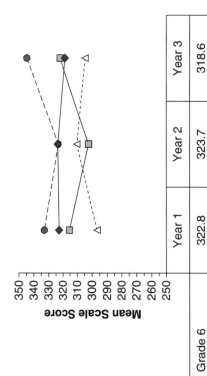

	Year 1	Year 2	Year 3
Grade 6	322.8	323.7	318.6
Grade 7	315.4	302.3	322.1
Grade 8 General	296.7	310.2	304.6
Grade 8 Algebra	332.9	323.4	344.6

Year

Observations

1. Grade 8 algebra and Grade 7 averages dip in Year 1 and then recover in Year 3.
2. Grade 6 drops in Year 3.
3. Grade 8 general math improves in Year 2 and then dips in Year 3.
4. Grade 8 algebra and Grade 6 are highest scoring; Grade 8 general math is lowest scoring.

Course Enrollment Data for Grade 8 Selective Courses

Data Review Questions

Does selectivity affect course performance?

Mathematics	Grade 8 General Math Enrollment	Grade 8 Algebra Enrollment
Year 1	67.10%	32.90%
Year 2	72.10%	27.90%
Year 3	73.50%	26.50%

Observations

1. Algebra enrollments are decreasing over time.
2. General math enrollment is increasing.

Examine Differences in the Proportion of High- and Low-Scoring Students by Grade Level and Content

The mean score provides a handy summary of grade-level performance but can mask large discrepancies within a grade level. For example, a mean score of 50 on the state mathematics test could mask the reality that almost half your students are scoring in the upper quartile and a nearly similar proportion are scoring at the lowest level. Your actions based on the latter would be very different than if most all students are scoring around 50. In other words, the same mean score can represent a score distribution where students are split into a high-scoring and a low-scoring group (bimodal distribution), or a score distribution where all students score pretty much near the average! Moreover, by looking at overall mean performance, we mask how students at various points of the score continuum are performing, for example, whether high-performing students are continuing to perform well, or whether low-performing students are improving. We need to examine how students' scores are distributed to discover potential discrepancies in performance, such as the one we hypothesize between Grade 8 Algebra and Grade 6 performance on the one hand and Grade 7 and Grade 8 General Mathematics on the other. Figure 4.2 presents the percentage meeting targets,

Figure 4.2	Three-Year Trends by Course for Students Meeting Targets Versus Lowest-Scoring Students

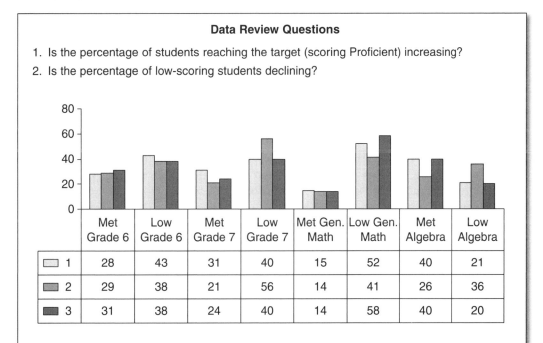

Data Review Questions

1. Is the percentage of students reaching the target (scoring Proficient) increasing?
2. Is the percentage of low-scoring students declining?

	Met Grade 6	Low Grade 6	Met Grade 7	Low Grade 7	Met Gen. Math	Low Gen. Math	Met Algebra	Low Algebra
1	28	43	31	40	15	52	40	21
2	29	38	21	56	14	41	26	36
3	31	38	24	40	14	58	40	20

Observations

1. Grade 6: Percentage meeting target slowly increasing over three years. Percentage scoring low dropping slightly.
2. Grade 7: Percentage meeting target drops significantly in Year 2 and increases slightly in Year 3. Percentage scoring low spikes in Year 2 but drops to Year 1 levels in Year 3.
3. General math: Percentage meeting targets small but unchanging. Percentage scoring low generally over 50% of class.

the percentage scoring Proficient, and the percentage of low-scoring students in each grade level at My Middle School.

An examination of the score distributions reveals that an unacceptably high percentage of students still score in the lowest categories at Grades 6 and 7, possibly indicating that mathematics scores at Grade 6 may be a result of the highest-scoring students "carrying" the entire grade level. Grade 7 appears not to remediate students nor prepare them for algebra, because we see that at Grade 8, where students are grouped by prior preparation, the underprepared in General Mathematics are disproportionately low scoring, and the highly selected population in Algebra has a distribution reflective of their entry-level scores. We still don't know what caused the Year 2 score dips in Grade 7 Mathematics and Algebra or why there was no dip in Grade 8 and General Mathematics! Is the problem a function of the tests at certain grade levels? How important is the dip for our planning?

Examine Trends for Subgroups and Compare With Your Benchmark School

What about the equity issues in our mathematics program? An important goal for all schools is reducing the achievement gap between traditionally low-performing groups of students—including students with disabilities, African American and Hispanic students, and students with limited English proficiency—and "mainstream," middle-class, White and Asian students. The difference between average performance of the mainstream group and traditionally low-performing groups is called the *achievement gap*. The comparison of the performance of some groups of students against White/Asian/middle-class performance is fraught with problems. Socioeconomic status is a strong predictor of school performance and is confounded with ethnicity for some groups. "Asian" includes historically low-performing groups (recent arrivals from rural or war-torn areas) as well as those from industrialized Asian nations with universal public education.

Perhaps the most straightforward way to reduce performance differences among subgroups of students in your schools is to work on accelerating academic growth for low-performing students, those below grade-level proficiency. At the same time, students who have mastered standards and are ready to work above grade level should be allowed to move ahead, even if their performance widens the achievement gap on your test scores. "Gap" politics can put schools in a tough position. Identifiable subgroups of students should not be consistently performing in the lowest proficiency ranges. The target is to have all students Proficient or above. On the other hand, the background factors that enabled some students to enter school advantaged continue to operate and may sustain the initial advantage.

We examine the gap between different subgroups and the school average as one method of defining an achievement gap. We also examine simultaneously the subgroup performance of our benchmark school as a way of defining what might be possible to achieve in our school. The simultaneous examination of a comparable school eliminates excuses and deflects blame from student populations to our program. Table 4.5 presents our most current subgroup mathematics data (Year 3) and identifies areas of performance inequity.

Table 4.5 My Middle School and Benchmark School Percentages Proficient in Mathematics by Subgroup, Year 3

Data Review Questions

1. Where are there achievement gaps between subgroups meeting the target and those not meeting it?

2. If some groups are scoring significantly lower than others, in which courses does this occur?

3. How does the performance of our subgroups compare with that of similar subgroups in our benchmark school?

My Middle School Percentage Proficient by Subgroup, Year 3								
% Proficient	All	SED	EL	African American	Asian	Latino	White	SWD
Grade 6 Mathematics	31%	32%	5%	24%	50%	29%	36%	3%
Grade 7 Mathematics	24%	23%	2%	24%	41%	21%	37%	3%
General Mathematics	14%	12%	2%	9%	7%	16%	19%	3%
Algebra	30%	26%	2%	None	46%	23%	7%	NA
The Benchmark School Percentage Proficient by Subgroup, Year 3								
% Proficient	All	SED	EL	African American	Asian	Latino	White	SWD
Grade 6 Mathematics	52%	51%	38%	44%	None	42%	None	0%
Grade 7 Mathematics	51%	49%	31%	32%		58%		12%
General Mathematics	38%	40%	28%	28%		17%		5%
Algebra	63%	64%	27%	67%		59%		0

Observations

1. The target for gap analysis is the percentage proficient for the school listed under All.

2. Grade 7 and general math have the fewest students meeting the proficiency target.

3. The largest gaps are for ELs and students with disabilities (SWDs). White and Asian students exceed the school average.

4. Asians, ELs, and African American students are below the proficiency average in general math.

4. Whites are below the proficiency average in Algebra. There are not enough African American students in Algebra to even "count."

5. The benchmark school has significantly larger percentages of proficient students in all subgroups and lacks traditionally high-scoring Asian and White subgroups.

6. General math students at the benchmark school, like ours, are the lowest performing.

7. The benchmark school also does much better than we do with ELs and SWDs, though they still score very low.

Note: SED = socioeconomically disadvantaged; SWD = students with disabilities; EL = English learners.

Summarize Your Review of State and Local Test Data

At the end of our review of state and local assessment data, we summarize our discussion in the same format we used for our accountability data review. Table 4.6 summarizes the findings, questions we raised, and lists of other data to examine that we generated during our investigation of subject, grade level, and subgroup performance. The most important items in the data summary are the questions raised and the need to examine other data. Your school's data team could and should continue the analysis and report to the group any contradictory or extended findings, but at this point, staff may be suffering data delirium and need a short break!

Table 4.6   Data Discussion Summary Table: State Assessment Results for My Middle School

Area	Data Used	Findings	Questions Raised	Other Data to Examine
Mean Score Trends	Mean scale score by grade level from state standards test	• Grade 6 scores were flat, and then dropped this year. • Grade 7 and Algebra scores dipped in Year 2, and then regained their Year 1 level this year. • General Mathematics scores increased for 2 years and then had a slight decline this year.	• Was it the test or the program? • Was it the test in Year 2 that caused the dip? • Did the additional enrollment in general math this year affect the average score, or was it the test?	• Technical manual for assessment • Benchmark schools average and state average to see if the "test effect" holds in these other places • District and local tests to corroborate achievement trends
Math Enrollment Trends	Enrollment numbers by grade level reported on state standards test	• In Grades 6 and 7, all students take the same course. • Grade 8 Algebra enrollment is declining.	• Why are we admitting fewer students into Algebra? • Why are there so few African American students in Algebra?	• Number of students enrolling each year or transferring out • Cohort size and subgroup size by year
Proficiency Trends	State standards test results by grade level for past three years	• Grade 6 percentage proficient is increasing. • Grade 7 percentage	• What is making the Grade 6 program stronger each year?	• Grade 6 math program: curriculum, instruction, tutoring, and so forth.

Area	Data Used	Findings	Questions Raised	Other Data to Examine
		proficient is declining. • Grade 8 General Mathematics proficiency is stable but low. • Grade 8 Algebra proficiency had a dip last year but is back to Year 1 levels in Year 3.	• Why are Grade 7 scores declining while Grade 6 scores are improving? • Is "tracking" an explanation for the General Mathematics versus Algebra performance difference?	• Grade 7 math program: curriculum, instruction, and prealgebra skill development • District end-of-course tests at Grades 6 and 7 • District quarterly exams for General Mathematics and Algebra
Subgroup Trends by Grade Level (Achievement Gap)	State standards test reports by grade level and subgroup	• Special education students and English learners haven't improved and are drastically underrepresented in the Proficient category. • African American students start out not too far behind in Grade 6, but by Grade 8 they don't score Proficient in Algebra. • Asian students in general math are very low performing compared to their subgroup trends.	• How much is the difference in subgroup performance due to motivation, attendance, or "tracking"? • Are the subgroup students who are not proficient pretty close to being proficient, or are they scoring in the Below Basic and Far Below Basic categories? • What is our policy for Algebra placement?	• Data about students from the student information system • Student placement procedures • State test data disaggregated for subgroups
Benchmark School	NCEA Just for the Kids website reports for comparable schools	• Benchmark school has a "tougher" demographic but does twice as well as we do.	• What is the math program in the benchmark school?	• Benchmark school curriculum, instruction, assessment system

CLARIFY AND CORROBORATE INSTRUCTIONAL FOCUS AREAS WITH LOCAL ASSESSMENTS

A review of accountability results and state and local high-stakes, high-quality assessment data help us identify areas of concern for individual grade levels, content or subjects, and subgroups. But these assessments, depending upon how they were developed and reported and how the information is made available to teachers, may not be fine-grained enough to help us answer two really essential questions:

1. Which skills are not being mastered?

2. Where is our curriculum out of alignment with state standards?

We look to local assessment results to corroborate our findings to this point and to clarify what needs improvement. Before using local assessments, be sure to check how well your local assessments are aligned to the state test. There are two strategies you can use:

Tool 4.4

1. Review state test blueprints and release items to determine how well your local test's standards emphasis, item types, and skills aligns to the state test. **Tool 4.4, Discussion Protocol: Reviewing Sample Items or Released Tests,** provides a discussion protocol for checking the alignment of a local test to a high-stakes test.

2. Your tests should cover the same range of standards that the state test covers. Assuming so, calculate a correlation between student performance on your local end-of-course or annual assessments and the state test results. A high correlation suggests good alignment.

Expert Help

You can use your individual student results from local assessments (the longer and more carefully crafted tests) to calculate a correlation coefficient with individual student results on the state assessment. The correlation coefficient will tell you how well a student's performance on your district or common assessment predicts performance on the state test. A math teacher and someone good with organizing large data sets can correlate your more-formal local assessments, or your district- or school-developed end-of-semester or annual tests, to high-stakes tests and let you know if your local tests can predict performance on the state tests.

Having confirmed the alignment between local and state tests, you're ready to move on to further analysis.

Use Local Assessments for Diagnosing Specific Learning Needs

Local monitoring assessments, such as benchmark or interim tests, may not stand up to psychometric scrutiny. Too often they have no technical manual, no clear description of what is being measured or how they were developed, no reliability or validity information, and no detail on how items were selected or on item difficulty. Not to worry! Coupled with teacher experience, these assessments can stimulate valuable discussions to identify curriculum areas in need of revision or improvement and to understand student needs. Local assessments, with just a little extra effort, can also clarify what the high-stakes assessments are really measuring. Your less-than-professional local tests, if well leavened with teacher expertise, can contribute to identifying your instructional focus.

Local monitoring assessments can help us address some of the following questions:

- At what point (early in the semester, midyear, later) do students start having difficulty?
- Are we delivering the curriculum at a pace that will enable students to be prepared for state assessments at the end of the year?
- Are all students mastering key competencies? If not, what alternative teaching strategies and opportunities to learn them do we provide?
- Based on test results, who are the students who need extra help? What interventions can we provide to ensure that students master key skills and don't fall behind?

When we reviewed local assessments at My Middle School and combined the information with our findings from the accountability system and state test, we identified several areas in need of improvement. The local tests included end-of-course mathematics assessments, quarterly tests, and math facts/integer fluency tests. Based on district reports and teacher experience, we revisited our data summaries from our analysis of state assessment results. The state data suggested that our students entered Grade 6 fairly well prepared but began slipping in Grade 7. By Grade 8, those assigned to general math fell further behind, and only the cream took Algebra, with poor results when compared with those of our benchmark school. We began our local test review with an eye to identifying which Grade 8 (both General Mathematics and Algebra) and Grade 7 skills needed additional attention. The results of our skill identification review provided us with our instructional focus description (see Table 4.7).

Table 4.7 Local Test Review Summary: My Middle School Instructional Focus Description

Grade Level and Content	Grade 7 Mathematics	Grade 8 General Mathematics	Grade 8 Algebra
Subgroups	All	All	All
Key Skills Needing Attention	• Add, subtract, multiply, and divide rational numbers (integers, fractions, and terminating decimals), and take positive rational numbers to whole-number powers. • Solve problems that involve discounts, markups, commissions, and profit, and compute simple and compound interest.	• Simplify numerical expressions by applying properties of rational numbers (e.g., identity, inverse, distributive, associative, commutative), and justify the process used.	• Solve two-step linear equations and inequalities. • Solve multistep problems that involve rate, speed, distance, and time.
Key Mathematics Reasoning Supporting the Skills (all courses)	• Use estimation to verify the reasonableness of calculated results. • Analyze problems by identifying relationships, distinguishing relevant from irrelevant information, identifying missing information, sequencing and prioritizing information, and observing patterns. • Estimate unknown quantities graphically and solve for them by using logical reasoning and arithmetic and algebraic techniques.		

REVIEW OTHER VALUED OUTCOMES

We have devoted the majority of our discussion in this chapter to reviewing test data. We do not for one minute believe that test scores define all or even most of the important outcomes in your school. The reality, however, is that if you, your parents, or the public perceive that your school needs improvement, test scores contribute a great deal to that perception. A great many other indicators exist to help you define your instructional focus. We have selected a few of the most frequently cited performance criteria, in addition to test scores, that you could review to establish your turnaround student performance goals.

Analyze Dropout Data

If you are a middle or high school, your dropout rates most likely are part of your state accountability system. Dropout rates have great political appeal and often are used to characterize schools as "dropout factories" by state and national politicians and advocacy groups. It is worth taking time to examine your school's dropout rates, not just because you are committed to graduating all students, but because they are so frequently misunderstood.

How is *dropout rate* defined by your state or district? Spend time finding the official definition used for your school, and then identify all the ways that you could improve your data collection and reporting system to eliminate errors in the reporting and calculation of the rate. Once you understand and have cleaned up the procedures associated with calculating your school's dropout rate, you will want to investigate the data to identify patterns in who is dropping out and possible precursors to it—for example, course failures, absence rates, grade retention, and the characteristics and pathways of those who persist to successful high school completion. Such analyses can reinforce or add to the instructional focus for your Turnaround Plan. For example, if students who fail Algebra twice are likely to drop out, intervention programs to promote Algebra I success may become a priority instructional focus. We have included **Tool 4.5, Analyzing Dropout Rates to Determine Instructional Focus,** to guide dropout rate data review should you serve students in the middle and high school grades.

Tool
4.5

Examine Progress on Student Preparation Goals

An instructional focus on preparation is implicit in all levels of schooling. Preschool implicitly prepares students for success in kindergarten. Elementary school implicitly prepares students for success in middle school, and so on: K–12 public education should prepare students for success in college, work, and life. While these ultimate outcomes might be weakly predicted by test scores, they are larger and more complex than test performance.

A first step in understanding how you are doing on your preparation goals is to identify them. If you work at a preschool, your preparation goals likely relate to preparing students for formal schooling (kindergarten) and literacy acquisition. If you work at an elementary school, you will prepare students for subject-based learning, which begins in middle school and is based on literacy, numeracy, study skills, and instilling efficacy and the belief that school completion is a personal benefit to a student. If you teach in a middle school, you are preparing students for high school subjects, high school persistence and graduation, and college or career goals. At the high school level, preparation might entail acquiring knowledge of subject matter that enables a student to successfully pursue college-level work or perform skilled labor, developing an ability to learn how to learn, acquiring study and research skills, persisting through obstacles, and setting clear postsecondary goals. Specialized athletic, performance, art, or vocational skill development could also be included in your school's preparation goals.

When you are reviewing data about how to improve student achievement, keep in mind that the construct that test scores attempt to predict is preparation. Until you define for your school the valued preparation goals, you will miss reviewing data central to the kinds of student outcomes all educators entered the field to promote. **Tool 4.6, Suggestions for Reviewing Progress on Student Preparation Goals,** provides an example of how you can use the preparation goals central to the grade span of your school to identify data central to defining key aspects of student achievement related to those goals.

Tool 4.6

Consider English-Learner Reclassification Rates

Helping immigrant students, and even native-born children from immigrant families, learn English is a central function of schooling. Title III funding requires that schools monitor and report the progress of ELs in acquiring English-language proficiency and achieving proficiency in the core curriculum. The federal government has timelines and targets for English acquisition for students in schools receiving Title III funding. If your school receives federal Title III funding, you will have accountability and reclassification rate targets for ELs. You will need to review data related to your Title III targets when considering the instructional focus for your turnaround work. Your data review could include the following:

- Results on state English-language proficiency tests: Are ELs making progress?
- State content assessment results for ELs
- Reclassification rates: How many students are reclassified, how soon after entering school, by what criteria?
- Long-term ELs: Are some students becoming "career" ELs?
- The performance of reclassified ELs (fluent English-proficient subgroup students) over time; that is, how do former ELs perform after they have transitioned to English-only status?
- Characteristics of more and less successful ELs

Be careful as you analyze results for your ELs: The group changes from year to year, as some students transition out and are redesignated, and other new ELs enter your school. A drop-off in EL state assessment scores from Grade 4 to Grade 5 may simply be the result of the higher-ability students having transitioned out of EL status in Grade 5, and thus their higher scores are no longer included among those of the ELs!

CHOOSE THE TURNAROUND FOCUS AREAS

Given all of the data you have now reviewed, the choice of focal areas for the Turnaround Plan becomes clear. Our sample data, which is real and current, indicate the following:

- My Middle School students are struggling in both English and mathematics, but the situation in mathematics is deteriorating and significantly worse than in English.
- Students who traditionally do better in mathematics than English, such as ELs, do not do well at My Middle School.
- All subgroups do worse in mathematics than English.
- Students do relatively well in Grade 6, but sometime in Grade 7, math achievement falls off and leaves students ill prepared for Grade 8 General Mathematics or Algebra.

While we would work on Turnaround Plans for all areas in which our school did not meet its targets, for purposes of making the process clearer, we will focus our Turnaround Plan on improving mathematics. Table 4.8 summarizes our turnaround focus. Specifically, we would like to improve the performance of all students in all subgroups in Grade 7 Mathematics, Grade 8 General Mathematics, and Grade 8 Algebra by increasing the percentage scoring Proficient by at least 20% in two of the courses and 30% in Algebra. We established this target goal as reasonable based on the performance of our benchmark school. We also used benchmark school course enrollment data to set targets for our Grade 8 Mathematics course enrollments. If our benchmark school can do it, so can we!

Table 4.8   Turnaround Focus Based on Student Outcome Data

Grade Level	Target Groups	Turnaround Focus
Grade 7 Mathematics	All SWD	• Increase percentage scoring Proficient on the state standards tests by 20%. • SWD goals to be determined after reviewing benchmark school's success with SWDs.
Grade 8 General Mathematics	All	• Increase percentage scoring Proficient on state standards tests by 20%. • Decrease course enrollment by 5% to meet percentage enrollment of benchmark school.
Grade 8 Algebra	All	• Increase percentage scoring Proficient on state standards tests by 30% to meet benchmark school outcomes. • Increase course enrollment by 5% to meet enrollment of benchmark school.

Note: SWD = students with disabilities.

Don't Move On Until You Have Identified Your Strengths

We have reviewed our accountability and assessment results and generated many questions about areas where we have failed to meet our targets or where our instructional program might be weak. Our school strengths have not clearly emerged from this analysis. If you have a low-performing school, the more general accountability summaries may not reveal school strengths. Areas of academic excellence are often buried in accountability indices. However, as soon as we begin to disaggregate data by subgroup, by grade level, and by content area, strengths are uncovered. The same students who in our example struggle in mathematics may very well excel in other areas. When you find subgroup or content strength—and you will—you can examine classrooms or content areas where performance is relatively strong and ask some intriguing questions: Is there more student engagement? Is instruction clearer? Do students feel less intimidated by the subject or the teachers? While there is much to explore, we do have some relative strengths upon which to build our turnaround efforts.

It may have been difficult to examine the overwhelming amount of data we have available to diagnose student learning needs. In the next step, we move into more comfortable territory, changing curriculum and instruction and providing support for these changes. However, much as we as educators find it easier to discuss our practice than student learning issues, we find that we have fewer data available for program redesign than we did for developing an instructional focus. One of the goals of our turnaround work is to remedy the lack of information we routinely gather related to curriculum and instruction. As we examine data to redesign our program, we can plan to collect data during our Turnaround Plan implementation that will allow us to make better decisions about program redesign in the future.

CHAPTER 4 TOOLKIT

IDENTIFY THE TURNAROUND FOCUS

The Tools for Chapter 4 can be found on the companion website for *The TurnAround ToolKit* at http://www.corwin.com/turnaroundtoolkit.

Tool 4.1   Performance Criteria for Reviewing Student Outcome Data

Tool 4.2   Understanding Your State Accountability System

Tool 4.3   Data Discussion Summary Template

Tool 4.4   Discussion Protocol: Reviewing Sample Items or Released Tests

Tool 4.5   Analyzing Dropout Rates to Determine Instructional Focus

Tool 4.6   Suggestions for Reviewing Progress on Student Preparation Goals

5

Redesign Programs to Address the Turnaround Focus

Don't tell me you believe all children can learn; tell me what you do when they don't.

—National Reform Faculty

Redesign: Use Data to Create the Turnaround Plan

Data

Identify the turnaround focus.

Redesign programs to address the turnaround focus.

Develop and implement the Turnaround Plan.

POCKET SUMMARY

Task	Major Activities	Purpose
Redesign programs to address instructional focus.	• Introduce the concept of *theory of action* early in the redesign process. **Tool 5.1 Toolkit Tutorial: Basing Our Turnaround Plan on a Theory of Action or Change** • Adopt an attitude of rapid-fire experimentation.	• Make cause-and-effect relationships explicit.
Clarify the turnaround focus.	• Specify how you will know you have met your long-term goals. • Identify short-term outcomes needed to accomplish long-term goals.	• Define expected outcomes.
Redesign the program.	• Begin redesign with curriculum, instruction, and staff development. • Build continuous improvement into teaching practice. • Select needs assessment questions for program redesign. **Tool 5.2 Needs Assessment Questions for Curriculum, Instruction, and Staff Development** • Review data to address needs assessment questions. • Consult experts to help address redesign questions. **Tool 5.3 Resources for Program Redesign**	• Identify instructional redesign. • Build in monitoring strategies.
Build program support into the redesign.	• Review school context variables that support instruction. **Tool 5.4 Needs Assessment Questions for School Context Variables** • Embed program support into the Turnaround Plan.	• Identify support needed for instructional program changes.

REDESIGN PROGRAMS TO ADDRESS INSTRUCTIONAL FOCUS

Introduce the Concept of *Theory of Action* Early in the Redesign Process

Program redesign begins at the end! Tell us where you want to go, and we will help you find your way there. The process of identifying the kinds of program changes needed to turn around student performance trends is one familiar to most teachers working in standards-based systems:

1. Identify the goal.

2. Write a clear statement of outcomes that lets you know you've reached your goal.

3. Identify the skills and knowledge students need to acquire on the road to achieving the outcomes, completing the course, and attaining grade-level proficiency.

4. Design and/or select the instructional materials, activities, assignments, instructional strategies, assessments, and other supports that will enable students to acquire the prerequisite skills and achieve the final outcomes.

Teachers call this process "backwards mapping," because they create an instructional route to a final desired destination. Some educators call this process "task analysis," because the final learning outcome is analyzed into the skills and component parts that students must learn en route to the outcome. The "tasks" along the way guide the design of curriculum and instruction activities to be used at each step until students have met the ultimate goal.

However, underlying the process of backwards mapping are human theories about how students learn particular subject matter or skills. These theories of cause and effect underlie all curriculum design and instructional programs. As you brainstorm solutions to address your turnaround focus, differences will surface among staff as to what should be done. These differences reflect different theories of action, theories of change, or hypotheses underlying staff's mental cause-and-effect models of what good instruction looks like and what the road to student success looks like. If your program is falling short, meaning students aren't attaining program goals, then you need to discuss these implicit mental models, both to improve them and to create a shared understanding of why certain changes need to happen. We, like many others, refer to the process of making explicit our thinking about what will "cause" the desired outcomes as a *theory of action*.[1] We will use a simple diagram to capture the links between our actions and intended outcomes and to help us through both the redesign and its subsequent evaluation process.

Using our My Middle School example, some teachers might say that students must master math facts to improve their performance. Others could hypothesize that students lack a conceptual understanding of the relationship between math algorithms and the logic of math problems. Still others might add that the achievement deficiency results from the disconnect between how math is taught and how it is assessed. All points of view have merit and reflect different theories of action. These internal theories play out in the classroom as different instructional approaches and curricular emphases. The purpose of discussions about theories of action is not to create uniform practice or search for the one right answer but rather to entertain multiple approaches to and perspectives on better addressing student needs.

At the same time, however, turnaround work requires a clear focus and a unified approach to improvement. The clear focus emerges when staff involved in implementing the Turnaround Plan share a common vision of what the implementation requires. Consensus on and common understanding of the theory of action underlying the redesign goes a long way toward successful implementation. A simple theory of action for your turnaround work could include the elements displayed in Figure 5.1. **Tool 5.1, Toolkit Tutorial: Basing Our Turnaround Plan on a Theory of Action or Change,** provides a brief explanation of the purpose of creating a visual diagram of your implicit theories.

Tool 5.1

| Figure 5.1 | Components of a Theory of Action or Theory of Change |

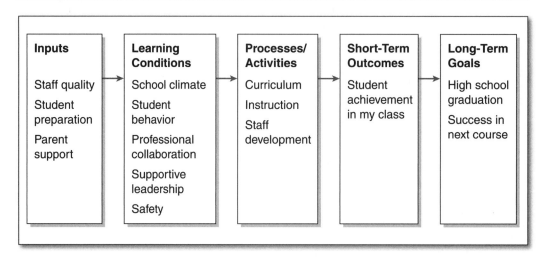

Inputs	Learning Conditions	Processes/ Activities	Short-Term Outcomes	Long-Term Goals
Staff quality	School climate	Curriculum	Student achievement in my class	High school graduation
Student preparation	Student behavior	Instruction		Success in next course
Parent support	Professional collaboration	Staff development		
	Supportive leadership			
	Safety			

Adopt an Attitude of Rapid-Fire Experimentation

In addition to having a shared understanding of how the program is supposed to address your instructional focus, staff needs to develop an attitude of pragmatism and experimentation. Turnaround work is distinguished by its urgency and its commitment to rapid-fire experimentation. Experimentation simply means that we try something, determine how well it is working, and continue using it, revise it, or drop the practice, depending upon how well students are progressing. Experimentation is pragmatic, not ideological. Our theories of action are usually based on our ideas of what is supposed to work. We may even have "faith-based" theories of action, such as those underlying the small learning communities movement. We "believe" small high schools will improve student achievement. Small schools are appealing and the concept is logical. However, we don't have strong data to support their success. Turnaround work requires teachers to check the theories underlying program design not only by adopting research-based practices but also by frequently assessing whether their turnaround activities are working. Given the urgency of our task, we cannot wait for a year or three to decide if we need to make changes. Change is imminent, ongoing, and based on data we are collecting throughout the program implementation process.

CLARIFY THE TURNAROUND FOCUS

Specify How You Will Know You Have Met Your Long-Term Goals

Once staff understands that the turnaround plan will be based on a theory (or theories) of action or change that will be tested as the plan is implemented, it's time for the backwards mapping redesign process to begin. We cannot emphasize enough how important it is that clear, long- and short-term outcomes focus your curriculum and instruction redesign work. Table 5.1 following summarizes the long-term goals for My Middle School Grade 7 Mathematics that we identified in Chapter 4.

The long-term turnaround focus exudes "faux precision": We have a target of a 20% increase in the number of students scoring Proficient on state tests but don't really have a concrete idea of what the increase entails. Specifically,

- What exactly must students do to score Proficient? What kinds of skills and knowledge indicate that a student is proficient? What level of standards test mastery indicates proficiency?
- In which areas are students deficient? Which skills have they not mastered that are interfering with their ability to demonstrate proficiency?

Table 5.1 Turnaround Focus: Long-Term Goals for My Middle School Grade 7 Mathematics

Grade Level	Target Groups	Turnaround Focus
Grade 7 Mathematics	All SWD	• Increase percentage scoring Proficient on state standards tests by 20% • SWD goals to be determined after reviewing benchmark school's success with SWDs
Grade 8 General Mathematics	All	• Increase percentage scoring Proficient on state standards tests by 20% • Decrease course enrollment by 5% to meet percentage enrollment of benchmark school
Grade 8 Algebra	All	• Increase percentage scoring Proficient on state standards test by 30% to meet benchmark school outcomes • Increase course enrollment by 5% to meet enrollment of benchmark school

Note. SWD = students with disabilities.

Identify Short-Term Outcomes
Needed to Accomplish Long-Term Goals

A test score target on a grade-level standards test is necessarily vague. A percentage Proficient score provides no guidance for teachers about what skills students have yet to learn and what they have already mastered. We must revisit our state standards test and our local assessments to identify the skill areas our students must improve to increase their scores. Table 5.2 identifies specific areas where students must improve to meet proficiency levels on the state standards test.

Perhaps a better criterion for identifying what you should be expecting from students as a result of your turnaround efforts can be captured by the term *generative outcomes*, outcomes that enable students to meet long-term learning goals. Important generative learning outcomes have three characteristics:

1. They build upon student prior knowledge.

2. They are used in other content areas at the student's grade level and/or generalize to life situations.

3. They become the foundation of future learning, from the next skill to the next unit to the next grade level.

All of the short-term outcomes listed in Table 5.2 are generative in this sense. For example, *estimation* builds on students' basic computation skills,

Table 5.2   Short-Term (Grade-Level) Outcomes for My Middle School Mathematics Program

Grade Level and Content	Grade 7 Mathematics	Grade 8 General Mathematics	Grade 8 Algebra
Subgroups	All	All	All
Key Skills Needed	• Add, subtract, multiply, and divide rational numbers (integers, fractions, and terminating decimals), and take positive rational numbers to whole-number powers • Solve problems that involve discounts, markups, commissions, and profit, and compute simple and compound interest	• Simplify numerical expressions by applying properties of rational numbers (e.g., identity, inverse, distributive, associative, commutative), and justify the process used	• Solve two-step linear equations and inequalities • Solve multistep problems with rate, speed, distance, and time
Key Mathematics Reasoning Skills (all courses)	• Use estimation to verify the reasonableness of calculated results • Analyze problems by identifying relationships, distinguishing relevant from irrelevant information, identifying missing information, sequencing and prioritizing information, and observing patterns • Estimate unknown quantities graphically and solve for them by using logical reasoning and arithmetic and algebraic techniques		

is useful across curriculum areas and in life, and supports metacognition and subsequent mathematics learning. As you list your most immediate student learning goals, evaluate their importance to long-lasting skills and dispositions.

Because we hypothesize that if students improve their test performance on the key skills identified in Table 5.2, they will increase their proficiency level on standards tests, we have made explicit one part of our theory of action: what end-of-course skills are needed for students to score Proficient in mathematics. This is specified in our program redesign diagram (Figure 5.2).

In addition to the short- and long-term outcomes you specified in your program redesign diagram (the theory of action), you will want to consider additional crucial grade-level outcomes that may not appear on a high-stakes test. While it's important in your analysis of curriculum and instruction to identify core (generative) competencies and background knowledge, you also will consider outcomes related to application of grade-level knowledge that are better assessed with projects, writing, or other performance measures than with the high-stakes test.

Figure 5.2 Specifying the Outcomes and Goals of the Theory of Action

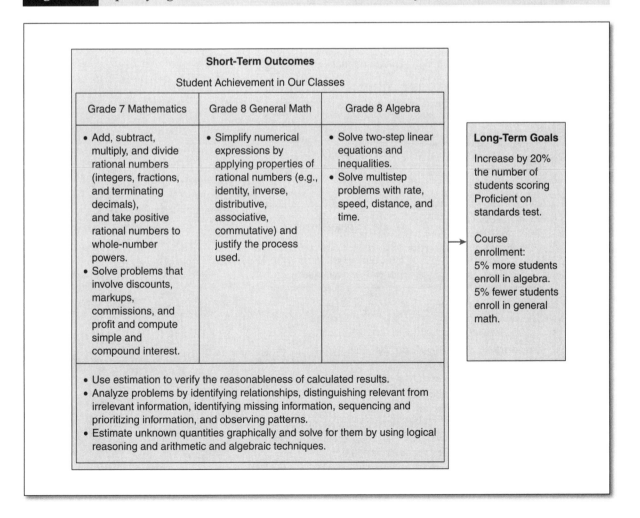

REDESIGN THE PROGRAM

Begin Redesign With Curriculum, Instruction, and Staff Development

We can see that our backwards mapping process, which began with specifying long- and short-term targets, has brought us squarely to the center of program redesign, the issues and activities that constitute curriculum, instruction, and staff development. These central activities are identified in the "Process" box in our theory of action diagram (Figure 5.1). The process part of our theory of action describes the exact activities and actions we will take to cause students to achieve our short-term, end-of-course outcomes, which then will enable them to reach our long-term goals. Figure 5.3 highlights key areas

Figure 5.3   Processes and Activities to Examine in Program Redesign

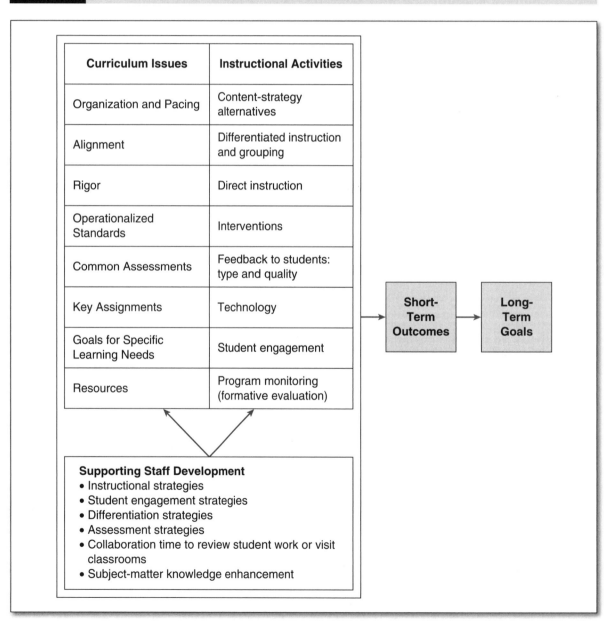

of curriculum, instruction, and staff development that you will examine and revise. The revisions in these three areas constitute your school's turnaround work. You will notice that Figure 5.3 outlines many possible changes to your program. You will not make changes in all of these areas, but prior to deciding on your turnaround activities, we urge you to examine a wide range of possibilities, much as you did when you reviewed student achievement data to identify the turnaround focus. You will also notice that many of these factors are intertwined. Alignment and rigor are difficult to separate. Differentiating instruction is accompanied by interventions and student engagement strategies.

Build Continuous Improvement Into Teaching Practice

It may come as a surprise that we included "program monitoring" as an instructional activity. By asking teachers to examine their practice through data on student work, as well as to frequently monitor student progress toward their short-term outcomes, you are redefining teaching as a continuous improvement process. You are sending the message that everything teachers do merits review, reflection, and revision. Assessment and revision of instruction are not commonly incorporated into teaching, even though most teachers understand that their instruction should be modified based on student learning. Unfortunately, with high-stakes assessments used to rate and rank schools, many teachers labor under the tyranny of the pacing chart. They may assess, but how do they take time to reteach and risk being off schedule in delivering content that surely will appear on the spring test?

A second problem is the sheer number of standards that constitute the curriculum. If you see that students do not understand a concept, and your curriculum is packed with many, many topics, concepts, principles, and skills, just where do you slow down and reteach, and what will you not cover as a result? Refocusing the curriculum on core competencies and content, while maintaining alignment to state standards that appear on the high-stakes test or that are central prerequisite skills in the subject, requires a deep understanding of the particular curriculum and how teachers can leverage instruction in a skill or topic to include other important skills and topics.

Turnaround work is conducted under the pressure of delivering rapid improvement. Yet the rather counterintuitive notion of having teachers frequently review data and then revise instruction is really the only way to prune the crowded curriculum and contain instructional impresarios who can get your redesign efforts detoured.

Select Needs Assessment Questions for Program Redesign

Just as you identified the turnaround focus by selecting questions to guide selection and analysis of student outcome data, you will identify redesign strategies by selecting data review questions that help you to analyze the strengths and weaknesses of your current program in your instructional focus area. One set of program needs assessment questions appears in **Tool 5.2, Needs Assessment Questions for Curriculum, Instruction, and Staff Development.** There are many, many other questions we could include.

Tool
5.2

We like to start with an examination of how our curriculum is organized and paced in conjunction with the teaching strategies that are used with foundational content and skills (curriculum—organization and pacing, instruction—strategies and alternatives). In our My Middle School example, we have identified key grade-level content and skills, the mastery of which should lead to improved performance on a wide variety of grade-level curriculum targets. (That's part of our theory of action: Make sure students are engaged in challenging instructional activities that enable them to develop the fundamental knowledge and skills they need to master grade-level proficiencies.) Therefore, we begin examining the parts of the curriculum and their accompanying instructional strategies related to these key skills. More to the point,

- Are the key knowledge and skills new to this grade, do they build upon prior learning, or is it assumed that they are foundational and are not taught this year?
- When are the knowledge and skills introduced or required for learning this year's content?
- How much time is allocated to their instruction, or how frequently are they used?
- Which materials introduce or employ the skills and knowledge? What is their quality (accuracy, clarity, effectiveness with students)?
- Which strategies are recommended for teaching these skills? What other strategies do we know?

You also may wish to investigate only a few aspects of curriculum and instruction, because those might be the only areas you have the power to change. For example, you may not be able to purchase more technology, change the kinds of interventions offered during the school year, or change instructional materials due to district directives or local budget issues. However, there are many aspects of curriculum and instruction directly under your control that have a clear impact on achievement. Revisable components include pacing, strategies, assignments, assessments, student engagement activities, direct instruction on key concepts, learning goals, differentiated classroom instruction, and use of formative assessment.

Review Data to Address Needs Assessment Questions

You can refer to your data inventory (see **Toolkit, Tool 2.7, Data Inventory Template**) to identify available data and create data summaries related to your needs assessment questions. Student outcome data are abundant, but unless your school planning process requires yearly parent, student, and/or teacher satisfaction surveys or you regularly collaborate to review assignment rigor, student work, or conduct classroom walk-throughs, you may have little useful information for determining just which parts of curriculum and instruction need adjustment to improve student performance. If you find that you have many questions for which no data exist, you may wish to have your data team or grade-level teachers conduct reviews of the quality of assignments and student work or conduct classroom walk-throughs to identify program weaknesses.

However, curriculum and instruction, unlike student achievement, have many unobservable components. Quantitative data won't address all

Tool
2.7

of your redesign needs. How content is understood and taught resides inside teachers' heads and is a product of knowledge and experience. Teaching decisions and acts can be observed and reported, but capturing this information is time consuming and expensive. When reviewing your program, you may also wish to include an expert to help you analyze materials and instructional strategies related to the content and skill weaknesses you have identified. Some of the most important curriculum and instruction questions require expertise and understanding of how students learn particular subjects. You might ask for help from individuals with expertise in learning theory, curriculum organization and development, and pedagogical content knowledge[2] as well as from teachers who have experience with the curriculum and instruction areas you are interested in.

> ### Expert Help
>
> Curriculum experts, along with professionals who understand what your standards tests emphasize as well as what is missing from those tests, could work with your staff to help clarify content and skill sequences, the depth needed to reach proficiency, and the common learning problems students have in a particular grade and with particular content. These experts can help teachers see the forest for the trees as well as give them permission to omit some topics, spend more time on others, or approach some in a way that may not be presented in their adopted materials. The experts are practiced in letting the outcomes determine the strategy: backwards mapping. Teachers very often get immersed in the strategies and what they are to do. Focused instruction requires that what students should be doing drives instructional decisions.

Let's see how a review of curriculum and instruction helps us with program redesign. We have identified a set of needs assessment questions for the mathematics program at My Middle School. In the last chapter, we discovered that our Grades 7–8 students were falling behind in mathematics, especially the African American, English learners, and special education subgroups. Our data discussion summary included questions about placement practices and motivation that we will address in our review of curriculum and instruction. We also found that the areas with the most emphasis on the test, number sense and algebra concepts, were areas where students struggled the most. Our local tests indicated that three mathematics areas were especially problematic for our students; these are summarized in Table 5.2. For our example, we are choosing only one grade level, Grade 7 Mathematics, to explore. Grade 7 is a key course in which students learn the prerequisite skills for algebra. Students who don't master those skills are programmed into Grade 8 General Mathematics. Therefore, an improvement in our Grade 7 math program should increase Algebra enrollment, increase the chances for success in algebra, and send better-prepared students to Grade 8 General Mathematics so that the rigor of that course can be increased. We are hoping to leverage our turnaround efforts by focusing on this one course.

We then used Tool 5.2 to select the needs assessment questions and data for our program review. Table 5.3 presents these curriculum, instruction, and staff development needs assessment questions with relevant data sources that we reviewed at My Middle School. These questions were selected specifically to review our Grade 7 Mathematics course. Our questions will differ by course and grade level, because each course serves a different student population and has a different preparation goal. You will notice that we reproduced our course-specific skills as well as the supporting skills required in all of our mathematics courses to help us focus our discussion. It quickly becomes apparent that much of the review depends on collaborative work to share exemplary lessons, to review

Table 5.3 My Middle School Grade 7 Mathematics Program Review Questions

Grade 7 Mathematics: Instructional Focus

- Add, subtract, multiply, and divide rational numbers (integers, fractions, and terminating decimals) and take positive rational numbers to whole-number powers
- Solve problems that involve discounts, markups, commissions, and profit, and compute simple and compound interest
- Use key mathematics reasoning skills (all courses)
- Use estimation to verify the reasonableness of calculated results
- Analyze problems by identifying relationships, distinguishing relevant from irrelevant information, identifying missing information, sequencing and prioritizing information, and observing patterns
- Estimate unknown quantities graphically and solve for them by using logical reasoning and arithmetic and algebraic techniques

Curriculum Needs Assessment Questions

Curriculum Organization/Pacing and Alignment

- What is the relative emphasis of content versus skills in the course?
- How much time should be spent on major units/topics/skills?
- Are the skills new to this grade, do they build upon prior learning, or is it assumed that they are foundational and are not taught this year?
- When are the skills introduced or required for learning this year's content?
- How much time is allocated to their instruction, or how frequently are they used?
- Which materials introduce or employ the skills and knowledge? What is their quality (accuracy, clarity, effectiveness with students)?
- Is the curriculum aligned with state standards?

Assignments

- Which assignments provide practice in skills identified in the turnaround focus?
- Do the assignments require students to apply their skills in a variety of contexts?
- Do the assignments ask students to explain their thinking?

Instruction Needs Assessment Questions

Content-Strategy Alternatives

- Which strategies are most effective in helping students master content?
- Do we have alternative strategies for key concepts and skills that are important or particularly challenging?
- Which strategies are recommended for teaching these skills? What other strategies do we know?

Staff Development Needs Assessment Questions

Subject-Matter Knowledge

- In which topics or content emphases do teachers require more background knowledge or pedagogical content knowledge?
- In which topics might teachers need help to differentiate instruction?

Strategies

- Which strategies are most needed to teach key Grade 7 math concepts and preparation?

assignment rigor, and to collect data on feedback. In addition, the need for a math expert quickly becomes apparent. The expert could be the most successful teacher in our school or district, a district curriculum coach, or a well-known mathematics education consultant. We need expert help to deepen our understanding of the mathematics we teach and to assist us with content emphasis, pacing, common assessment item types and content, assignment content and rigor, well-constructed lessons for different purposes, and content and student preparation levels.

Our data discussions for program revision were based primarily on documents (archival data), with some local assessment, student work, assignment rigor review, and classroom walk-through data. We included the mathematics department and all teachers of Grades 6–8 Mathematics as well as the English-learner department chair and special education teachers, because we had struggling subgroups of students who were being served in programs other than mathematics. The results of our needs assessment are summarized in Table 5.4. You can infer that the data review required teachers to apply their expertise and experience to interpret the information and create hypotheses about what was causing students to do poorly in mathematics. You can also see that many of the unanswered questions emerging from our discussions require expertise beyond the school level.

Table 5.4 Data Discussion Summary: Curriculum, Instruction, and Staff Development for Grade 7 Mathematics Program

Curriculum				
Area	**Data Used**	**Findings**	**Questions Raised**	**Other Data to Examine**
Organization, Pacing, and Alignment	• Expert and teacher review of instructional materials, pacing charts, student performance on class work, and tests	Pacing guides move too quickly to develop student competence in number sense and facility with problem solving. We need to delete some topics and focus on fewer units.	How have students fared with revised pacing guides?	• Visit benchmark school to see how they outperformed us with same students.
Assignments	• Classroom assessments • Assignments keyed to standards • Collaborative teacher review of major assignments	Classroom assignments and tests don't ask students to estimate or show mathematical reasoning. Not enough monitoring of	If we deviate from "book" assignments, what is a good source to provide better preparation?	• Expert math education consultant • Examples from benchmark school

Table 5.4	(Continued)

Area	Data Used	Findings	Questions Raised	Other Data to Examine
	• Data from assignment rigor review	student errors in problem solving Students don't do homework regularly		

Instruction				
Area	Data Used	Findings	Questions Raised	Other Data to Examine
Content-Strategy	• Expert-teacher discussion of current practice • Teacher review of research-recommended lessons	We have "remedial" units, but in the computer age, these aren't appealing to students. Is there some online work that would fit the bill?	Which math topics are best taught by computer, and which are best taught by teacher, and to whom?	• Expert math educator suggestions • Math research review • Text publisher support

Staff Development				
Area	Data Used	Findings	Questions Raised	Other Data to Examine
Subject-Matter Knowledge	• Walk-through lesson observation • Teacher self report	We need to understand relationships between calculation and application. We need to understand how to analyze math problems and then explain to students	Who is best to help us develop deeper understanding in these areas?	Identify experts: • National organizations such as Association for Supervision and Curriculum Development and the National Council of Teachers of Mathematics • Local universities • Outstanding teachers in our school and benchmark school
Strategies	• Expert-teacher review of research-based math teaching strategies • Data from highest-performing classrooms— teachers share strategies	What new approaches can we use to reteach and reinforce operations with rational numbers, problem solving, and prealgebra concepts?	No new questions	• Use list above

The data discussion summaries provide a clear indication of what kinds of program changes we could make, but they do not tell us *how* exactly we could improve our work. For example, our classroom assignments are not complex enough, they lack practice in essential estimation skills, and they don't provide enough feedback to students about their learning errors. However, as we revise those assignments, we could approach the problem in a number of ways. We could use online assignments with built-in feedback for selected answers (in either a multiple-choice or free response format). We could have fewer assignments with more complexity, or have a graduated set of assignments for which students practice individual steps and are not allowed to move on until they master the skills of each step. We could use existing texts and assessments or find new ones. Thus, while the process of examining program data and thinking deeply about the relationship between program and outcomes might appear to "create" a Turnaround Plan, there are still many important instructional decisions in the hands of staff. The quality of those decisions and the accuracy of staff hypotheses about what will make learning improve determines the effectiveness of your turnaround efforts.

Consult Experts to Help Address Redesign Questions

The program redesign needs assessment has identified specific changes for your program and revealed areas where your school will need assistance. While the process to this point may appear tedious, with its cycle of questions—data review—more questions—more data review—in fact, many of the questions can be dealt with together, much of the discussion will address multiple needs assessment questions, and the issues that emerge and require further information can be charted in one meeting and addressed by the second one. The narration of this process makes it look more linear and sequential than it plays out in real life. However, many of the unanswered questions in our program review point to the need for some outside help from subject-matter experts, from teachers who have devised lessons and strategies with under-prepared students, and from mathematics education experts. Important decisions about content emphasis, problems students have in learning key content, multiple strategies for introducing challenging content, feedback methods, and devising efficient and effective assignments and assessments almost always call for some outside expertise or points of view. **Tool 5.3, Resources for Program Redesign,** summarizes some of the most well-known and long-standing sources for deepening content and pedagogical expertise.

Tool 5.3

In our My Middle School example, we referred to the work of a university mathematics education professor whose research focused on teaching middle school math, to our district math curriculum coach, and to a prominent middle school mathematics textbook author who had been a teacher, a president of the National Council of Teachers of Mathematics, and a school superintendent. We chose our expert trio for their ability to speak with teachers, their experience in debugging student learning problems and crafting teaching solutions, and their deep understanding of school mathematics content. Based upon their expert advice, we identified several program redesign initiatives, of which the following are representative:

- Build fluency in rational number operations by having students practice and complete computer-based drills.

- Test fluency quarterly until all students are proficient.
- Use specially developed "real-world math" lessons to teach the reasoning behind and operations needed for discounts, markups, interest, commissions, and related topics.
- Have the community businesspersons volunteering in our after-school math "intern" program engage students with and provide feedback on the kinds of problems encountered in class: computing discounts, commissions, markups, and the like.
- Introduce all new content with multiple representations and multiple problem-solving strategies—arithmetical, algebraic, and geometric (graphic)—and then require students to use at least two approaches on every assignment.

Given the new curricular emphases and skills to be taught, staff development activities will focus on developing teacher content expertise in the relationship between mathematical operations and their applications in financial and commercial transactions as well as on practice in teaching multiple strategies for problem solving.

After we identified our program redesign activities, we entered them into our theory of action to be sure that our new activities were indeed linked to our targeted student outcomes (see Figure 5.4).

Figure 5.4   Theory of Action: Processes Linked to Outcomes

Process/Activities	Short-Term Outcomes	Long-Term Goals
Curriculum and Instruction Revision • Build fluency in rational number operations by having students practice and complete computer-based drills. • Test fluency quarterly until all students are proficient. • Use specially developed "real-world math" lessons to teach the reasoning behind and operations needed for discounts, markups, interest, commissions, and related topics. • Have the community businesspersons volunteering in our after-school math "intern" program require students to perform the kinds of problems encountered in class: computing discounts, commissions, markups, and the like. • Introduce all new content with multiple problem-solving strategies—arithmetical, algebraic, and geometric (graphic)—and then require students to use at least two approaches on every assignment. **Staff Development Revision** • Content expertise in operations related to real-world math problems. • Instructional strategies for multiple representations of math problems.	• 100% of students are fluent in math operations. • 90% of students score Proficient on end-of-course real-world math test. • 90% of students correctly solve end-of-course problems with two methods.	• Standards test Proficient increase 20% • Increase of 5% in algebra enrollment

Once you have tentatively identified the instructional intervention or program changes you want to make to achieve the goals you have established for your instructional focus area, you will want to examine ancillary and contextual school factors to support your program redesign work. It is impossible to revise curriculum and instruction without considering the school context.

BUILD PROGRAM SUPPORT INTO THE REDESIGN

Review School Context Variables That Support Instruction

While it may seem that school context variables, with perhaps the exception of the "staff" category, aren't directly related to student achievement, when we think carefully about why students are struggling in school, issues of parent involvement, health, safety, and even students' valuing their time at school come to the surface. As we delineate our turnaround work, we want to have a comprehensive understanding of student learning needs and the kinds of support that will make a difference. In our theory of action, the majority of program support will fall into "Inputs" and "Learning Conditions" boxes (see Figure 5.5).

Figure 5.5   Theory of Action: Program Supports Linked to Processes

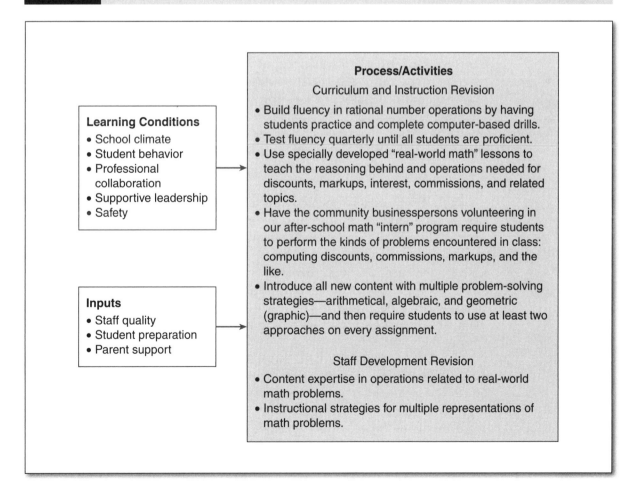

Instructional problems may be exacerbated or can be addressed in part by attending to aspects of school climate, staff training and attitudes, or parent and community support. If students in the Grade 7 Mathematics classes, for example, tend to be truant or not engaged during instruction, if the math staff needs resources to reach the more underprepared students, if parents can be involved in supporting the use of homework through a parent-training program, the success of instructional changes is more assured and won't be undermined by factors all teachers know exist but do not have much time to consider in depth. From both the student outcome data review and the review of curriculum and instruction, we have identified several contextual areas of concern:

- Student behavior problems, such as truancy, homework noncompletion
- Staff expectations for special education and English-learner students
- Staff failure to collaborate in continuous improvement cycle
- Parent and community involvement getting students to school and getting homework done

As you review your own school context, you will want to consider more than issues of curriculum and instruction in your efforts to identify what is impeding student learning. Changes in how we teach mathematics will involve changes in relationships between students and teachers, training for parents, and perhaps even some community resources to make mathematics more relevant and engaging.

Tool 5.4

We recommend you consider a variety of the school contextual variables listed in **Tool 5.4, Needs Assessment Questions for School Context Variables,** and add some of your own. At this initial stage of your turnaround efforts, it pays to take a broad view of your work, to entertain all possible causes for student achievement problems and all potential solutions, no matter how out of the box these solutions might be. After you have created your data summaries for the school context variables, you can revisit your analyses and strategically focus on those problem areas and potential solutions that will have the best result.

Table 5.5 presents selected aspects of school climate, staff characteristics, and parent/community involvement that My Middle School identified to support its program redesign. Again, the data to address these questions are often not immediately available. However, most of the needs assessment questions lend themselves to student, teacher, and parent surveys, focus groups, or interviews. These data can be collected on a relatively short time frame if you have parent volunteers to help conduct evening telephone surveys with parents and if you involve teachers in surveying their students.

The My Middle School staff developed a brief 10-item survey to be given to teachers, parents, and students in Grades 7 and 8 about the Grade 7 mathematics program. Questions about positive relationships, high expectations, learning support, communication, and involvement were the same on all three versions of the survey. The teacher survey also included additional questions related to expertise and support for

Table 5.5 School Context Needs Assessment Questions for the Grade 7 Mathematics Program

Area	Needs Assessment Questions
Positive Relationships	Do teachers, students, parents, and administrators report they have positive working relationships and methods for dealing with disagreements?
High Expectations	Do parents and students perceive staff as supporting high levels of achievement: holding high expectations, delivering a rigorous curriculum?
Learning Support	Are staff seen as being available to provide help and providing clear feedback to students?
Expertise	Are staff assigned in their areas of expertise? Do all meet Highly Qualified Teacher criteria? Do some have National Board certification?
Support for Professional Growth	Are mentors, coaches, and/or curriculum experts available to support staff?
Communication	Does the school have a system for regular communication with parents about student progress (online access to assignments, progress reports, e-mail communication with teachers)? Do staff notify parents about student progress and involve parents in supporting student class work?
Community-Based Programs	Does the school take advantage of community-based programs to leverage learning?

professional growth. Data related to community-based programs that would support development of Grade 7 mathematics skills were collected by asking the chair of the Parent Advisory Committee to visit community service clubs and service organizations to determine the kinds of programs they might have for underprepared middle school mathematics students. The entire process of data collection, from survey development to data summarization, took about one month, and the data were used to review each of the school context needs assessment questions. A summary of data discussions about program support initiatives is shown in Table 5.6.

Table 5.6	Data Discussion Summary: School Context Support Variables for the Grade 7 Math Program			
Area	**Data Used**	**Findings**	**Questions Raised**	**Other Data to Examine**
Positive Relationships	Survey (Parent, Student, Teacher)	Parents uniformly reported positive relationships, as did teachers. Student patterns differed by subgroup, with English learners and African American males reporting 60% of the time that "my math teacher doesn't like me," "my teacher doesn't explain assignments clearly," and "my teacher sometimes embarrasses me in front of the class."	What is the relationship between achievement and negative ratings on relationships?	Grades for students reporting very positive and very negative survey results
High Expectations	Survey	Parents answered this question with mostly "somewhat agree" or "don't know." Teachers were uniformly in agreement that they held high expectations. Student responses varied, with the lowest-scoring subgroups responding that teachers did not hold high expectations for them.	How do we better communicate our expectations to parents? Why do our lowest-scoring students think our expectations are low?	Responses from a parent focus group and low-scoring student focus groups
Learning Support	Survey	All students reported that they didn't always know how to improve their grades or assignment scores. Students reporting that math was their favorite subject agreed that teachers were always available to help. Among the low-scoring groups, answers were mixed depending upon the individual.	How do we help students understand that we are available to help at any time? How can we encourage them to come for help?	Responses from low-scoring student focus groups
Expertise	Survey	None of the Grade 7 teachers was a math major. Most had a knack for math or interest in it or had taught elementary school math. All expressed frustration in teaching key mathematics reasoning skills and the use of exponentials.	Who would be best to help teachers deepen content knowledge?	List of experts created during program needs assessment

Area	Data Used	Findings	Questions Raised	Other Data to Examine
Support for Professional Growth	Survey	None of the teachers knew about the district math coaches.	How do we get math coaches for our school?	Availability of coaches from district and benchmark school
Communication	Survey	Phone survey to parents indicates that they don't access online classroom assignments and grade reports regularly; they don't know about them or have no Internet access.	How do we get Internet access to all parents? How do we train parents to use online grade system?	School or district sources of computers and Internet service for parents; sources for donated computers and Internet service
Community-Based Programs	Phone Interviews	Several local companies will offer math internships to students a few hours a week after school to demonstrate math in action. Local Kumon academy will provide 10 scholarships to neediest seventh graders.	How do we organize connections between students and community offerings—transportation and so forth?	Details about community offerings and how to access them

Embed Program Support Into the Turnaround Plan

The data discussion summary for program support indicates several areas that could support student math achievement, most notably teacher-student relationships, staff expertise, and parent communication. School context variables related to achievement can often be incorporated into curriculum, instruction, and staff development redesign and not require separate action. For example, the staff development devoted to deepening content expertise and improving instructional strategies could easily embed techniques for improving student relationships (e.g., avoiding sarcasm, using positive language, not singling out students for praise or criticism). The staff assigned to create community connections could also work on solving the technology issues impeding parent involvement; both of these activities provide direct support to the instructional program by improving homework completion and attendance and by helping students understand that both parents and teachers are keeping an eye on their mathematics progress. Once program supports are identified, you can complete your theory of action by adding the "inputs" and "learning conditions" boxes to your diagram.

Figure 5.6 presents our completed theory of action. We hypothesize that if we address the core knowledge and skills that students need to reach proficiency and improve teacher-student interactions in mathematics classrooms, and if teachers provide clearer feedback, learning conditions will improve. Concurrently, we will marshal our community resources to bring technology to parents so that they can be a resource for monitoring and motivating their Grade 7 students. Given these two

Figure 5.6   Theory of Action: Grade 7 Mathematics

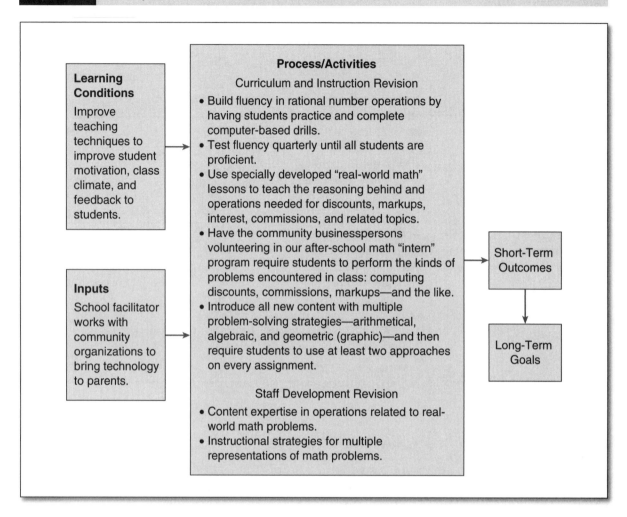

program supports, the actual curriculum will focus on three key content areas: fluency in a comprehensive set of numerical operations, focus on real-world math problems needed for finance and commerce, and multiple approaches to problem solving. The math internships in community businesses can be considered part of the instructional intervention, but they are also a program resource or "input." The theory of action diagram has three important uses:

1. It makes clear to all involved in turnaround work what we will do and what results we expect; essentially, it presents our Turnaround Plan.

2. It captures the target of our formative evaluation—what needs to be implemented and monitored during implementation of our plan.

3. It helps build a common understanding of our turnaround work.

SUMMARY OF THE REDESIGN PROCESS

We have spent every minute up to this point focused on data. How to find it, how to interpret it, how to prepare summaries and displays, how to select questions for analyzing data, and how to use data to identify student learning needs and program redesign strategies. It is now time to act! The time invested up to this point is time well spent, however. Our thorough familiarity with the kinds of data available, with the kinds of questions we might need to answer to serve students better, and with what our data really say (and don't say) will shorten the amount of time we need to spend designing our formative evaluation for refining the program. In the next chapter, we will create and implement the Turnaround Plan for program redesign that we specified in our theory of action—or rather, we will develop a flexible working document to guide implementation activities (which we refer to as a "plan") and then describe implementation milestones we will use to assure that program activities are of high quality.

CHAPTER 5 TOOLKIT

REDESIGN PROGRAMS TO ADDRESS THE TURNAROUND FOCUS

The Tools for Chapter 5 can be found on the companion website for *The TurnAround ToolKit* at http://www.corwin.com/turnaroundtoolkit.

Tool 5.1   Toolkit Tutorial: Basing Our Turnaround Plan on a Theory of Action or Change

Tool 5.2   Needs Assessment Questions for Curriculum, Instruction, and Staff Development

Tool 5.3   Resources for Program Redesign

Tool 5.4   Needs Assessment Questions for School Context Variables

6

Develop and Implement the Turnaround Plan

The map is not the territory.

—Alfred Korzybski, semanticist

Redesign: Use Data to Create the Turnaround Plan

Data

| Identify the turnaround focus. | Redesign programs to address the turnaround focus. | Develop and implement the Turnaround Plan. |

145

POCKET SUMMARY

Task	Major Activities	Purpose
Develop the Turnaround Plan.	• Translate your theory of action into a plan. • Avoid overly elaborate plans. • Include program redesign, management, and monitoring activities in your plan. **Tool 6.1 Turnaround Plan Template**	• Develop an action-focused, list-style plan.
Implement the Turnaround Plan.	• Carry out activities listed in your plan. • Collect monitoring data during implementation. • Monitor the quality of teaching and learning. **Tool 2.3 Program Quality: Assignment Rigor** **Tool 2.4 Program Quality: Protocols for Looking at Student Work** **Tool 2.5 Program Quality: Classroom Walk-Through Guidelines** • Monitor staff development needs. **Tool 6.2 Staff Development Survey Template** **Tool 6.3 Survey Development Cheat Sheet** • Monitor student learning frequently and informally. **Tool 6.4 Teacher Test Analysis Procedures** **Tool 6.5 Student Test Analysis Procedures** • Consider implementation challenges. • Document your successful efforts.	• Focus on doing, monitoring, and revising.

DEVELOP THE TURNAROUND PLAN

Translate Your Theory of Action Into a Plan

By the time you have reviewed your curriculum, instruction, and school context, you will have created a list of solution strategies that involve changes in teaching and learning as well as in how your school involves teachers, parents, and students in the change process. The program redesign activities and their relationship to desired outcomes will have been documented in your theory of action, which will be some version of the diagram in Figure 6.1.

The specific activities that appear on your theory of action diagram are the core of your Turnaround Plan. In addition, it will include arrangements

| Figure 6.1 | Simplified Theory of Action |

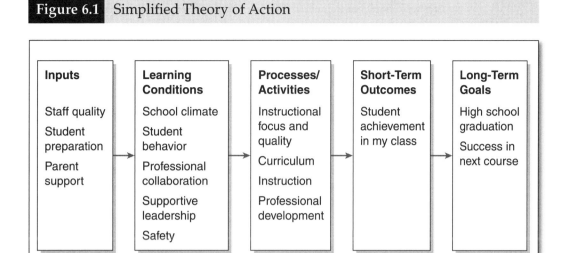

to manage who will do what and when, and to monitor the data you will collect to assess program quality and student progress.

Avoid Overly Elaborate Plans

You don't want to be mired in plans and lose you focus or momentum.

A Turnaround Plan is not a strategic plan, though it is strategic. It is more surgical, formative, and flexible than strategic plans, which are characterized by formal indicators of success in many areas and are designed to measure long-term progress. The Turnaround Plan captures the changes your school is going to make and what it takes to implement those changes in the immediate future. It is a working document (or electronic spreadsheet) designed to help people clearly understand "who's on first." Your Turnaround Plan has three major functions that guide program implementation:

- It describes your program activities: What are we doing?
- It provides a management plan: Who is doing it? When? What are the resources needed?
- It incorporates a monitoring system: How are we doing?

Unlike your school plans or formal documents developed to meet compliance demands for federal or state programs, the Turnaround Plan is more of a to-do list or an action checklist. Table 6.1 compares a strategic plan with a Turnaround Plan. It is quite possible your district has a strategic plan. Your school might even have a School Improvement Plan. Yet these plans have not enabled you to make the progress you need. If you wonder why that might be the case, we recommend you read Mike Schmoker's "Planning for Failure? Or School Success?"[1] In a sentence, to paraphrase Schmoker, strategic plans do not

Table 6.1   Strategic Plan Compared With Turnaround Plan

Component	Strategic Plan	Turnaround Plan
Purpose	A road map for improvement	Documentation of key responsibilities in the collaborative process of changing instruction
Identification of Strengths and Weaknesses	Environmental scan and comprehensive data review (covering both student outcomes and school context)	Assessments of student outcome data to identify instructional focus and of program data to describe instructional practice
Vision, Mission, Values	Statement of your institution's purpose, who the clients/customers are, what you'd like to be "tomorrow"	(Implied: increase achievement in identified instructional focus area)
Timeline of Objectives	Yearly (or long-term) objectives	Instructional focus: specific student outcomes to be addressed this year
Action Planning	Description of desired results, obstacles, and support	Description of instructional changes to be made, who will do them, and when
Implementation Process	Interim checkpoints of implementation: who will do what by when	Monthly or quarterly check points for implementation and student progress
Evaluation and Measurement	Reported results on key indicators of the Balanced Scorecard that capture achievement of objectives (A Balanced Scorecard is a specific strategy for summarizing organizational vision, goals, and measures, and for monitoring progress toward meeting goals. Many larger districts use this particular format to report progress. More information about this particular approach to monitoring change may be found at www.balanced scorecard.org.)	Formative evaluation of the program change using implementation data, student progress data, and year-end student outcome data
Plan Communication	Formal communication through website and documents posted on walls	Informal working group document used by participants and modified frequently

create change; only a team of teachers meeting regularly to design and test lessons and adjust their lessons and strategies in light of their results can turn around a school. Strategic plans encompass too many goals, have too many promises, use vague language, and are owned by no one. Turnaround Plans, by contrast, are lean and action oriented. They cut directly to the student achievement problem, apply remedies, test them, and require revised actions should initial activities not improve achievement. Turnaround Plans involve every member of the school team in the design, implementation, and evaluation of their planned activities. We use the term *Turnaround Plan* in a metaphorical sense. We believe, like Mike Schmoker, that spending time creating elegant goals, flow charts, and courses of action interferes with the forward movement and urgency associated with making immediate and visible improvements in learning.

Include Program Redesign, Management, and Monitoring Activities in the Plan

We like a less-is-more approach to documenting planned activities. As Alfred Korzybski reminds us, "The map is not the territory." More directly, the plan is not the program. You have spent much time in preparing for action, diagnosing student learning needs, and identifying gaps in curriculum, instruction, and school context that need fixing. It is time for action. Your plan is really a sophisticated to-do list that guides your work. There are many possible plan formats, but we like a tabular plan that lists only essential information: task, who's responsible, when, and how monitored. An additional column to code the task type (for example, staff development, materials, technology, monitoring, administration/management) will allow you to record your plan on a spreadsheet and then sort by time, person, or task type so that you can print and distribute to-do lists to the staff responsible for the work. Keep it simple; keep it clear. Focus on action. Do not overwhelm people with information, lofty rhetoric, and aspirational documents. Turnaround Plans should not be overly formal, nor should they be in a medium that cannot be altered, such as a laminated poster or a bronze plaque!

You already have a diagram, or perhaps a chart or table, summarizing your theory of action. In your diagram or theory, you have listed many of the activities you need to carry out in order to turn around student achievement. These activities are categorized as processes (program changes), learning conditions (school context), and inputs (school context) causing short- and long-term student outcomes. To create your Turnaround Plan, you will simply copy the short- and long-term outcomes from your theory of action into the top of a table to remind yourselves of your turnaround focus, and then list more specifically the activities that you need to carry out in order for the more general changes listed in your theory of action to occur. In addition, the plan embeds data collection to monitor the quality of program implementation and student progress toward short-term outcomes. While you can identify your program redesign implementation activities directly from your theory of action, the monitoring activities emerge from two sources, program implementation activities and the formative evaluation of your plan. Therefore, as you develop your plan, you can identify monitoring activities for each implementation task. After you have designed your evaluation (see Chapter 7), you will need to revisit your Turnaround Plan and add monitoring activities and program evaluation management tasks previously not identified.

We suggest that your plan include at a minimum the components presented in Table 6.2.

| Table 6.2 | Turnaround Plan Components |

Plan Component	Contents
Turnaround Focus	• Restate specific goals for improving student outcomes
Instructional Focus	• All learning skills and knowledge identified in the turnaround focus
Program Redesign Activities *This is the program redesign.*	• Program activities designed to address the specific objectives of the instructional focus • Curriculum, instruction, and staff development and program support activities • Examples: instructional strategies, student engagement strategies, direct instruction topics, common assignments, common assessments, specific staff development sessions, school or classroom climate changes, parent involvement, community resources, coaching, visits to benchmark schools, and so forth
Program Monitoring Activities *Monitoring activities will be revised based on the evaluation design.*	• Data collection activities designed to monitor quality of program implementation and student progress • Examples: assignment review sessions, sessions for looking at student work, classroom observations, reviews of common assessment data, parent-teacher-student surveys
Management Activities *Management activities will be revised based on the evaluation design.*	• Who is responsible for which redesign and monitoring activities • When these activities take place • What resources or additional support are needed for the activities

Let's see how a plan emerges from our My Middle School Grade 7 Mathematics example. Figure 6.2 is a reproduction of the last stage of program redesign that we outlined in Chapter 5. We will now convert our diagram from Figure 6.2 into our Turnaround Plan, using **Tool 6.1, Turnaround Plan Template.**

Tool
6.1

Figure 6.2 Theory of Action: My Middle School Grade 7 Mathematics Program Revision

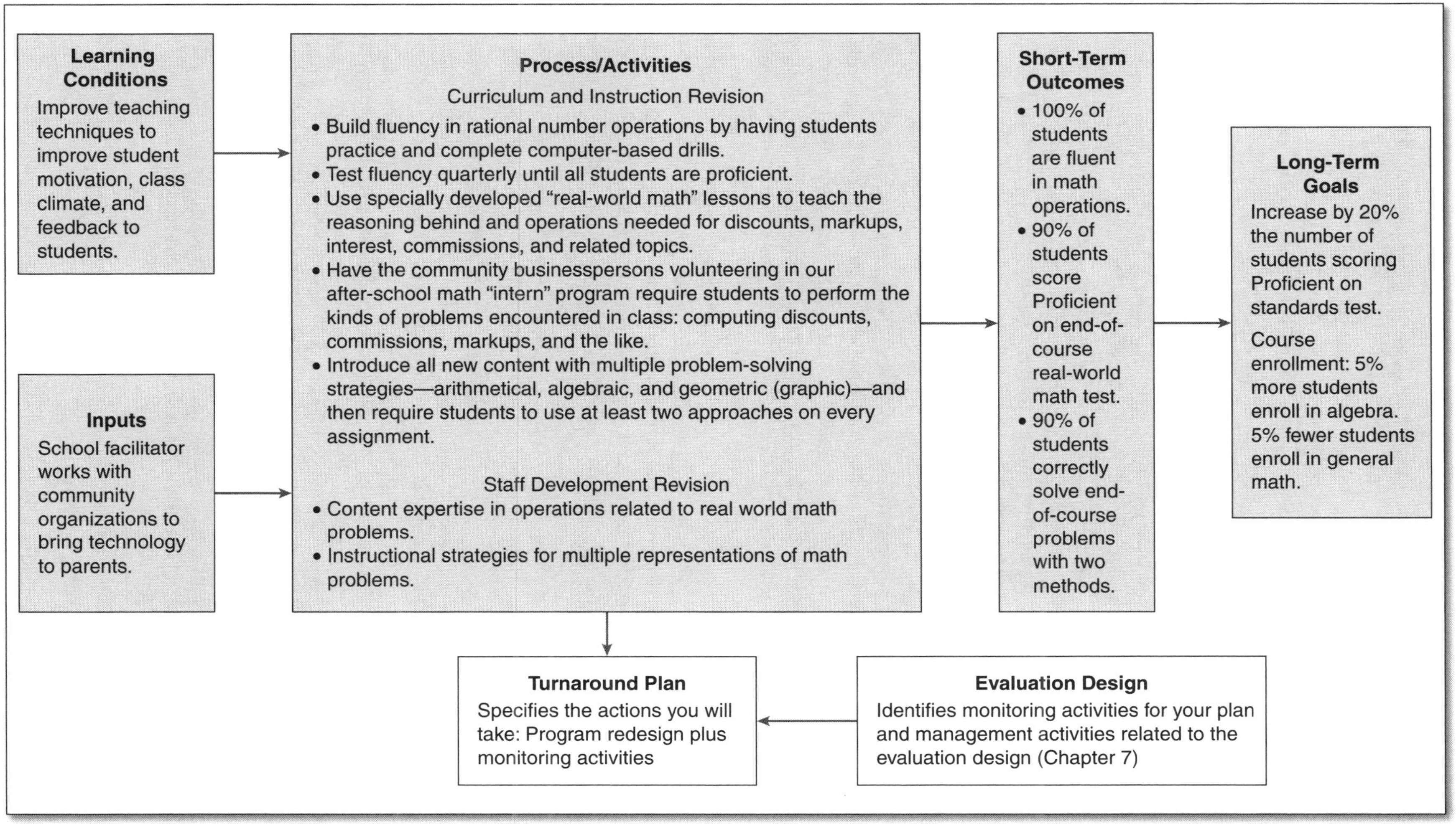

Learning Conditions

Improve teaching techniques to improve student motivation, class climate, and feedback to students.

Inputs

School facilitator works with community organizations to bring technology to parents.

Process/Activities

Curriculum and Instruction Revision

- Build fluency in rational number operations by having students practice and complete computer-based drills.
- Test fluency quarterly until all students are proficient.
- Use specially developed "real-world math" lessons to teach the reasoning behind and operations needed for discounts, markups, interest, commissions, and related topics.
- Have the community businesspersons volunteering in our after-school math "intern" program require students to perform the kinds of problems encountered in class: computing discounts, commissions, markups, and the like.
- Introduce all new content with multiple problem-solving strategies—arithmetical, algebraic, and geometric (graphic)—and then require students to use at least two approaches on every assignment.

Staff Development Revision

- Content expertise in operations related to real world math problems.
- Instructional strategies for multiple representations of math problems.

Short-Term Outcomes

- 100% of students are fluent in math operations.
- 90% of students score Proficient on end-of-course real-world math test.
- 90% of students correctly solve end-of-course problems with two methods.

Long-Term Goals

Increase by 20% the number of students scoring Proficient on standards test.

Course enrollment: 5% more students enroll in algebra. 5% fewer students enroll in general math.

Evaluation Design

Identifies monitoring activities for your plan and management activities related to the evaluation design (Chapter 7)

Turnaround Plan

Specifies the actions you will take: Program redesign plus monitoring activities

First we will transfer the course (short-term) outcomes to our plan for our turnaround focus. We next copy each of the activities implied or stated in our Inputs, Learning Conditions, and Process boxes to the "Activities" column in the template. We assign responsibilities for these program redesign activities and schedule them using the "Person(s) Responsible" and "When" columns. We also label and perhaps code them for sorting in a spreadsheet so that we can print task lists for individuals and groups.

Finally, for each redesign activity, we have planned a monitoring activity to ensure that the specific redesign is taking place and to determine how effective it is; these are shown in the "Monitoring" rows. You will notice that many of the expected changes in instructional practices will be monitored by classroom walk-throughs. One walk-through could serve several purposes. Our walk-through focus is determined by our monitoring needs. We also have added a Student Opportunity to Learn survey to monitor implementation of instructional strategies and content. We can ask both students and teachers how often they do certain activities and what they are required to do in the way of problem solving. Again, the long list of monitoring activities becomes consolidated.

The translation from theory of action to Turnaround Plan required only three new tasks: identification of responsible personnel, and scheduling and creation of monitoring activities, which will be discussed again in the next chapter. Table 6.3 presents our first-draft Turnaround Plan, which we will implement beginning August 15. However, based on the information we collect after the first staff development session, our plan could be revised as early as August 16. Activities could be added, such as coaching particular teachers or providing counseling services to particular students. Others, such as the staff development session to strengthen staff content expertise on September 8, might be revised or rescheduled or dropped altogether. Our plan is not the territory; it is not even a complete map. And our plan certainly is not a mandate—it's an experiment.

Table 6.3   My Middle School Grade 7 Mathematics Turnaround Plan

Turnaround Focus	<ul><li>100% of students fluent in math operations</li><li>90% of students score Proficient on end-of-course real-world math tests.</li><li>90% of students correctly solve end-of-course problems with two methods.</li></ul>		
Activity Type or Code	**Activity**	**Person(s) Responsible**	**When**
Staff Development	Improve teaching techniques to improve student motivation, class climate, and feedback to students	Math department chair and Myra Magic, national student attitude consultant	Aug. 15, opening teacher meeting
Monitoring	Staff development evaluation survey	School data team	Aug. 15, data summarized in one week

Activity Type or Code	Activity	Person(s) Responsible	When
Staff Development	Improve teaching techniques for student engagement, monitoring participation, and giving students feedback	Math department chair and U Will Learn Associates	Sept. 5, first week of school
Monitoring	Classroom walk-throughs	Expert friends team and math department chair from benchmark school	One month after staff development and monthly thereafter
Staff Development	Improve teachers' content expertise in operations related to real-world math problems.	Dr. M. A. Thematics, local university math education professor	Sept. 8
Monitoring	Staff development evaluation survey focus group with Dr. M. A. Thematics	Focus groups to be announced by math department chair	Sept. 8
Staff Development	Improve instructional strategies for multiple representations of math problems	Dr. M. A. Thematics, local university math education professor	Nov. 1
Monitoring	Classroom walk-throughs (Tool 2.6) Student Opportunity to Learn survey (report their problem-solving requirements)	Expert friends team and math department chair from benchmark school	One month after staff development and monthly thereafter
Curriculum and Instruction	Use specially developed real-world math lessons.	Grade 7 teachers	At least two times a week beginning Sept. 5
Monitoring	Classroom walk-throughs Student Opportunity to Learn survey (report their problem-solving requirements)	Expert friends team and math department chair from benchmark school	One month after staff development and monthly thereafter
Instruction	Introduce all new content with multiple problem-solving strategies—arithmetical, algebraic, and geometric (graphic)—then require students to use at least two approaches on every assignment	Grade 7 teachers	At least two times a week as part of the real-world math lessons

(Continued)

Table 6.3   (Continued)

Activity Type or Code	Activity	Person(s) Responsible	When
Monitoring	Student Opportunity to Learn survey (report their problem-solving requirements) Assignment Rigor Review (Tool 2.3) and Looking at Student Work (Tool 2.4)	For student surveys, data team For review of assignments and student work, math department chair and Dr. M.A. Thematics	One month after staff development and monthly thereafter
Curricular Focus	Build fluency in rational number operations by having students practice and complete computer-based drills	Grade 7 teachers	Weekly math integer assessments, beginning Oct. 1
Monitoring and Instructional Strategy	Test students quarterly until fluency improves	Grade 7 teachers	Oct. 15, Dec. 12, Jan. 28, Feb. 15
Monitoring	Teacher Test Analysis (Tool 6.4)	Data team with Grade 7 teachers	Quarterly, Oct. 16, Dec. 13, Jan. 28, Feb. 16
Community	Community businesses create math "intern" program that requires students to perform the kinds of problems encountered in class: discounts, commissions, markups, and the like	School facilitator	Business internships to begin in November and be completed in June. Individual students serve for at least 10 weeks sometime during this period.
Monitoring	Teacher, student, parent survey of impact of internship (Tool 6.3)	Data team	Feb. and June
Parents	Community organizations to bring technology to parents	School facilitator	Sessions in September, October, November, January, February, and March
	Inform parents how to monitor students' math learning online	Math department–parent meeting	Oct. 1
Monitoring	Parent survey Online audit for parent use	Data team	Dec. 1

IMPLEMENT THE TURNAROUND PLAN

Carry Out Activities Listed in Your Plan

As part of our preparation for turnaround work, we developed a willingness to engage in rapid-fire experimentation. We committed to collecting data and monitoring the effectiveness of our changes, and then either revising the new practice or continuing to implement it as initially proposed. The intense period of learning, changing roles and responsibilities, rethinking all we do, and questioning every aspect of our weakest programs is over. We are now ready to implement our turnaround proposals and examine their impact. Our implementation will be guided by a revisable, brief Turnaround Plan with built-in monitoring activities.

Implementation is simply performing the actions you listed in your Turnaround Plan. However, all program implementation has a series of simultaneous activities, as does your plan:

- Acquiring materials and other resources needed by students and teachers
- Providing staff development if changes in teaching practice or curriculum are indicated
- Involving parents in supporting the change, and the community when possible as well
- Delivering instruction using the new materials, curricular emphases, and instructional strategies, and engaging students in more effective learning activities
- Monitoring all of the new activities, reviewing the monitoring data, and changing course when indicated

Collect Monitoring Data During Implementation

Monitoring your implementation plan is really conducting the formative evaluation of your turnaround work. Thus, as you include your specific monitoring activities in your Turnaround Plan, you will need to consider your formative evaluation design and data needs. (We discuss monitoring activities more fully in Chapter 7.) After you have considered how you will evaluate your plan, you can go back and add needed monitoring or data collection activities so that all your work is available in one source. However, monitoring and revising your work is part of the implementation process. (After all, it's the work, not the plan, that we are committed to.) In fact, it's a very large part of the process, because it includes ensuring that activities take place, determining the quality of implementation and the need for further support, and establishing the effectiveness of activities. One half of program implementation consists of doing something or using new materials, assignments, or assessments. The other half consists of evaluating what we do and seeing how we can do it better.

Monitor the Quality of Teaching and Learning

You will find monitoring tools throughout this book. Strategies for assessing program quality, which appear in Chapter 2, are particularly relevant to

**Tools
2.3–2.5**

monitoring how well teachers are changing practice and engaging students in more rigorous activities. **Tool 2.3, Program Quality: Assignment Rigor, Tool 2.4, Program Quality: Protocols for Looking at Student Work,** and **Tool 2.5, Program Quality: Classroom Walk-Through Guidelines,** provide simple, straightforward techniques to help teachers review the quality of their efforts and discuss needed midcourse corrections.

Monitor Staff Development Needs

**Tools
6.2 & 6.3**

Teacher staff development is a central turnaround activity. Often we do not know what we need until we have begun to implement a program and have a good idea of where we would like more support or resources. Surveying teachers or conducting focus groups about needed staff development is an essential part of planning how to support teachers engaged in changing their practice. **Tool 6.2, Staff Development Survey Template,** and **Tool 6.3, Survey Development Cheat Sheet,** will help you develop short, focused, and useful teacher surveys (or interviews) that ensure what you provide is actually what is needed to move the professional staff forward in their program implementation work.

Monitor Student Learning Frequently and Informally

**Tools
6.4 & 6.5**

Turnaround is generated by a school's performance on high-stakes accountability assessments. However, both the timing and the content of these tests make them useless for classroom decision making. Both teachers and students can be engaged in reviewing assessment results on a regular basis. The best assessments for this purpose are the formative classroom exercises or quarterly common assessments that provide feedback about progress on local learning goals. We have provided **Tool 6.4, Teacher Test Analysis Procedures,** and **Tool 6.5, Student Test Analysis Procedures,** to help both teachers and students discuss the results of local assessments and to communicate to students that they are responsible for understanding their own learning issues and sharing this knowledge with their teachers.

Monitoring program implementation is an integral part of your turnaround evaluation. Our discussion in this section provides a preview of some of the evaluation activities you will build into your formative evaluation, which will be presented in Chapter 7. It's a reminder that processes are not linear (even though books are) and that activities embedded in a process can have multiple purposes and yield data useful for multiple decisions.

Consider Implementation Challenges

In addition to adopting new practices, using new materials, and monitoring your work, an important part of implementation is adapting to unanticipated challenges. The effectiveness of your program design depends not only upon excellence of execution (not the life-ending kind!) but also on the cleverness of midcourse corrections. Consider the following common impediments to educational change:

- *Political circumstances change.* The union decides that teachers cannot participate in collaborative meetings because of contract issues. Leadership changes and is less committed to the work. National policy requiring immediate correction of student achievement trajectories changes, and funding is not available for your work.
- *Resources are inadequate.* Costs rise for teachers, for materials, for consultants. Activities take longer than anticipated. More staff development is needed on the same topic. Coaches are needed. More release time is needed.
- *Your theory of action is faulty or incomplete.* Your redesigned activities should result in desired outcomes. But you may find that there are intervening or prerequisite skills that need to be included for your theory to yield results. This adds a requirement for additional staff development in new teaching practices, which elongates the anticipated timeline.
- *Despite having developed a theory of action together, participants do not all understand the work in the same way.* Thus, you will have some staff thinking they are implementing the program, but in fact their practice has not changed (the old-wine-in-new-bottles syndrome). Or there will be other staff who don't help students make explicit connections from their work to their achievement, because they can't articulate these connections themselves, or because they don't think in terms of cause and effect but rather see teaching and learning as "experiential."
- *Leaders conduct their work in silos.* You have distributed leadership and responsibility for tasks and have even pressed others outside of your school—experts, district office support, community members, et cetera—into service. However, if they don't communicate and coordinate their work, staff is inundated with initiatives and directives and will drown in confusion.

Implementation requires the prescience to consider possible challenges and the flexibility on all parts to stop, think, modify, throw out, add, or reconsider. These verbs are not often found in the language of school reform or teaching, where the dominant metaphor is the fast-moving train on its way to a well-known destination.

Document Your Successful Efforts

One of the most important products of your turnaround work, after increases in student achievement, is a description of your program that would enable others to replicate your success. Your Turnaround Plan has identified your program goals, the program components, even the kinds of assessments students will use; however, you will also want to keep notes about more specific training strategies, materials, instructional processes, direct instruction lessons, grouping practices, assignments, assessments, and so on that are linked to the successful student outcomes. Your notes can easily be translated into a program description or turnaround manual that other schools could use (or use as a starting point) in their turnaround efforts.

SUMMARY

This chapter was short in length and long on action. Your plan will be short and mutable and include program redesign and monitoring activities. Management or leadership is essential for success; however, leadership's role is to support changes in practice, collaboration, and plan revision as well as to provide resources and encouragement. Your planned work is not entirely complete until you consider the formative evaluation design, data collection, analysis, and revision work in more detail. These follow in Section III, Refine.

CHAPTER 6 TOOLKIT

DEVELOP AND IMPLEMENT THE TURNAROUND PLAN

The Tools for Chapter 6 can be found on the companion website for *The TurnAround ToolKit* at http://www.corwin.com/turnaroundtoolkit.

Tool 6.1   Turnaround Plan Template

Tool 6.2   Staff Development Survey Template

Tool 6.3   Survey Development Cheat Sheet

Tool 6.4   Teacher Test Analysis Procedures

Tool 6.5   Student Test Analysis Procedures

Section III

Refine

Evaluate and Revise the Turnaround Plan

Innovation never happens as planned.

—Gifford Pinchot, first chief
of the U.S. Forest Service

In this section, we ask you to halt the forward momentum of your work for a brief time to refine the monitoring and management activities in your Turnaround Plan. We then jump past the implementation work you have begun and move forward to the point in your work where you have collected monitoring data and now need to analyze and use it to either do a midcourse correction or evaluate the entire year's efforts to begin the program redesign process anew. The findings from your evaluation drive the next cycle of turnaround work. We call this phase Refine because the work of designing an evaluation, analyzing the resulting data, and reflecting on our turnaround efforts is in the service of refining or revising our turnaround activities. One of the most significant aspects of refining and revising is the third step of this section, reflecting on our efforts and sharing lessons learned.

This last section has three chapters, each focused on procedures for refining your program during implementation and revising it yearly. The concluding chapter invites you to reflect upon your work and plan how you will share the lessons learned with colleagues engaged in the difficult work of turning around student achievement and sustaining gains amidst the ever-changing political and financial challenges faced by schools today.

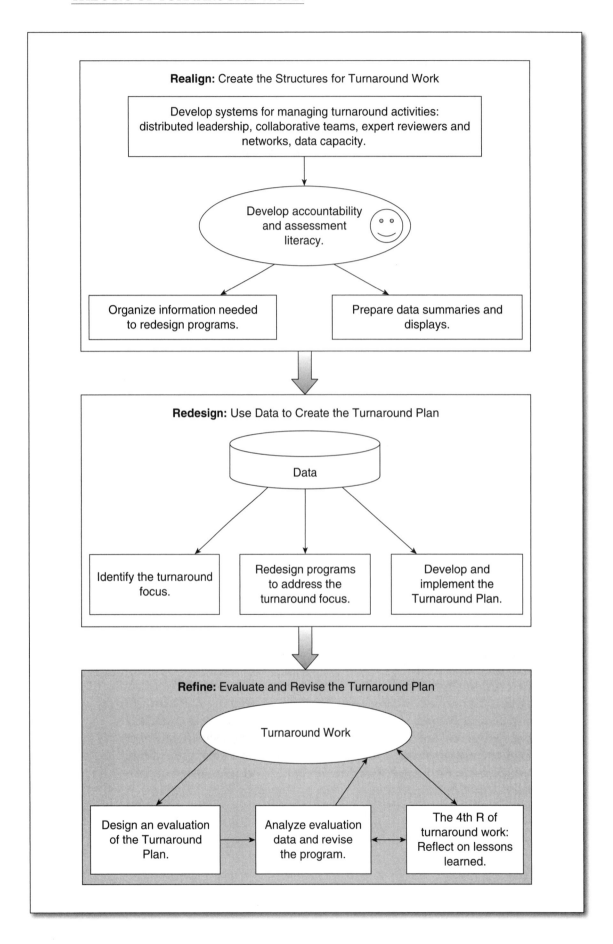

CHAPTER 7 ■

DESIGN AN EVALUATION OF THE TURNAROUND PLAN

The evaluation is actually part of our Turnaround Plan. However, evaluation and program implementation are parallel activities. The evaluation itself assesses our work and provides information for improvement during the year and for refinement and revision at the end of the year. Therefore, prior to implementing our Turnaround Plan, we stop and consider the formative evaluation. This process produces changes to our monitoring and management activities in the Turnaround Plan.

CHAPTER 8 ■

ANALYZE EVALUATION DATA AND REVISE THE PROGRAM

Data analysis is simply the process of transforming responses or electronically scored measures into useful information. Analysis requires selecting appropriate scores to address your evaluation questions, using descriptive statistics to summarize scores, displaying the results in tables and graphs, and organizing data summaries by evaluation questions. The second part of data analysis is really the data use function: Use logic to interpret and apply findings. You will use data to refine the Turnaround Plan during program implementation and to revise the program and planned activities at the end of the year. Finally, your use of data requires that you communicate what you are learning to interested stakeholders, both while you are engaged in implementation and after you have evaluated your yearlong efforts.

CHAPTER 9 ■

THE 4TH R OF TURNAROUND WORK: REFLECT ON LESSONS LEARNED

This last chapter has no toolkit, although we contemplated including a mirror to help with "reflections." We present examples of lessons learned from psychology, educational research, a measurement expert, our own work in a large urban school district, and the Chinese. These examples are meant to spark reflective discussions and make the point that what we learn from reflecting on what we do may be as important as the results of our efforts.

7

Design an Evaluation of the Turnaround Plan

Make the measurable things important but make the important things measurable.

—Unknown

PROGRESS MAP

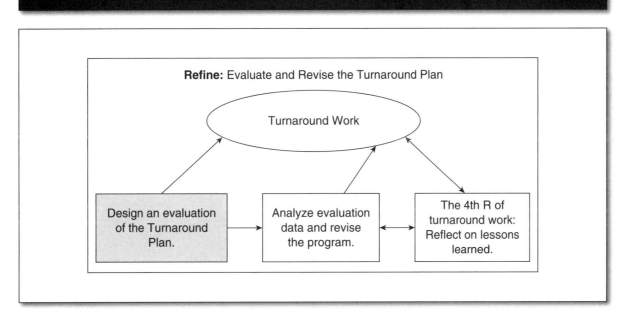

Refine: Evaluate and Revise the Turnaround Plan

Turnaround Work

Design an evaluation of the Turnaround Plan.

Analyze evaluation data and revise the program.

The 4th R of turnaround work: Reflect on lessons learned.

POCKET SUMMARY

Task	Major Activities	Purpose
Understand the role of evaluation in turnaround work.	• Evaluation distinguishes turnaround work from less-urgent reform. • The turnaround evaluation is formative. • The elements of evaluation design.	• Understand multiple uses of formative evaluation.
Identify evaluation questions.	• Start with the theory of action or Turnaround Plan. **Tool 7.1 Formative Evaluation Questions for a Turnaround Plan** • Make questions specific to your work. • Consider a range of questions; then prioritize. **Tool 7.2 Template for Prioritizing Evaluation Questions**	• Use your theory of action and/or your Turnaround Plan to develop evaluation questions.
Create a sampling plan.	• Decide whether you need a comparison group. • Consider sampling versus census data collection.	• Consider how generalizable you need your evaluation results to be. • Determine from whom you need to collect data.
Select or develop measures to address evaluation questions.	• Identify the data needed. • Consider a range of measures or data sources. **Tool 7.3 Advantages and Limitations of Common Data Collection Techniques** • Create blueprints or specifications for instrument development or selection. **Tool 7.4 Blueprint Components for Common Measures** **Tool 7.5 Test Evaluation Criteria for Published Achievement Tests** • Employ multipurpose measures. • Use multiple measures when feasible. • Consider trade-offs between feasibility and credibility in selecting instruments. • Convert measures into monitoring activities.	• Select or develop measures and data collection strategies.
Specify data analysis strategies and decision rules.	• Plan data analysis strategies for summarizing and interpreting data. • Establish decision rules for judging implementation quality and student progress.	• Choose data summary strategies that answer questions. • Know in advance what success means.

Task	Major Activities	Purpose
Flesh out the management plan.	• Review and revise the Turnaround Plan management activities. **Tool 7.6 Template for a Data Collection Management Plan** • Distribute responsibility for data collection. • Avoid preventable data collection disasters. **Tool 7.7 A Catalog of Data Collection Disasters**	• Identify management activities to support data collection and analysis, and embed them in Turnaround Plan.
Document your evaluation design.	**Tool 7.8 Template for a Formative Evaluation Design**	• Document plans, and establish checklist of evaluation tasks that need to be completed.

UNDERSTAND THE ROLE OF EVALUATION IN TURNAROUND WORK

Evaluation Distinguishes Turnaround Work From Less-Urgent Reform

Your Turnaround Plan is really a grand experiment based on the theory of action or change that links your hypotheses about program activities that are needed to produce improvements in student outcomes. You are experimenting, because what you have done in the past has not worked as well as you had hoped. You are doing rapid-fire experimentation, because your school has no time to wait the usual three to five years, or some say ten years, for a new program to show effects. Your timeline is short, because your school may have not met state or federal accountability targets, you face competition from local schools due to school choice policies, or your community is demanding and expects your school to be high performing. In this chapter, we examine how the monitoring activities embedded in the Turnaround Plan can be used to address the primary research and evaluation questions for turnaround:

- Is the Turnaround Plan being implemented as planned? Is the program implementation of high quality?
- Are students making progress?

Here, the program implementation monitoring activities you generally scheduled in Chapter 6 provide data you need for refining or revising the Turnaround Plan and program. Monitoring activities not only are part of our daily work but also constitute a parallel activity: research and empirical review to continuously improve our effectiveness. Hence the term *rapid-fire experimentation.*

The Turnaround Evaluation Is Formative

As we have noted, the data-guided, continuous improvement process built into turnaround work is an example of formative evaluation. Formative evaluation is designed to answer questions about how programs can be improved; it contrasts with summative evaluation, which serves the purpose of determining the *value* of a program. Summative evaluations focus on questions such as, "Is this program effective?" or "Is Program A better than Program B?" When most of us think of program evaluation, we think of the large-scale, headline-making studies that tell us whether programs are successful for large segments of the student population in different parts of the country. The famous comparisons among literacy approaches—Success for All, Reading Recovery, and Accelerated Reader—featured on the What Works Clearinghouse website (www.ies.ed.gov) are good examples of summative evaluations. These studies were conducted over long periods of time, used sophisticated research designs and scientific sampling methods to represent a range of different kinds of school sites, and employed state-of-the-art statistical models with large data sets to evaluate program effects.

While formative and summative evaluations encompass the same general phases of activities, they have very different purposes, which shape how these activities are designed and carried out. Summative evaluations, because they seek to identify practices that generalize across settings and students, are more formal and require certain kinds of designs and sampling plans (random assignment when possible), documented measurement quality, and advanced statistical analysis techniques. Formative evaluations, which are used locally for the purpose of creating a program or making it better, do not require elaborate sampling strategies or statistical inference tests. Both formative and summative evaluation studies, however, typically are developed to test a theory of action and to assess both the quality of program implementation and effects on outcomes, so that results are supported with valid and useful evidence.

The Elements of Evaluation Design

An evaluation, regardless of focus, is an applied research study. It is developed in the same fashion as all research. Evaluation and applied research studies start with an inquiry process to define specific hypotheses or questions, drawing on available research, perhaps a needs assessment, observations, or case studies. In school settings, the hypotheses may center on a theory of action about how to improve student learning and school quality and what it will take to get from where we currently are to where we want to be. The hypotheses are turned into questions that guide the evaluation inquiry process. The next step is the identification of data sources or measures that can help to address the questions. Once data are collected, they are analyzed to help answer each question, and findings stimulate discussion and may provide recommendations for next steps.

The management function associated with formative evaluation is simple to lay out, and practitioners understand its necessity, but it is an often-neglected aspect of school program evaluation. Management must ensure that measures are selected or developed, data are collected at the right time, tests are scored and surveys summarized, interviews or case studies are coded, data displays and tables are created, and meetings are held to interpret the results and identify implications for action.

Like all research, our formative evaluation design for turnaround work incorporates the following design elements:

- Theory of Action—A theory-based set of assumptions or hypotheses that describe expected relationships we intend to investigate. In an experiment, these are hypotheses. In evaluations, the objects of investigation are the hypothesized causal relationships between what happens in a program—its professional development, instructional materials, teaching strategies, parent and community involvement strategies, and other aspects of the teaching-learning process—and intended teacher and student outcomes. The hypothesized cause-and-effect relationships between our program or activity and outcomes are captured in graphic form as a theory of action or logic model.
- Evaluation Questions—A set of research questions determined by the evaluation's purposes, summative or formative.
- Design and Sampling Plan—A plan that determines from whom data should be collected. If a large number of subjects are to be included in the study, it may not be necessary to include all; participants may be randomly sampled.
- Measures—Measures or data collection techniques to inform the research questions.
- Data Analysis and Decision Rules—Analysis strategies to summarize data and address evaluation questions. The data analysis plan also includes specifying criteria for judging whether the results meet an acceptable threshold to be considered significant or important.
- Management Plan—A plan describing data collection timelines, resource budget, personnel assignments, and training of data collectors (if needed). The management plan assigns responsibilities and deadlines for each element of the evaluation process.

Each design element will be considered in this chapter along with how the element can be incorporated into your Turnaround Plan. Your evaluation provides a decision-making framework to monitor and improve the effectiveness of your efforts. The time to design your evaluation is *after* your Turnaround Plan is created, because the plan describes the "thing" you will be evaluating. However, you will begin your evaluation activities *at the same time* you begin your turnaround activities. Table 7.1 shows how the Turnaround Plan and the evaluation combine.

Table 7.1   How the Turnaround Plan Encompasses Formative Evaluation

Turnaround Plan Activity	Evaluation Activities Embedded in Turnaround Work
Develop a new or redesigned program to address student achievement goals.	Document a theory of action stating how the new or redesigned program will cause improvement in student outcomes.
Implement new or redesigned program: • Staff development • Teacher and student changes in instruction and learning activities • Materials and other resources	Monitor implementation quality and impact.
Determine program effectiveness.	Collect data to judge whether program attained desired outcomes.
Redesign program based on data.	Revise theory of action, design program changes, and identify data to collect for monitoring program implementation and outcomes.

IDENTIFY EVALUATION QUESTIONS

Start With the Theory of Action or Turnaround Plan

Your theory of action diagram is actually the organizer for both your Turnaround Plan and your evaluation questions. You used the theory of action diagram to develop your Turnaround Plan and to define what you think it will take to improve student learning in your area(s) of focus. For example, your plan lists your hypotheses about

- changes in teacher knowledge and practice, curriculum, and opportunities to learn content that are necessary to improve achievement;
- changes in parent involvement and community support that are needed to support learning; and
- improvements in course-level learning that will result in improved attainment of long-term goals.

These hypotheses about how to improve achievement were the basis for your Turnaround Plan and the specific program changes you plan to implement. They point to four foci for your evaluation questions:

1. How well are we implementing the Turnaround Plan?
2. How are student knowledge and skill attainment improving (or not) in response to the program redesign?
3. Is there a relationship between our turnaround activities and student achievement?
4. What are the implications for action?

Table 7.2 presents a set of evaluation questions that can be tailored to most turnaround efforts. This chart also appears as **Tool 7.1, Formative Evaluation Questions for a Turnaround Plan.**

Table 7.2 Formative Evaluation Questions for a Turnaround Plan

Program Implementation Quality
• How is the program being implemented? Which components are well implemented, minimally implemented, or not implemented at all? (To answer this question, you'll need to consider what good and minimal implementation are supposed to look like!) Have some components or strategies been adapted to work even better than originally planned? • How well did professional development and other training and orientation activities go? Did teachers attend? Acquire the knowledge and skills they need to change their practice? Buy-in to needed changes? What about parent, administrator, and/or other training and orientation efforts that may be part of the redesign? • How is the professional development changing teachers' practice? What aspects are they incorporating, which not? Which are working well, which not? What changes are needed? • What changes in teaching do you observe? In student engagement? In assignments? Assessments? Class or school climate? Student skill acquisition? • How well are teachers implementing and adapting other components of the program? Who's resistant or having difficulties? Who are the adept implementers? • How well are program activities for parents or others working? For example, has parents' understanding or involvement in their children's learning improved as planned? • For each major program activity or component, what factors are contributing to quality implementation? What barriers or obstacles to implementation occur?

Student Progress
• How well are students acquiring the knowledge and skills that are the immediate learning targets for the redesigned program? What learning problems continue to occur? Why might this be so?

Linkages With Theory of Action
• What is the relationship between specific redesign activities and student short-term outcomes? • What is the relationship between specific changes in staff expertise, parent involvement, student behavior (and so on), and student short-term outcomes?

Make Questions Specific to Your Work

When you are monitoring specific and targeted program changes, you will want to create evaluation questions that will help you debug your theory of action. Instead of, "Is our math program accomplishing better results?" more useful questions would be, "Does an additional 10 minutes a day of homework result in increased fluency in math facts? In better understanding of core math concepts?" You especially will want to pay attention to the specifics of program implementation:

- Are all teachers making the intended changes?
- If not, what is getting in the way?
- How does implementation differ by teacher?
- Is the amount of time spent on the priority instructional objectives similar across classrooms?
- Do teachers all define "group work" in the same way?
- How do classroom assessments differ in length, rigor, and skills tested?

Posing specific questions ensures that the data you collect will be useful and that staff involved in implementation have a shared understanding of what that implementation entails.

Consider a Range of Questions; Then Prioritize

After you have generated your list of formative evaluation questions, review them to be sure they are clear and specific. Work with your collaborative groups to clarify your evaluation questions so that they are concrete and there are no big inferential leaps as to what information is needed to answer them. Discuss what the expected program implementation will look like and what you will see when implementation is successful. Then create a chart to identify those priority questions requiring immediate data collection and those for which data can be gathered later in the year or over time. You can then create a set of priority rankings for your questions based on immediacy and importance. Limit your formative evaluation, high-priority questions to a manageable number (three or four at most). Remember, you are working on a rapid experimentation cycle and can address additional or different questions at the next turnaround review session.

How do you decide which questions are more important than others? While no one answer fits all situations, we have found some of the following criteria useful in setting priorities for formative evaluation:

- Which changes are most complex or difficult to accomplish (and may therefore need fine-tuning early on)?
- Which changes do we hypothesize as most central to changes in outcomes?
- Which changes leverage multiple outcomes and therefore are more generative? An example would be a program where writing instruction across the curriculum is being used to improve reading fluency, reading comprehension subject, matter understanding, and writing.
- Which changes are most resource intensive or require extensive training?
- Which changes might cause the most resistance and need a longer time to get stakeholder buy-in?

Table 7.3 presents an abbreviated example of prioritized questions based on our Grade 7 My Middle School example. It is for purposes of illustration; we have not included all of the evaluation questions. A template for prioritizing evaluation questions appears in **Tool 7.2, Template for Prioritizing Evaluation Questions.**

Tool 7.2

Table 7.3	Selected Grade 7 Mathematics Evaluation Questions With Priority Rankings			

Program Component and Question	Rank 1 Required	Rank 1 Essential and Immediate	Rank 2 Essential but Not Time Sensitive	Rank 4 Nice to Know
Student Outcomes: How has the addition of 20 minutes of weekly computer lab time with Powersource affected student mastery of math facts?		√		
Student Outcomes: What changes in student self-reported perceptions of math ability and motivation have occurred since we introduced group work?			√	
Curriculum: Which enrichment needs to be offered to students who quickly master course standards?	√			
Curriculum: What required math computer programs should be retained and which should be dropped?			√	
Instruction: What will engage African American males more in course content and give them a desire to do well on course tests?	√			
Parents: What do parents really define as "supporting my child in school," and how can we capitalize on that definition?				√

CREATE A SAMPLING PLAN

A sampling plan describes what information you will collect and from whom to be sure you have useful information to address each of your evaluation questions. The "from whom" question involves two central decisions: Will you collect data only from those directly participating in your turnaround efforts, or will you also include a comparison group of those who are not involved? In addition, how much data do you need to answer each question? Will you collect the responses of all participants—for example, all teachers, all students, all parents—or will you collect them from only some—ideally, a random sample of the whole? Like most everything else in turnaround, there are no easy answers here; rather, you'll need to resolve obvious tensions and trade-offs in making these decisions.

Decide Whether You Need a Comparison Group

At times, you will use a targeted strategy, focusing only on students or teachers directly involved with your turnaround efforts. At other times, you may wish to collect data to compare results between those involved in turnaround activities and those not participating to determine whether your efforts are making a difference. When you expand your data collection to a comparison group, it allows you to consider competing alternate hypotheses for any results you find. For example, imagine that your first-quarter test results show that students involved with your new math strategy are performing pretty well—they averaged 75% correct. Before you declare victory, you might want to consider how students did who were not participating in the new strategy—for example, last year's students or students in a school similar to yours. Evaluations that compare results from students receiving an intervention with those receiving a different program yield stronger evidence about an intervention's effects since they offer data about what happens in the absence of the intervention. However, with small sample sizes, results can be difficult to interpret, and such designs take more time, more resources, and more sophisticated data analysis techniques than designs that include data from only those directly involved in the program. The trade-off is between cost and confidence in your results. For most of us, available resources will constrain our sampling plan decisions.

Consider Sampling Versus Census Data Collection

Do you want data from all students, parents, teachers, and others involved or expected to be affected by the Turnaround Plan, or will a sample suffice? As a general rule, more is better, and some complex data analyses require hundreds of responses. However, there almost always are difficult trade-offs between the technical quality of your data and available resources to collect and analyze them. You will need to balance the needs for highly credible data with the costs, including the cost of student and teacher time, specialized data collector costs for observations or interviews, and direct costs of materials, training, scoring, and reporting. For formative evaluation purposes on a quick collection-review-revise program cycle, you most likely will choose to minimize costs rather than maximize statistical estimates of reliability, validity, or power.

There are statistical programs that provide power analyses to estimate the sample sizes you need to detect differences in performance or that tell you how likely you are to detect a difference (if one exists) with specified sample numbers. As a general rule, if you have a small program serving fewer than 100 students, you would not sample. When you are dealing with students in intact classrooms, it is easier to administer a survey or test to everyone than to sample. However, when you are considering potentially expensive data collection from a large population, such as the parent population of a 4,500-student high school, sampling may be the only affordable alternative. For example, you may consider randomly sampling half or a quarter of the parents and carefully following up to get responses from as many as possible. The sampling plan, whether it includes all respondents or a subset, should be created to respond to this question: How many responses do I need to believe that these results represent what is really occurring?

SELECT OR DEVELOP MEASURES TO ADDRESS EVALUATION QUESTIONS

Identify the Data Needed

The "data needed" is the evidence needed to specifically address each of your evaluation questions. Sometimes, the data needed and the results from a specific measure are one and the same, such as student test results. At other times, it's important to identify first what information you need and then decide how best to get it. You will notice how specific data sources or measures almost jump out from the data needed once you have been specific about the evidence requirements of your question. Taking the time to consider what data are needed can help you select the best measures or data sources for your monitoring activities. From Table 7.4, we see immediately what we need for our Turnaround Plan at My Middle School.

Expert Help

At this point, you may wish to bring in a member or two from your expert friends group or from the district office to identify data sources for the information you need to address your monitoring questions. This group can provide useful advice about efficient methods for collecting, summarizing, and reporting the data.

Table 7.4	Data Needed for My Middle School Grade 7 Mathematics Turnaround Plan

Evaluation Question	Data Needed	Data Source or Measure
How has the addition of 20 minutes of weekly computer lab time with Powersource affected student mastery of math facts and core concepts?	• Evidence that students spend 20 minutes a week on self-assessments • Evidence of student facility with math facts and conceptual understandings	• Powersource log-in and use data from computer • Quarterly tests of math facts and conceptual understanding
What changes in student self-reported perceptions of math ability and motivation have occurred since we introduced group work?	• Amount of time students work in groups; what are the group work topics? • What are students' attitudes toward and interest in math?	• Student math attitude survey • Teacher lesson plans • Student Opportunity to Learn survey with group work questions
What will engage African American males more in course content and give them a desire to do well on course tests?	• Evidence that African American males attended the project team's group counseling sessions • Evidence of engagement during math • Evidence of math attitudes	• Project team's appointment log, meeting attendance, field trip roster • Powersource log-in and use data from computer • Student math attitude survey

Consider a Range of Measures or Data Sources

Tool
7.3

An important concept in selecting a data collection strategy or measure or a data source is to select the methods that will yield the most valid information that you can afford; that is, maximize data quality, but you cannot ignore costs. With few exceptions, there is more than one way to obtain the information you need to answer your evaluation questions. **Tool 7.3, Advantages and Limitations of Common Data Collection Techniques,** presents the trade-offs among different types of measures or data sources to help you determine which are best for your particular monitoring activities.

Most of us are more familiar with data from student assessments than we are with other types of data sources, such as archival information or data from phone interviews or focus groups. The first data collection strategy that often comes to mind is to get information directly from students by administering a test or collecting assignments, or to get data from teachers by conducting an observation or a survey. But data collection methods extend far beyond what we normally see in a school. If you first think about the *purpose* of the measure—for example, to find out how people feel, or to identify what they would like changed, or to measure how well they understand the causes of the Civil War—you will soon see that you can think of many, many strategies for obtaining information.

Good measurement, like a good life, is purpose driven. It's best to begin your consideration of what evidence you need by brainstorming all possible methods and then selecting those that best meet your standards for feasibility and credibility before you settle definitively for one method. Table 7.5 lists the various measures, data sources, and data collection strategies you might use for each of several common data needs.

Table 7.5 Multiple Measures for Common Data Needs

Data Needed	Possible Measures, Data Sources, and Data Collection Strategies
To determine what students know and can do	Standardized tests, classroom tests, school-developed common assessments, student assignments, performances, projects, portfolios
To determine how students, parents, or teachers feel, what they value, or what they like or dislike	• Online or paper-pencil selected-response surveys • Online or paper-pencil open-ended survey questions • Phone surveys (read from a script) • Phone interviews • In-person interviews or focus groups • Notes from parent meetings • Computer-administered surveys • Behavioral observations (school spirit, classroom engagement, etc.)
To determine whether teachers are implementing the turnaround strategies	• Lesson plans • Assignments and scoring guides • Student Opportunity to Learn surveys • Walk-throughs or other observations • Teacher self-report surveys

We suggest you brainstorm possible measures for each of the data needs listed for your evaluation questions, then review the monitoring strategies in your Turnaround Plan. If you find more cost-effective, accurate, or valid measures than ones you have tentatively considered, then you can either augment or replace your weaker monitoring strategies with better ones.

> **Tech Tip**
>
> When identifying how you will obtain data, think about where it might be stored currently, how you will add it to your own data files, and what kinds of automated reports you can create to maximize time spent reviewing and using data versus time spent in data collection and presentation efforts.

Create Blueprints or Specifications for Instrument Development or Selection

The match between your evaluation questions and the content of your instruments is a central requirement for gathering valid data. One way to assure that your data sources will give you the information you need is to create instrument blueprints that specify the content and issues that each instrument is intended to and must address to answer your evaluation questions. If you are developing your own assessments, the blueprint is a necessary first step, because you will select or write test items, writing prompts, or other kinds of exercise descriptions and scoring rubrics based on what you have specified in your blueprints. If you are purchasing instruments or using archival data, the blueprints will provide a checklist for reviewing the data source to see if it really adequately addresses your evaluation questions. Whether you develop or select your data collection instruments, you need to pay attention to important issues in data quality: validity, reliability, test administration considerations, and appropriateness for your population. Blueprints can capture guidelines that improve data quality in all of these areas.

What should a blueprint contain? There are many different formats that might be appropriate for your blueprints. When you develop or select a measure, you will need to have a clear idea of what is being measured. The blueprint provides you with a description of what is measured that also helps you to interpret the scores that result from the instrument. Table 7.6, which is also reproduced as **Tool 7.4**, **Blueprint Components for Common Measures,** presents some categories of information you will want to either describe when you develop your own measures or ask about should you select already-developed instruments. These blueprint categories are suggestive, not exhaustive. Without clear descriptions of what is being measured, you have little information about whether any measure or instrument can meet your decision-making needs.

Tool
7.4

If you take the time to clearly describe what your measures should contain, even if you do not develop your own assessments, you will have better guidelines for reviewing surveys, interview protocols, rubrics, and other measures of program processes and outcomes. When selecting a commercially published standards test or norm-referenced test, in addition to your blueprint, you should also have a list of review questions that point you to the qualities those tests should

> **Expert Help**
>
> Expert help in the development or selection of instruments is almost always essential. Experts can help you develop test blueprints or specifications to guide item writing, they can point you to sources of widely used or research-based measures, and they can ask terribly hard questions of test publishers to determine exactly what you are getting in terms of information from a test score or score report.

Table 7.6	Blueprint Components for Common Measures

Data Type	Blueprint Information
Student-selected or brief-response assessment	• Content to be sampled • Concepts and skills to be assessed • Expected levels of cognitive demand (e.g., recall, application, problem solving) • Item format • Rules for writing distractors • Number of items per skill • Total number of items
Student essay or performance assessment	• Content to be sampled • Concepts and skills to be assessed • Expected levels of cognitive demand (e.g., recall, application, problem solving) • Rubric scale • Type of rubric: holistic versus analytic • Rubric dimensions
Student, teacher, parent self-report survey	• Concepts and topics to be assessed • Response scale • Number of items per topic/concept • Number of items per survey
Archival data: student information system (attendance, grades)	• Kind of data • Rules for data collection • Data calculation (if applies) • Data verification method
Archival data: documents (teaching guides, lesson plans, etc.)	• Kind of data • Topics and themes to review • How data will be summarized
Archival data: records from online learning modules	• Topics, content, skills • Time allocated for module • Number of practice items • How items are scored or feedback is provided online

Tool 7.5

possess in order to be useful for program improvement. **Tool 7.5, Test Evaluation Criteria for Published Achievement Tests,** provides a set of review questions designed for selecting tests that yield instructionally useful information.

Employ Multipurpose Measures

You will notice that some of the same instruments, such as the student or teacher surveys, are used to address different evaluation questions and appear as monitoring activities for several different aspects of program redesign activities. A final step in instrument selection is to consolidate your data sources to reduce the testing burden on teachers, students, and parents. The same survey can be designed to monitor multiple program redesign activities and multiple evaluation questions. While your monitoring activities may include a student survey or parent survey for several different activities, in fact, one survey with questions addressing each activity may be all that is required.

Some data sources will be relevant to only one evaluation question. When this is the case, you should ask yourself if this unique data source is really necessary or if needed information could be collected nearly as well through another strategy that might be more cost-effective. For example, pacing information can be extracted from teacher lesson plans instead of through a separate measure. Instead of preparing a separate survey to assess whether students have had adequate opportunities to learn the content, you could insert student Opportunity-to-Learn (OTL) questions on your quarterly assessment. Figure 7.1 provides an example of embedding survey items with content assessments to reduce the testing burden. The advantages

Figure 7.1	An Example of Combining Opportunity-to-Learn Items With a Content Assessment

Question 1. Number Sense: Rational Numbers

Helen is buying a pair of jeans that regularly cost $45. They are on sale for 15% off. If the tax rate is 9%, what is the sale price of the jeans including tax?

A. $38.25

B. $41.69

C. $40.95

D. $47.70

Opportunity-to-Learn Questions That Could Be Attached to the Item

Ask students to rate each of the following statements on a scale that includes Never, At Least Once, 2 to 5 Times, More Than 10 Times:

1. I have practiced problems like this in class.

2. I have completed homework items like this.

3. My teacher has explained how to do problems like this.

4. I have practiced calculating the percentage of a number.

5. I have practiced calculating discounts.

6. I have practiced calculating taxes.

Ask students to rate each of the following statements on a scale that includes Not At All, Maybe a Little, Definitely, This Is a Priority for Me:

1. I feel I need more practice to understand problems like this.

2. I feel confident I understand problems like this.

3. I feel this problem tests something important that I should know.

of embedding OTL questions with actual items on your district monitoring assessments are several:

- Students understand exactly what kind of practice they would need to answer the item.
- Teachers get immediate feedback about student homework habits and perceptions of instruction as well as the extent to which students value what they are learning.
- A sprinkling of OTL questions routinely embedded in a few items for each assessment make explicit to students the importance of information being tested and their teachers' concerns that they understand what they are learning.

Use Multiple Measures When Feasible

As you identify the kinds of evidence (data) you are going to collect, you need to keep in mind an important principle of all research studies: Use multiple sources of information to address each evaluation question. There is no such thing as a perfect measure. (Does your bathroom scale come to mind?) Even the best data collection instruments contain some measurement error or inaccuracy. (Again, the bathroom scale should come to mind!) Each information source has its particular weakness as well as its singular strength. To counter these measurement flaws, use several sources. When the data you obtain from several measures provide similar results, you will have more confidence in your findings, and your results will be more credible to external audiences. For example, in assessing whether students are making the progress you expect, you might consider teachers' classroom tests as well as quarterly benchmark data. To know how well teachers are implementing changes, you might conduct observations and get specific feedback through teacher meetings and focus groups. Tool 7.3, Advantages and Limitations of Common Data Collection Techniques, presents some well-known trade-offs of commonly employed data sources.

The same survey questions can be given, with some adjustment in wording, to multiple participants—teachers, students, and parents—and can be used to cross-validate responses. While student self-report data are not always the gold standard in reliability and validity, when these data are combined with other information, such as test results and teachers' reports of what they are doing and how they assign work, the surveys provide another view of your efforts. When you ask students, for example, how well they did on unit assessments, and their responses don't correspond to the actual scores, you have important information. Have students not received their results? Do they not know the performance level they are expected to meet? Do students not think results are important enough to remember, or do they not realize that knowing their results is key to taking responsibility for their learning? Discrepancies between student self-report data and other data can help you identify some of the expectations, motivation, and study habit issues that need to be addressed if achievement is to improve.

In our experience, when we ask both students and teachers to report on what learning activities they engage in and how often, there is a discrepancy in responses. Teachers invariably report that students have more practice, and practice more often, than students report. However, they are nearly always identical in how they *rank* the relative frequency of their classroom opportunities to learn. Thus, the activities that teachers report they assign most frequently are the same ones student surveys show as being most frequently engaged in. Unfortunately, the teachers may say the activity occurs ten times and the students three times, but the ranking is invariably identical. Is it that students are not always aware of the purpose and goals of their classroom activities? Are students confused about what they are doing? Might teachers overestimate how often they engage students in critical learning? Might the discrepancy be some combination of these and other factors?

Consider Trade-Offs Between Feasibility and Credibility in Selecting Instruments

No one data collection strategy or measure is perfect for all situations. Issues of data quality and the credibility of the information you collect will help determine which strategy you select. Unfortunately, information that is credible to one group may not be as important to another. A good example is standardized test results. The community and parents often put a lot of faith in state or national test scores. However, teachers who are familiar with the limitations both in test content and testing motivation for these tests often feel that the utility of these scores is quite limited. On the other hand, teacher observations and evaluations of student work have a lot of credibility for teachers and administrators, but they are difficult to summarize for outside audiences, who may even suspect these data as being "subjective." Although you will want to be responsive to your stakeholders' views of what constitutes high-quality data, time, cost, and availability of measures will impose limitations on which instruments you select for your evaluation.

Central to the concept of credibility is instrument validity. Validity is largely a question of whether a data collection instrument actually captures what it was intended to measure with results that yield accurate information for the decisions at hand. A key validity concern is the match between your evaluation questions and the information provided by the instrument. For example, if we wish to capture the impact of our number sense intervention in Grade 7 with a norm-referenced standardized test, an available test may not provide a valid inference about whether students have mastered the particular concepts we taught in our program; there may be few items on the test, or its purpose may be to compare students to each other rather than to assess whether students have achieved curriculum learning goals. Without a match to our program, the test information is irrelevant to our concerns. The sensitivity of our instruments to what we are trying to accomplish is central to validity. It is also critical to our ability to demonstrate program impacts and ferret out strengths and weaknesses.

While the usefulness of data, its validity, and its credibility are paramount, as long as we are living in a world of limited resources, time, money, patience, and expertise, we must also take into consideration the feasibility of our data collection strategies. Using already-developed tests, surveys, and observation checklists saves much time and money in instrument development and may also save time in scoring. The trade-off, however, is the sensitivity of these methods to school goals and intentions and the credibility to local audiences.

Often concerns for credible, yet feasible, measures are in conflict. Feasible often means inexpensive, quick, something that we can integrate into existing work. Very often we rely on school-developed instruments that have not been guided by formal assessment development techniques or subjected to technical scrutiny. An expert from the district or your expert friends group can be helpful in navigating the shoals between credible and feasible.

Convert Measures Into Monitoring Activities

Collection and analysis of the measures you select become the monitoring activities for the Turnaround Plan and are embedded into the turnaround work of teachers and other staff. You already have indicated a monitoring activity for each program redesign component in your Turnaround Plan. However, these activities were generic placeholders for the instruments and data you finally choose based on your evaluation plan. Go back to your Turnaround Plan and replace "Student Opportunity to Learn" survey with the name of the actual instrument you have developed, such as "embedded OTL items on quarterly assessments." List the focus areas for specific classroom walk-throughs, which, like surveys, can be used to address multiple evaluation questions and activities. You also may find that you want to expand the sample for certain monitoring activities that address your specific evaluation questions, such as asking teachers and/or parents the same questions about an activity. Indicate that information on your Turnaround Plan as well. The first draft of your Turnaround Plan lists the kinds of monitoring assessments you are considering. After you have designed your formative evaluation, you will name specific assessments or strategies.

SPECIFY DATA ANALYSIS STRATEGIES AND DECISION RULES

Plan Data Analysis Strategies for Summarizing and Interpreting Data

It may seem premature to consider how you will analyze, summarize, and perform relevant statistical analyses on your data prior to data collection. However, if you don't consider the kinds of analyses you need to answer your evaluation questions, you will not know if you are collecting appropriate information and how best to store it nor how to manage the collection and analysis process, including finding appropriate staff or experts to analyze the data and create appropriate summaries and displays. For example, if you are concerned about improving the achievement of a particular subgroup and want to know whether parent involvement and a special counseling program has helped students from the subgroup to improve academically, you will need to set up your parent and student surveys for this group (and all others as well) in a way that lets you identify the individual student responses on the survey and link these electronically with each individual's performance on particular academic assessments. To make the link happen, you would be best served by having student identification data on surveys bar-coded or having respondents identify themselves by name on the survey. Moreover, your data analysis for turnaround work will be focused on growth and improvement, which require a longitudinal tracking system to record trends over time. Given that you are focusing on individual students, the data system will need to store data by student, linked to teacher, not just as classroom-level summaries. If you do not know in advance that individual student data linked to teacher is the building block of your analysis, you may not collect the necessary information to monitor your turnaround efforts.

The use of student data linked to teachers and parents brings up issues of student confidentiality and perhaps clauses in the teacher contract. You can keep data confidential by assigning unique identification numbers, and then use the IDs to analyze data for particular demographic groups, teachers, or grade levels. However, you will want to spend time helping teachers understand why individual data are needed, what the methods are for protecting confidentiality, and exactly what decisions the data will inform (and not inform).

Establish Decision Rules for Judging Implementation Quality and Student Progress

Our final consideration related to data analysis is to determine how we know we are making progress. What are our criteria for determining whether the program implementation is "high quality," whether student performance has "improved," whether student attendance is acceptable, or whether we were successful in improving parent involvement? While it might seem premature to discuss the performance standards we expect to attain, it is not. Our criteria for judging progress help clarify goals and help staff monitor day-to-day classroom practice and student work. Typically, progress is measured in one or more of the following ways:

- Change Over Time—Are we approximating our program vision in increasing performance? In improving implementation?
- Improvement Relative to a Comparison Group—Is our practice similar to what is considered "best practice"? Are our student test results approximating those in our benchmark schools?
- Matching a Predetermined Performance Standard—Are we providing feedback on five writing assignments a month? Have all students scored Proficient on the number sense section of the state assessment? Are all teachers able to demonstrate how to teach a particular concept in more than one way?

Most evaluators use several approaches to judging success. In this age of standards-based accountability, it might seem counterintuitive to judge as successful any effort that does not meet a predetermined "standard of excellence." However, how much student love of mathematics is reasonable? Would it be better to have a standard of "significant" improvement over time, or even a "norm" by which your school's Grade 7 Mathematics students' attitudes are compared with those of students in your benchmark schools? Normative data actually are the standard for much of human behavior. Mental health and social behavior diagnoses are made not on the basis of an absolute standard but on norms, and culturally determined norms at that. Comparisons, norms, or even "better than before and enough to be noticeable to us" are all valid standards for judging your work.

Too often an arbitrarily selected criterion, such as 90% of the students master 90% of the work, provides no information at all. Why are 10% left behind? Why is 100% important (especially in light of the extra time it would take to hit the perhaps unattainable 100% mark)? If you are looking at specific performance targets, take some time to research where these came from, how realistic they are, whether these targets need to be attained for students to be successful on your long-range goals, and what you might be sacrificing to meet these targets.

Another example of this arbitrary target issue is often seen in math placement. Students who receive a grade of C in a mathematics class get full credit and are told their work is "average." Yet in some schools, you cannot enroll in the next level of mathematics (say, geometry) unless you earn a B or better. What does it mean to pass a course yet not be ready for or be considered acceptable to take the next mathematics course? This practice is especially egregious, because it dooms students to repeating courses they supposedly have completed satisfactorily. We do know that repeating Algebra I in high school is correlated with poorer, not better, performance as well as with high school dropout rates.

The criteria for determining progress, when set in advance of our turnaround work, also have an impact on teacher expectations for both themselves and their students. Just as students need to know what is expected of them to be able to take responsibility for their own learning, so too do teachers and school administrators need to be clear on what success looks like so that they can be thoughtful, purposeful, and accountable in pursuing and achieving it.

FLESH OUT THE MANAGEMENT PLAN

Review and Revise the Turnaround Plan Management Activities

You would not be working on a Turnaround Plan or improving student achievement if your school were not attentive to local, state, or national accountability requirements. Your school is already heavily committed to assessing students, collecting data, and reporting results. Try to leverage your data collection efforts from already-scheduled events. Whether you create or select existing data sources, you will need to consider the following management and budget issues related to data collection:

- If you create your own assessments or data sources (such as a database of student attendance or parent participation), you will need a timeline for development, pilot testing, and implementation. Be sure to leave adequate time for any proofing, expert review, and printing you intend to do, or for mounting the database online.

- If you are using existing data sources such as published tests, available surveys, district databases, and the like, be sure to leave yourself adequate time for ordering, receiving, and distributing materials or for setting up systems for collecting archival and electronic data.
- If data collection requires special skills, such as making classroom observations, rating essays, judging performances, or summarizing meeting notes into themes, build in time to train scorers, judges, or data analysts, and create a system for capturing their ratings that is easily accessible to all throughout your work.

Before you exit at this point for a strong headache remedy, remember that while we are describing a start-up data collection operation, you most probably will have existing data sources: required school site plan surveys, state and district assessments, curriculum-embedded assessments tied to instructional materials, and routinely collected archival data, attendance, grades, credit accumulation, teacher staff development hours, and the like. For most of us, instrument development means finding and adapting existing surveys, content assessments, and interview questions so we can meet the specifications of our blueprints. If you are developing measures from scratch, you should add an additional six months to a year for

- writing items,
- conducting item reviews to match items to specifications,
- testing items with students or intended respondents and revising them,
- creating assessment administration guidelines,
- pilot-testing instruments and calculating reliability, and
- creating, producing, and distributing final instruments.

We have included **Tool 7.6, Template for a Data Collection Management Plan,** in the Toolkit to help you organize your data collection management activities.

Tool
7.6

Distribute Responsibility for Data Collection

If staff availability or resources permit, select one person to coordinate data collection; train administrators, observers, interviewers, and/or scorers, if necessary; and supervise materials distribution, administration of measures, answer sheet collection, data cleanup, and other required activities. If you have a data-savvy coordinator, you will eliminate headaches caused by inconsistent administration methods, or, worse, responses influenced by the data collector. Data collection coordinators should be people who have a passion for operational and systems work, are good at details, and are careful to keep opinions to themselves. The person who will have access to student, parent, and teacher responses to surveys should be seen as someone who is good at keeping information confidential and is not aligned with any one staff faction or ideological stance. The objectivity of your coordinator will enhance the credibility of your data.

Avoid Preventable Data Collection Disasters

When it comes to managing data collection, scoring, and reporting, it's always wise to have a belt and suspenders. There are many challenges in the data collection cycle, and Murphy's Law prevails. Why, for example, are important accountability tests given in the spring, when chicken pox is most likely to strike? Why do you not notice that a test is an instructional mismatch until a shockingly low result motivates you to examine the assessment with a critical eye? It's always wise to build in practices that will help you avoid some of the more common data collection disasters. **Tool 7.7, A Catalog of Data Collection Disasters,** provides descriptions of disasters we personally participated in creating; these include measurement mayhem, language landmines, data collection dilettantes, passionless participants, wretched return rates, and no suspenders.

Despite all of the things that can go wrong, and will, at one or more points during your data collection cycle, we have salvaged the moment by getting a little help from our friends. Have on speed dial your district office person in charge of the student information system and testing, the county office person in charge of training teachers for the state tests, and the state department of education person in charge of high-stakes assessments and data collection for the state longitudinal databases. These folks spend their lives dealing with data collection and analysis issues and are likely to have a response that will fix whatever local problem you encounter.

DOCUMENT YOUR EVALUATION DESIGN

What? Another plan? We have insisted throughout this book that the focus of our work is on doing, not documenting. We have a Turnaround Plan that incorporates the measures, timelines, and management responsibilities you would find in an evaluation plan. Why, then, another document?

Formative evaluation plays two roles in turnaround work: (1) It is used to make program revisions during program implementation, and (2) it is used to evaluate progress over longer time periods, most commonly at the end of the year. Your annual evaluation of turnaround work will use data collected about program quality and link it to student outcomes to determine what refinements are needed in your theory of action, which then drives revisions of program activities for the coming year. The evaluation design would most reasonably be the responsibility of your school data team, a district official responsible for supporting your turnaround work, or the evaluator hired by an agency supporting your turnaround efforts. The staff should know its contents, but it doesn't need to know every detail, nor do all aspects of the design need to be incorporated into the Turnaround Plan. We have included a template for summarizing and documenting your formative evaluation design in **Tool 7.8, Template for a Formative Evaluation Design,** and include an abbreviated example of the template in use in Table 7.7.

Table 7.7 Formative Evaluation Design: Grade 7 Mathematics

Evaluation Questions	Data Needed	Data Source	Sample	Data Collection Strategy	Criteria for Judging Progress
Are classes allocating more time to developing number sense?	Individual classroom pacing guides Time allocation for lessons	Student OTL survey Teacher pacing charts	All Grade 7 students All Grade 7 teachers	Teachers file weekly time allocations electronically Students complete OTL surveys electronically	Percentage of students understanding number sense increases; 80% score mastery.
What materials are being used and how?	How and when students use materials	Computer logs of student completion of Powersource activities Student OTL survey	All Grade 7 students	Powersource logs participation Students complete OTL surveys electronically	Common materials in all classes
How much training have teachers had?	Teacher sign-in sheets for PD	Sign-in sheets and district PD automated course sign-ups	All mathematics teachers, all grade levels	School secretary creates PD attendance file	All teachers at least 3 hours
What training do they need?	Teacher feedback about needed PD Teachers use of new strategies	Teacher PD evaluations Classroom observation of teacher use of strategies	All mathematics teachers, all grade levels	Grad student summarizes PD evaluations Mentor teachers conduct walk-throughs	Majority of teachers report improvements in knowledge All teachers are using the new strategy; majority (8/10) following guidelines.
How many parents are using our homework monitoring module, and is it making a difference?	Computer logs for parent log-in by date, grade, and student Correlation between parent log-in frequency and student results	Computer logs from parent module	All parents regardless of grade level	Computer logs parent use of homework module	Percentage increases to 75%
How are students doing on quarterly assessments? End-of-course assessments?	Assessment results	Classroom assessment results for individual students by test type over time	All Grade 7 students	Grad student prepares spreadsheets of series of test scores converted to percentage correct, sorted by student and classroom	20% improvement in proportion of students proficient on number sense

Note: PD = professional development; OTL = opportunity to learn.

SUMMARY

This chapter has described the core work for your turnaround monitoring activities, which we have referred to throughout this book as formative evaluation. You have taken the monitoring questions you identified in Chapter 5 and in this chapter have identified the kinds of information you need to address each one:

- You have identified how you will obtain data, from your district databases to published tests and locally developed measures.
- You have scheduled when you will collect data.
- You have scheduled scoring and analysis of data so that your collaborative teams can take action to improve your turnaround efforts, both in the short term and over time.

At the site level, all of these activities must be managed, coordinated, implemented, and completed, which is why we have grouped them into the process of designing an evaluation of the Turnaround Plan. Some of the work in carrying out evaluation requires expertise in instrument development and review, selecting appropriate scores, and creating summaries and analyses that will aid appropriate data interpretation. We recommend allocating resources, time, and expert help to the tasks of monitoring, evaluating, and managing your turnaround work so that the quality of your decisions is the best possible.

CHAPTER 7 TOOLKIT

DESIGN AN EVALUATION OF THE TURNAROUND PLAN

The Tools for Chapter 7 can be found on the companion website for *The TurnAround ToolKit* at http://www.corwin.com/turnaroundtoolkit.

Tool 7.1   Formative Evaluation Questions for a Turnaround Plan

Tool 7.2   Template for Prioritizing Evaluation Questions

Tool 7.3   Advantages and Limitations of Common Data Collection Techniques

Tool 7.4   Blueprint Components for Common Measures

Tool 7.5   Test Evaluation Criteria for Published Achievement Tests

Tool 7.6   Template for a Data Collection Management Plan

Tool 7.7   A Catalog of Data Collection Disasters

Tool 7.8   Template for a Formative Evaluation Design

8

Analyze Evaluation Data and Revise the Program

There are no facts, only interpretations.

—Frederick Nietzsche (1844–1900)

PROGRESS MAP

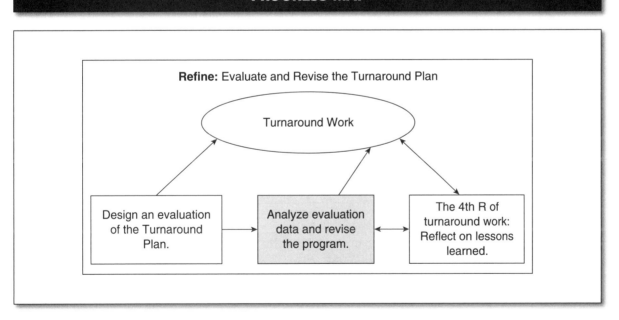

POCKET SUMMARY

Task	Major Activities	Purpose
Analyze evaluation data.	• Know the score (meaning). **Tool 8.1 Score Summary Methods for Common Measures** • Summarize results for each measure using descriptive statistics. **Tool 8.2 Descriptive Statistics for Common Measures**	• Transform raw data so that it is more useful in addressing evaluation questions.
Create data tables and displays.	• Consolidate data related to the same evaluation question. **Tool 8.3 Mapping Measures to Evaluation Questions for Data Analysis** • Summarize data in multiple ways. • Summarize evidence of practical significance.	• Simplify the presentation of multiple measures related to the same question.
Refine the program: Make midcourse corrections.	• Check to be sure you are implementing the program. • Identify indicators sensitive to short-term redesign activities. • Check the relationships in your theory of action. • Use data to make midcourse corrections.	• Achieve the rapid-fire experimentation cycle.
Revise the program.	• Annually examine long-term impact. • Begin your yearly review by judging findings in terms of prespecified criteria. • Look at trends over time. • Corroborate findings with multiple indicators. • Examine subgroup performance. • Test relationships in your theory of action. • Revise to address weaknesses. • Revise to build upon strengths. • Consider a new plan.	• Revise and redesign annually.
Communicate the results of your turnaround efforts to stakeholders.	**Tool 8.4 Communication Considerations** • Base communication on audience needs. • Plan to provide data for formal reports. • Incorporate reporting activities into your Turnaround Plan. **Tool 8.5 Communications Calendar Template**	• Build support for your work.

ANALYZE EVALUATION DATA

Data analysis is simply the process of transforming raw data into useable information. It has two phases, data distillation and logical analysis. The distillation phase requires that you take the raw information you have collected and summarize it in ways that relate to your evaluation questions. The logical analysis is using the findings to make decisions on how well the program is working and on whether and what program refinement and/or revisions may be needed. This second step, of course, is the essence of formative evaluation: to make decisions that will improve your program and, by extension, your Turnaround Plan.

Your transformation process from raw to useful data is straightforward:

- Review all of the evaluation questions a particular measure was designed to address, and select the kinds of category coding scheme—such as percentage reaching proficiency, percentage correct, or total raw score—needed to inform the evaluation questions.
- Summarize results with descriptive statistics: distribution shapes, measures of central tendency, and score dispersion.
- Define how you will establish practical significance (confidence intervals or other statistical tests, criteria for judging success).

However, each of these steps requires some knowledge and experience to be executed well. We begin by deciding how to "score" each measure and determining what the scores mean. We then summarize the scores using descriptive statistics, aided by the "statistics" function in your Excel or other spreadsheet software. Finally, we create tables or graphs to present the score distributions, trends, or comparisons that will inform our evaluation questions.

Know the Score

All data you collect will be raw data. Raw data, like their slightly provocative name, are simply data that haven't been "cooked" by any summarization or a score transformation. Observation and interview notes, focus group records, and written responses on surveys are raw data until they have been organized by categories, or coded, and summarized either by theme or by tallying similar responses. Test or qualitative data yield raw scores, which are rarely interpretable on their own. A raw score might be the number correct on a standards test, a tally on a classroom observation checklist, or a rubric score on an essay or project.

Each data source or measure, assessment, survey, performance, observation, work sample, or archive can produce multiple scores. Among the most common scores are categories like Proficient/Not Proficient, percentage correct, percentiles, normal curve equivalents, and scale scores. When you consider how you will summarize data to share with your staff, you must always keep in mind what questions you wish to address and what the scores mean. The bad news is that the kind of score scale underlying your results is not always easy to determine. The better news is that because you are interpreting scores in your local context and know the group producing the scores, if you perform some operations that your measurement level won't support, you will probably not be led too far astray if you interpret the performance in light of what you know from other sources of local information.

Choose the score summarization method based on your data interpretation needs. Here is an example of how data use drives summarization method. You have developed a rubric for evaluating persuasive essays. It has a score scale from 0 to 4, with 0 meaning "no response," 1 meaning "developing," 2 meaning "nearing proficient," 3 meaning "proficient," and 4 meaning "professional quality." It looks like an interval scale where the achievement difference between each scoring level 0, 1, 2, 3, and 4 is "one unit" and equal in meaning. However, let us not be fooled!

Most essay scores on a 0–4 rubric are not of equal intervals. Students who score a 1 may have produced only two or three sentences, may not have addressed the prompt at all, or may be unable to write a literate sentence. The student who scores a 2 is most likely able to string sentences together and allude to the topic. However, students who score 2 are much further below those who score 3 than students scoring 3 are from the 4 group. We also find that rubric scoring tends to place the majority of scores in the "just about made Proficient" group, or in our case, the 2 group. If we calculate class average rubric scores, as opposed to presenting the distribution, we will find very small differences among classes. We could also obscure important information. For example, which of the two following data summaries is more useful? Ms. Smith's class averaged 2.2 on the rubric, and Ms. Jones's class averaged 2.4. Or, 50% of Ms. Smith's class scored in the 1 and 2 categories and 10% scored 4, whereas no one in Ms. Jones's class scored below 3, but no one scored 4. For instructional purposes, knowing the score distribution on the rubric is usually more useful than knowing the average score. We should have this "best score" discussion for each of our measures prior to selecting the score we will use in our data summaries. You can reference **Tool 8.1, Score Summary Methods for Common Measures,** to help you select the kinds of scores you need to answer your evaluation questions.

Tool 8.1

Summarize Results for Each Measure Using Descriptive Statistics

Descriptive statistics simply capture how a group performs on a particular measure. Using the raw, percentage correct, standard, or scale score, you will calculate numbers that summarize the average score for the group, the distribution of scores, and the extent to which scores vary. Perhaps you also will categorize levels of performance, such as Not Proficient, Proficient, and Exemplary, by calculating the number or percentage of students whose scores fall into each category. **Tool 8.2, Descriptive Statistics for Common Measures,** presents a simplified example of a student assessment that can be used with survey data or other quantitative measures. We used Excel to perform all calculations; however, complete and engaging descriptions of how to calculate descriptive statistics from test or survey scores appear in our favorite measurement resource, *Assessment for Educational Leaders* (Popham, 2006).

Tool 8.2

CREATE DATA TABLES AND DISPLAYS

You have already been introduced to guidelines for creating data summaries, tables, and displays in Chapter 3. Even though the focus in Chapter 3 was on preparing data summaries to answer needs assessment questions, the procedures for summarizing data to answer program implementation and student progress questions are exactly the same. Because you have control over the amount and kind of data you collect in an evaluation, you have a more complete data set than is normally available for needs assessment activities. To organize the sheer amount of information you could find yourself having to summarize, we have added two additional guidelines: (1) Organize data from separate measures or sections of measures by evaluation question, and (2) summarize data to address multiple perspectives on a question.

Consolidate Data Related to the Same Evaluation Question

One of the most common mistakes in summarizing data is getting overwhelmed by the sheer volume of information. It is easy to spend so much time summarizing several different kinds of scores on a single instrument, or on several different measures, that you shift your attention from answering evaluation questions to reporting on the measures themselves. You have spent time organizing your formative evaluation plan so that you would have multiple measures for each question. Keep your eye on the prize! While it may seem more logical to organize data that you share with staff based on the measure, such as the interview, walk-through summaries, survey, or assessments, very often these measures really contain several component measures related to more than one evaluation question. For example, your parent survey may ask about homework support, use of the online parent portal, and feeling welcomed at school as well as parents' observations about their student's attitude toward mathematics. Those four survey questions each address four different evaluation questions. Thus, the items and sections of the survey should be presented with the other data related to the four separate topics: parent involvement, parent use of technology, school climate, and student attitude, rather than as the "parent survey data."

Tool 8.3, **Mapping Measures to Evaluation Questions for Data Analysis,** will help you consolidate results from multiple measures for each evaluation question. In addition, you might consider documenting some of the circumstances of data collection that could help you better interpret the meaning of the data. For example, you might have noticed that several of your weakest students completed the quarterly assessment rapidly, because they didn't read the questions and were guessing. Or your parent survey results were unrepresentative because only 10% of the parents returned surveys. Perhaps on your walk-through debriefing you noticed observers had contradictory views of what they saw. This information about context will add to the accuracy of your interpretations.

Tool
8.3

Expert Help

You may wish to call in an expert for help in selecting appropriate scores and clear data summaries. The expert can also help with more technical analyses for measuring year-to-year growth and making comparisons with benchmark schools or state averages should these be needed.

Summarize Data in Multiple Ways

Your data summaries and how you organize them to present to staff for interpretation should take into account that your audience will be considering the data from multiple analysis perspectives. For each evaluation question, they could consider

- trends over time,
- comparisons between similar groups (classes, schools),
- comparisons between benchmark groups (high-scoring schools, state or national groups, or high-scoring student subgroups within your school),
- comparisons to a standard or accountability target,
- comparisons among subgroups, and
- relationships between program activities (processes) and outcomes (test, survey, or other results).

Summarize Evidence of Practical Significance

As you examine your data, especially when you are making comparisons over time or between groups, you will want to know, "Is the change significant?" The concept of significance has at least two meanings: (1) The change is statistically significant, not attributable to sampling error, and (2) the change is educationally or practically significant; it represents observable differences in classroom practices and/or student performance.

Practical significance is conventionally measured by calculating a confidence interval to determine whether a change is greater than what would be expected by measurement error, or effect size. *Effect size* is simply the amount of change from a pretest to a posttest measure translated into standard deviation units. What effect size means is that the posttest score distribution has shifted upward, or improved from the pretest score distribution, by an amount that is greater than would be expected by chance.

Under some circumstances, rarely encountered at the school level with smaller sample sizes, scores can be statistically significant without having any practical significance. When samples are large, a small difference will be registered as statistically significant. For example, if the average percentage correct for Proficient on the state assessment ($n = 400,000$ students) is 30% in Year 1, and the average moves up to 30.2% in Year 2, that difference could be statistically significant due to the large sample size. However, in Year 2, teachers would not likely notice improved classroom performance from that 0.2% increase.

Although you will not likely be running statistical significance tests on your short-term, quarterly data, there may be occasions when you will want to know if your long-term outcomes with important political consequences (dropout rates, graduation rates, SAT scores, etc.) have improved significantly in both senses of the word. When you have high-stakes, public and politically important measures, you may want to hire an expert to calculate whether the gains you observe, or the differences between subgroups reported, are both statistically and practically significant.

Statistical significance tests will let you know whether the differences you observe are due to some sort of measurement error or chance. Practical significance tests, which take into account statistical significance, along with your own observations about what differences in test scores between groups mean in the classrooms at your school, will be far more important in judging the effectiveness of your turnaround work. You will want evidence that supports your year-end test results to be able to say, "Yes, we have made visible educational progress that is not due to yearly or chance fluctuations in scores."

In addition to statistical methods, there are two logic-based strategies for assessing practical or educational significance. Did your student scores improve as much or more than those of an important comparison group? We have urged you to use data from benchmark schools (schools like yours but doing much better) to help set standards for your turnaround work. If your year-end results are as good as or better than those of the benchmark schools, you can argue that your gains are practically significant, that they have real-world meaning. A second strategy is for your staff to use its expertise to define performance levels on important assessments that map onto their observations of what constitutes proficiency or better. You could even develop rubrics with rich descriptions of what students can do when they score at certain levels to create a growth scale useful in determining how much gain is meaningful.

REFINE THE PROGRAM: MAKE MIDCOURSE CORRECTIONS

You will be examining data summaries quarterly, if not more often, to assess your progress in two areas: (1) program quality and (2) student progress toward course or grade-level-defined outcomes. Program quality refers to how well program redesign activities are being carried out and how many staff members are implementing the redesign as planned. You will use data summaries from classroom visits, teacher focus groups, samples of student work, and assignments to ensure that your Turnaround Plan actually is being implemented. You will examine student assessment results at the classroom and school levels to determine whether students are making progress under the program redesign.

Check to Be Sure You Are Implementing the Program

One of the most common mistakes we make in evaluating our turnaround efforts is to assume that, because we call an initiative a "program," it actually exists. You will have quarterly data from classroom visits (walkthroughs), professional learning community meetings, and teacher and student surveys that can be used to indicate differences in implementation levels and strategies across classrooms. The differences do not necessarily mean that some teachers are doing it "wrong." It means that you need to explore the differences, connect them to desired student outcomes (attitudes, attendance, and formative assessments as well as results from high-stakes tests), and determine how you will define appropriate implementation for your particular school.

Identify Indicators Sensitive to Short-Term Redesign Activities

Some changes must be implemented for longer than others to show an impact. In a skill-based curriculum, such as mathematics or foreign language, students may struggle on skill assessments until they have had time to gain fluency (number facts, language pronunciation, and the like). The skill-development curve is not linear and incremental but almost like a step function, where one day things come together and the student "gets it." Thus, early and short-term measures, while helpful in improving instruction and a good way to assess and respond to student progress, may not be the best predictor about whether your efforts will ultimately be successful.

How do you determine whether disappointing quarterly data indicate that a change is needed? We have some suggestions:

- Consult research.
- Check with experts.
- Visit other schools that are successfully implementing the same changes.
- Rely on professional judgment.

If you choose to continue without changes, be sure to revisit your decision at your next quarterly review.

Check the Relationships in Your Theory of Action

Your theory of action may need a tune-up. Catch flawed assumptions early, and change your activities to maximize your chance of improving student achievement. Your quarterly reviews should address what the data show, raise questions about the quality of program implementation, and raise questions about the validity of the student outcomes and implementation data. Do they square with what the team sees? What do they reveal about gaps in the program strategy, in the sufficiency of new materials and/or professional development activities, or in the shortcomings of the data? The discussion will lead to ideas about whether and how best to stay the course, or what changes may be needed in the classroom, in staff development, in parent involvement, and in other areas of curriculum, instruction, and school climate.

Many instructional programs produced today are based on theories of how students learn to read, or understand mathematics, or comprehend history and science; or of how curriculum should be organized to maximize student learning. Some theory-based program activities you might consider, along with related changes you might look for, include the following:

- Grouping students in different ways, for example, into heterogeneous groups instead of needs-based groups, may lead to more positive attitudes.
- Using calculators may affect acquisition of number facts.
- Integrating subjects or using a multidisciplinary approach may improve reading comprehension.
- Differentiated staff development may lead to more complete program implementation.

The list is endless and will be informed by published research, practices observed at successful benchmark schools (schools like yours but outperforming your school), and current trends in curriculum and instruction.

Table 8.1 reproduces the processes and short-term outcomes from My Middle School's theory of action for Grade 7 Mathematics, which underlies its Turnaround Plan and evaluation design. The theory of action is based on four assumptions or cause-and-effect hypotheses:

- A new curriculum with more student-sensitive pacing of topics will be more engaging and improve student attitudes.
- More assessment and reteaching will improve student number sense proficiency.
- Staff development focused on formative assessment of number sense concepts will improve teaching and learning of number sense.
- Implementing online access to class work will improve parent support.

Table 8.1   Excerpt From the Theory of Action: My Middle School Grade 7 Mathematics

Processes	Short-Term Outcomes
Curriculum • Revised pacing guide • New number sense teaching modules	• Improve student attitudes toward math
Instruction • Frequent postinstruction assessment and regrouping • Multiple methods for explaining content	• Number sense proficiency
Professional Development • Powersource training • Professional learning communities • Walk-throughs and peer observations • Content: prealgebra core concepts • Parent online access to class work and homework	• Students engaged in explaining their work • Instruction connected to major mathematics principles • Teacher provides regular feedback • Teacher uses data to respond to student learning • Increase parent awareness and support for homework

In our review of the theory of action, perhaps we find that students still hate mathematics. What, then, would improve engagement and attitude? Better pacing and more accessible instruction could be part of the solution, but perhaps our assumptions need to be augmented with some feedback from students. Why is mathematics so difficult? Why do you find it so boring? It is possible students would say that they have a history of failure in mathematics and are used to being lost and confused. These answers can help us devise ways to make instruction more clear, to frequently check for understanding, and to provide success experiences both in class and on assessments for students. Quarterly checks of the assumptions underlying our turnaround work supported by easily collected and perhaps informal data can leverage our chances for a successful turnaround.

Use Data to Make Midcourse Corrections

Your analysis of program quality and quarterly data on student outcomes will likely focus on one or more of the following issues for midcourse correction:

- Usefulness of the quarterly assessments
- Extent of program implementation
- Need for additional staff development or support to better implement the program
- Improvements in student behavior, attendance, attitude, and engagement

And, perhaps the most useful, the mysterious category of

- unanticipated challenges and triumphs.

Table 8.2 presents a range of review areas and discussion questions for making changes during the implementation process.

Table 8.2   Focus Areas for Midcourse Corrections

Review Area	Discussion Questions
Usefulness and accuracy of student assessments	• Are our quarterly assessments providing diagnostic information? • Do the assessments capture important instructional targets? • Do they differentiate well between students doing well and those struggling with the concepts tested? • Are the assessment results corroborated by teacher observation and class performance?
Extent to which program is being implemented	• Do all teachers have the necessary materials for program implementation? • Have all teachers attended program-related staff development? • What percentage of the program has been implemented thus far? • Have all classes implemented the program to the same extent?
Staff development needed	• Do walk-through observations indicate a need for staff development? • Does the extent of program implementation indicate a need for more or different staff development? • Do teachers request more support in program implementation?
Incremental improvements in student behavior, attendance, and motivation	• Do walk-throughs indicate students are engaged? • Do informal student interviews or focus groups indicate students understand content, assignments, and how to improve their work? • Do attendance, tardiness, and behavior data show some improvement for all classes?
Unanticipated challenges and triumphs	• What do staff report as a continuing challenge to be addressed? • What positive changes has staff observed (anything from enjoying teaching more to more enthusiastic students, more parent contact, better student performance, or something else)?

REVISE THE PROGRAM

Annually Examine Long-Term Impact

Your quarterly data reviews rely on short-term assessments, many of which may have been locally developed, and on informal observations, such as walk-throughs, interviews, and focus groups and perhaps some computer-based surveys administered to parents and students. These indicators are useful but do not provide the measures by which your school is judged by the larger community. The real test of your work will be the high-stakes accountability measures reported to the public, from tests to graduation rates and college readiness indices, and more formal parent, student, and teacher surveys administered for program evaluation. At your yearly data review, you will focus on whether you met your goals and hypothesize how you could improve. Your yearly review, because it relies on formal data provided by the state and perhaps outside vendors, could take place at the end of the year or the beginning of the next school year. The timing will depend upon when data are available to your school and when staff can be assembled.

Your yearly review essentially repeats the work you performed in Chapter 4, identifying an instructional focus based on high-stakes student outcome data, and Chapter 5, creating a Turnaround Plan based on a review of data about school context, curriculum, and instruction. The yearly revision cycle is both an evaluation of your past efforts and a needs assessment for your future efforts. But the needs assessment you conducted in Chapters 4 and 5 was unstructured and required you to consider all factors; in contrast, for your revision planning, you now have both a Turnaround Plan and an evaluation design to point you to a small number of review questions and issues.

Begin Your Yearly Review by Judging Findings in Terms of Prespecified Criteria

Your evaluation design specifies which formative questions about your Turnaround Plan you will answer, what data you will review to answer the questions, and what the targets are for determining how successful your work has been. Now it is time to use your success criteria as a guide for analyzing the data presented in your data summaries for the purpose of deciding what is working, what is almost working, what is worthless, and what is missing.

Table 8.3 reproduces the evaluation questions, data sources, and criteria for success for My Middle School Grade 7 Mathematics that we created as part of our evaluation design (Chapter 7), but for purposes of clarity omits information about the sampling plan and schedule for data collection. Our yearly data review begins with each question, considers the scored and summarized data for each data source, and determines whether we met our criteria for success.

When you review your data in the context of prespecified success criteria, you will notice that the discussion does not get mired in the "How good is good enough?" bog and moves quickly to "Why didn't we meet our goal?" or "How can we improve?" If you did meet your goals, you might even be fortunate enough to have staff ask, "Did we set our success

Table 8.3	Formative Evaluation Design Excerpt: My Middle School Grade 7 Mathematics	

Evaluation Questions	Data Source	Criteria for Judging Progress
Are classes allocating more time to developing number sense?	Student Opportunity to Learn survey, teacher pacing charts	Percentage of students understanding number sense increases and is maximal
How much time is allocated to Powersource modules?	Student Opportunity to Learn survey, teacher monthly assignments for specific skills	Minutes reported >20
Which students are making progress on the modules?	Teacher monthly assignments for specific skills	Increase in number of English learners and African American students scoring at or above Proficient
What materials are being used and how?	Computer logs of student completion of Powersource activities, Student Opportunity to Learn survey	Common materials in all classes
How are students doing on module tests?	Data file from computerized assessments	Increase in number of number sense scores above Proficient
How are teachers using results?	Professional learning community meeting notes summarized by topics	Results used weekly to revise lessons and regroup students
How much training have teachers had?	Sign-in sheets and district professional development automated course sign-ups	All teachers at least 3 hours
What training do they need?	Teacher professional development evaluations	Most teachers confident in their knowledge of formative assessment and number sense; few need additional content training
How many parents are using our homework monitoring module, and is it making a difference?	Computer logs from parent module	Percentage increases to 75%
How are students doing on quarterly assessments? End-of-course assessments?	Classroom assessment results for individual students by test type over time	20% improvement in proportion of students proficient on number sense

criteria high enough?" These kinds of questions emerging from a data review provide the impetus for your revised Turnaround Plan and drive the continuous improvement process.

Look at Trends Over Time

Although your year-end data from both tests and surveys provide a single-year measure of your efforts, your goal is to sustain progress over time. Did performance on key indicators improve over the past three to five years? By taking a longitudinal perspective, you are in a better position to identify whether improvements observed in the current year are caused by your turnaround work or some outside factor. A change in staff, student population, number of dropouts (fewer dropouts means you are retaining more struggling students), or competition from local charter schools could have affected your results. In your first year of data collection, you create a baseline against which to compare future progress. While you should not be too hasty in making judgments about your efforts with only one year's worth of information, turnaround work, by its very nature, requires some quick wins. Search for changes in long-term trends that reverse declines. The U-turn is a requirement of successful turnaround, and you'll need longitudinal data to find one.

Corroborate Findings With Multiple Indicators

Even if this is your baseline year, if you have used multiple indicators to monitor your work, you will be more confident about your conclusions. Longitudinal data provide multiple measures, but different data sources about the same outcome also help with corroborating results. For example, suppose our number sense strategy included having students solve problems and explain their solutions. If only 12% of the students in Grade 7 Mathematics reached the goal for this activity by being able to write out clear explanations for their problem-solving strategies, you will want corroborating information before you decide that this goal was not attained. Do your classroom observations indicate that students were asked to write out explanations for problem-solving strategies? Do teacher, student, or parent surveys suggest that explanation was expected of students on a regular basis? If all of these data sources indicate that, yes, students indeed received repeated instruction and multiple opportunities to explain and receive feedback on their work, you can conclude that this remains an area of weakness. However, if survey responses and observations indicate that problem-solving explanations and feedback were not a regular activity, you have information for program revision.

Examine Subgroup Performance

NCLB has heightened educator sensitivity to achievement gaps between different subgroups of students. Even in a post-NCLB world, the focus on eliminating gaps will remain. We challenge you to examine subgroups *not* reported in your state accountability results if those subgroups represent traditional achievement inequities. For example, if you have a very small number of African American students at your school, your accountability reports will not summarize data for them as a significant subgroup. You should still examine performance for these students and compare it to school averages or a proficiency target to identify any possible achievement gap. Another example is gender. Girls have been underrepresented in both mathematics and science in college. Boys tend to do worse on the verbal section of the SAT than girls. You could compare test results by gender to catch these inequities and address them in your turnaround work. Examining parent and teacher survey data, or even Student Opportunity to Learn and attitude survey results by subgroups, can be very revealing. Differences in parental support, motivation, homework completion, and other school context factors by subgroup can lead you to craft interventions for specific populations to help level the educational playing field.

Test Relationships in Your Theory of Action

Annual high-stakes assessment and survey data need context to be useful. They indicate *what* has occurred but not *how* or *why*. The advantage of monitoring your turnaround work with a formative evaluation is that the data you collect, both quarterly and yearly, are designed to address these really important questions: "How did we get these results?" "Why (or why not) were we successful?" Your data related to program implementation, student behavior, school climate, staff development, curriculum implementation, and instructional strategies will be used to identify areas in your plan that need revision. During your yearly review of school context and process data, you will consider what cause-and-effect links in your theory of action may be faulty and where your theory and/or your program activities need revision.

The human brain is a pattern-making organism. We survive on our ability to organize information, connect it to what we already do, and make successful predictions about what our assumptions will produce. In the quarterly reviews, staff has been examining the cause-and-effect assumptions of their theory of action. The yearly review is a time to test more formally some of the relationships between the data and outcomes. Each turnaround change you implement will be attended by its own set of assumptions that need testing. In our Grade 7 Mathematics example, we are trying to prepare students for algebra by involving parents in homework monitoring, altering the pacing chart so that students thoroughly master number sense standards, and changing the problem-solving curriculum. Several questions beg for our attention:

- Does the emphasis on college readiness push students out of school or motivate them?
- Does asking parents to monitor completion of homework through an online system lead to better completion and higher-quality work?
- Does deviating from the pacing chart in order to reteach a concept result in lower yearly test results?
- Do the new problem-solving content, materials, and teaching strategies result in improved state test scores?

Your data from student and parent surveys, online audits of parent access, and teacher reports of allocated instructional time can be linked to test results and algebra enrollments (and later success) to verify your assumptions (theory of change) or identify areas requiring revision. At least once a year, consider summarizing your data formally and conducting appropriate statistical analyses, such as correlations, or asking an expert to review your qualitative findings, to see whether your data show expected relationships. For example, are teachers who participated in all professional development activities more likely to implement the new program? Is better implementation related to higher student performance?

Revise to Address Weaknesses

Weakness is a term with many meanings. If you are a high-achieving school with broad community support, your challenge will be to sustain your achievement and to identify areas of improvement that most schools do not have the luxury of addressing. Even high-achieving schools serve "forgotten" students. Do you need to improve your counseling services for students without college aspirations? Do you need to explore ways to offer vocational training or arts enrichment to more students? Do you need to connect your students, who are quite able, to the community through service projects? Do you need a character education program to help students develop ethical behavior? There is always something to improve, even in the best of schools.

Revise to Build Upon Strengths

As you reviewed your annual data, you identified what was working well. More importantly, as you examine relationships between your theory of change and student outcomes, you garnered empirical evidence of potentially successful program activities. Use these program successes as the basis of your continuing work. If, for example, you find a positive correlation between the number of times a parent logs onto the online homework system and the students' quarterly assessment scores as well as their number sense subscores on the state assessments, then you will want your efforts to focus on assuring that more parents and more classrooms are using the tool and involving parents.

If your Turnaround Plan was successful, you will want to plan how to sustain your success while moving into other instructional focal areas. Ideally, our focused improvement strategy has paid off. A small need has been addressed. Now it's time to expand your Turnaround Plan. It must sustain your gains while addressing a new need. This is a balancing act for allocating resources and time. How much of your time and money should be allocated to the initial area of instructional focus and how much devoted to new areas? Here is where your yearly review of the relationships between your turnaround activities and student outcomes will be essential. Identify the most powerful relationships you found between activities and outcomes. Are these institutionalized? If so, you can pull back a bit on monitoring those and allocate time and effort to other areas. Perhaps the relationships you identified can serve as interventions in other curricular areas. If you revised professional development (i.e., teacher learning) to focus on building teacher capacity to supplement, differentiate, and adapt instruction to student needs in math, then you might use that approach to support another curricular area where students are struggling.

Evidence of success also enables you to improve your school's image in your community and gain political capital as well as seek funding for your efforts—hard-cash capital. If you are improving despite budget cuts, changes in mandated curriculum and assessments, changing student enrollment or community needs, then inform your public, the media, and even the online school ratings organizations. Invite a university researcher to document your efforts in the coming year and disseminate your findings. If you have evidence of success in many areas, you could consider applying for a state, federal, or private foundation grant. Your quick wins and successes are an important engine of change.

Consider a New Plan

If you find many weaknesses, and your Turnaround Plan is in tatters, then focus on revising your theory of change. When your house has fallen down about you, call in some carpenters and an architect or two to help you re-vise (root word: *vision*). Step away from the Turnaround Plan monitoring data and from crafting tools, and return to your schoolwide data on achievement and context. Begin again with identifying instructional issues and describing your efforts to address them with changes in curriculum, instruction, student behavior, climate, and/or parent/community involvement. Your job is to reconstruct, not expand. In the case of major changes in your school, staffing, budget, student population, curriculum, or assessment, you may well find that despite your best efforts, you do not see results. In such cases, do not tinker with a focused Turnaround Plan that did not produce any results. Create a new one with as much outside support as is available to you.

COMMUNICATE THE RESULTS OF YOUR TURNAROUND EFFORTS TO STAKEHOLDERS

Forgive us for addressing how you will weave communication of your turnaround efforts throughout your work at the very end of the revision process. Communication is not an afterthought, nor is it the last activity in the turnaround process. However, effective communication very much depends upon having a message, being aware of your audience, and addressing a specific purpose. Until you had read about all of the elements of the turnaround continuous improvement cycle, the message was not completely formed. At this point, you have read about the purpose, activities, and structure of a turnaround improvement process. You now have an understanding of the work about which you will communicate to your stakeholders. **Tool 8.4, Communication Considerations,** summarizes important communication considerations discussed in this section.

Tool
8.4

Base Communication on Audience Needs

Different audiences have different levels of sophistication when it comes to understanding both your turnaround efforts and the data you will report. Parents' first concern is with the experiences of their own children, and then with how their school measures up. Our experience with parents in high-achieving schools is that they demand improvement and want specific evidence of excellence despite the school's proven track record of college acceptance or high test scores. Such parents are skeptical of reports containing only good news and are ever on the lookout for a whitewash. At the same time, these parents will rally to improvement efforts and will lavish time and money on their child's school. Parents whose children attend low-achieving schools have identical concerns with a different twist: In addition to hearing about all of the weaknesses and all of the special programs designed to improve their schools, these parents need to be made aware of their school's special strengths: particular teachers, an award-winning sports team, strong community-based programs. Parent audiences need balanced reporting that includes strengths and weaknesses accompanied by what the school is doing to improve. Concrete examples of what is changing or what is new appeal to parent audiences.

Teachers want to know how their own students are doing, whether their change efforts are paying off, and even how they measure up, despite the professional taboo against comparing teachers. Teachers who see no need to change need evidence that the change has positive results. Teachers who eagerly embrace change seek validation for their efforts. The biggest difficulty in sharing evidence with teacher audiences is that the data don't always provide clear answers. A recent study investigating the impact of research results on policymaker decisions found that these decisions were little influenced by evidence, and in fact, the more sophisticated the audience, the more critical it was of empirical studies. Teacher audiences mirror this finding. Their experience and underlying knowledge make them excellent critics of data and more skeptical of research results. Teachers can become discouraged with data-driven decision making and the evaluation process and may remain unconvinced that information collected outside of their own classrooms is useful. Descriptive, nonjudgmental findings supported by measures internal and external to the school and evidence of the relationships between activities and outcomes can help teachers accept changes more readily.

Political audiences, the board of education, the press, and community members who do not have students attending your school are less interested in the details of your work than in sound-bite-sized findings. Messages that garner the attention of political audiences must be both important and credible. These audiences are likely to want explanations and recommendations supported by data. They view your successes with pride and may widely publicize them. Therefore, you should have solid substantiation of your results, lest you be embarrassed in the future should outcomes plummet or you face reversals.

The audience most likely to be interested in the specifics of your Turnaround Plan will be your board of education. It is also the group most focused on the quick-win aspects of turnaround and least patient with the use of educational jargon or having nothing to show for your efforts. Your turnaround monitoring plan—we call it your formative evaluation—will likely provide at least one area of potential success, because you are asked to consider factors such as climate, student behavior, and parent/community involvement in addition to changes in curriculum and instruction.

Plan to Provide Data for Formal Reports

You perhaps would not be engaged in turnaround work were it not for the federally required, state-issued formal reports to the public on the status of your school's progress toward meeting accountability goals. Your turnaround efforts are designed to obtain better results on those reports and therefore more favorable judgments of your school. State accountability reports are not reports you will participate in producing; however, you may have local accountability requirements and local "accountability report cards" that you must complete yearly to satisfy state or district requirements. Most of the components of these reports are dictated by agencies outside your school, even though you provide the data. Once you have begun turnaround work, you might consider attending meetings of the agencies creating these reports, your district balanced scorecard committee, or the state school accountability report card working group, and attempting to add a category for turnaround work reporting, which can highlight your efforts as well as your achievements.

Another avenue of formal reporting is your local newspaper. Your media debut often occurs with the release of state test results, but not because you have called a press conference. It's time to seize the agenda. Get to know your local education reporter. Education reporters often feel that school people talk in jargon, are afraid to reveal problems, and aren't always responsive to the short deadlines reporters face. You can correct that image, and while it won't ensure that all press accounts of your school are positive, it will ensure that you get your side of the story heard. Some local reporters need help understanding accountability policies, test scores, or even "school reform" undertaken in "failing" schools. You can describe your efforts to the reporter along with how those efforts will lead to achievement gains, you can explain test score fluctuations and the difference between educationally significant changes and random error score changes, and you can provide concrete examples both of the curriculum and of what is being assessed. In addition, you are in a unique position to provide data about your school's other successes or unique school programs that will give reporters a more complete picture of your school than yearly scores. An important example of how having a relationship with the press provides a better picture of school turnaround has been the *Los Angeles Times* editorial board reporting on school reform at one of Los Angeles's lowest-performing high schools. The reporter spent the entire year highlighting improvements in student behavior and attendance and cautioning that achievement would not likely improve that year, because more students were coming to school and taking tests rather than opting out. The reports were supportive and sympathetic, even though test scores were dismal. Finally, connect your local reporting to the Hechinger Institute on Education and the Media at Columbia University. This organization provides training for educational journalists and keeps them up to date on changes in educational policy and practice. An educated reporter is an ally.

Incorporate Reporting Activities Into Your Turnaround Plan

Although formal reports will be prepared after yearly data are collected and interpreted, school constituencies—parents, teachers, and students—will find information most useful if feedback is provided quickly and fairly close to the time that the data are collected. Teachers are the most important audience for reporting results, as we are asking them to incorporate findings into ongoing work. Quarterly data review sessions and year-end reviews are built into the Turnaround Plan. Reports to teachers, however, should remain descriptive rather than evaluative and avoid premature conclusions or unsupported generalizations, as these act as deterrents to participating in evaluation.

Parents will be interested in results from any parent surveys. Online surveys often provide immediate feedback, but not all parents will have access to computers to participate. They also need some context for interpreting data as well as information about how you will use their feedback. Otherwise, why should they take the time to participate? You also might consider holding parent meetings that coincide with the reporting of student test scores. These provide you with opportunities to educate parents about what is being assessed by showing sample items and by explaining how difficult the assessments have become (they have!!), how to interpret scores, and, most important, how you will use the scores. Parents are often very anxious about how schools use test scores to advantage (place in advanced classes) or disadvantage (place in remedial classes) their children. Parent meetings provide opportunities to assure parents that students are judged on multiple criteria and are provided multiple opportunities for success. Parent forums also provide opportunities for you to present school results in context, to display your progress over time, and to discuss what you are doing about achievement weaknesses. You can use student score report meetings to entice parents into discussions of the larger issues affecting their students' education and to build support for the school and its Turnaround Plans.

You will want to provide frequent, informal reports to parent groups, advisory committees, and groups funding your work. These groups are interested in hearing about your efforts as they relate to group interests and in seeing data that validate the benefits of their support. Advisory and support groups appreciate concrete examples both of the questions guiding data collection and the measures. They need clear explanations of what the findings do and do not indicate and how the results guide your work. These groups are school advocates, so any examples you have for dissemination of clear findings and descriptions of your work will help them carry your message to other audiences.

We do not like generating lots of written documents or spending time planning instead of doing. However, if your school is under siege or has a particularly sophisticated parent community, investing time in thinking about what you will share with whom, and when and how, could help you build support and reap rewards. Even if you do not choose to create a formal communication plan, keeping in mind the information needs of different

Tool
8.5

audiences—addressing those needs will support your turnaround efforts. We have included a template for a communications calendar in **Tool 8.5, Communications Calendar Template,** should you find it necessary to keep track of your communications efforts.

Summary

We have traveled from the concrete task of converting a score into useful information to the rather airy world of communication. In this chapter, the work requires juggling and integrating a variety of disparate activities requiring very specialized skills, including data analysis, facilitation of data use discussions to refine and revise programs, and communicating well with different audiences for different purposes. One aspect of your turnaround work that would be well worth communicating to colleagues, to supportive stakeholders, and among yourselves is a reflection about the work itself, not just the results. Communication activities provide opportunities for you and your team to reflect on your work, how it is organized, whether the theory of action is well considered, whether your data sources are of high quality, and which data are most informative. It also affords opportunities to discuss challenges, lessons learned, and insights about practice that emerged during the year.

Turnaround work is so focused on results and so action oriented that it is only when you stop to consider what you will communicate, or what the message will be, that you allow yourself to reflect on your work in ways that can improve not only what you do but how and why you are doing it. In the last chapter, we share reflections from our own work and from others involved in school improvement to help you think about your own reflective discussions. Perhaps all that remains, once goals are achieved, are the lessons.

CHAPTER 8 TOOLKIT

ANALYZE EVALUATION DATA AND REVISE THE PROGRAM

The Tools for Chapter 8 can be found on the companion website for *The TurnAround ToolKit* at http://www.corwin.com/turnaroundtoolkit.

Tool 8.1   Score Summary Methods for Common Measures

Tool 8.2   Descriptive Statistics for Common Measures

Tool 8.3   Mapping Measures to Evaluation Questions for Data Analysis

Tool 8.4   Communication Considerations

Tool 8.5   Communications Calendar Template

9

The 4th R of Turnaround Work

Reflect on Lessons Learned

Plan to be better tomorrow than today, but don't plan to be finished.

—Carol Ann Tomlinson, U.S. educator

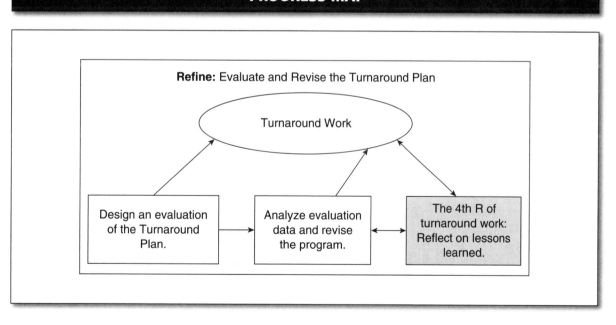

POCKET SUMMARY

Reflections About...	Major Lessons	Impact on Turnaround Work
Turnaround Process Versus Turnaround Dispositions	• Teachers feel responsible • Sense of urgency • Flexible practice based on frequent evidence-based reviews	Dispositions change, so changes in practice and responsibility become embodied in staff.
Turnaround as a Recipe Versus the Turnaround Way of Doing Business	• Begin at any time during the school year • Focus on repeating the cycle	Goal setting, monitoring, reviewing data, and refining work are institutional characteristics.
Lessons From Large-Scale Studies on School Turnaround	• University of Virginia case studies of 15 elementary schools that sustained turnaround for two years • RAND study of data-driven decision making	Research findings can inform work, but progress is messy and irregular.
Lessons From a Measurement Expert	• Too many curricular targets • Underutilization of classroom assessment • Preoccupation with instructional process • Absence of affective and other valued outcomes/measures • Instructionally insensitive accountability tests	Tough love about testing.
Lessons From a Broad Prize–Winning Urban District	• Driven by vision and inquiry • Powered by outside experts • Required curricular, pedagogical, and data expertise in central office • Required collaborative culture at all levels of the system • Cultural shift to taking risks	Lessen the stress of turnaround work.
Sustaining Turnaround Gains: The Zhuan Ji State of Mind	• Bring zhuan ji to your school	Problems are new beginnings, not obstacles.

TURNAROUND PROCESS VERSUS TURNAROUND DISPOSITIONS

We have used the term *turnaround* throughout this book to refer both to a process of continuous improvement focused on obtaining immediate improvements in student achievement and to a set of dispositions about school improvement. What has been lacking in the school reforms of the past 20 years, from "school improvement" through "whole-school reform" through using accountability measures to identify failing schools, are three important dispositions about our work: personal responsibility for student outcomes, a sense of urgency, and a commitment to continuous improvement. Turnaround work requires all three dispositions to effectively engage in identifying learner needs, attempting solutions and judging their effectiveness, and revising until we meet our goals.

These dispositions represent a change in how schools do business. Preservice teacher training typically focuses on what teachers do, with some attempts to address curriculum development and how assessment works, and some information about how students learn. Many teachers enter the profession committed to helping students by being culturally responsive and focused on social justice and by implementing a research-based curriculum or instructional strategies. However, a shift in perspective needs to be added to teaching: The teacher's work is defined by student needs (not curriculum pacing guides and decontextualized "best practices") and evaluated by student outcomes. We use the term *outcomes* to mean a wide variety of desirable results, which can include social justice; which must include attainment of academic knowledge, skills, and the ability to apply them; and which should include important student dispositions. Outcomes are never limited to standardized test results, though realistically, test results will always be part of the picture.

Second, teachers and other school staff, because they work in an enduring and revered institution, rarely feel the sense of urgency that defines private sector enterprises. Public schools have an important role in preparing citizens for democratic participation, so their historical perspective and measured response to current imperatives (which in many cases meet the "this too shall pass" test all too well) are what make public education effective. However, the public education system has been under attack for being inadequate to meet modern challenges since *A Nation at Risk* was published in 1983, over a quarter of a century ago! A sense of urgency about our work and an ability to share results on valued student outcomes is overdue and would go a long way toward silencing our critics. America is a young, impatient, and free-spirited country. Not for us the centralized, government-controlled curriculum and schooling of Europe that has changed little since the end of the 19th century! Not for us the state-controlled schools of current and former communist nations such as Russia, Cuba, and China, where reform was enforced, not incentivized! How do we obtain the high literacy rates with impoverished groups that we see in Eastern Europe, China, and Singapore without resorting to a one-size-fits-all national system? One approach is to adopt a sense of urgency to commit to showing results not after students complete higher education but now, for all students, every year.

Finally, we adopt a disposition of continuous improvement rather than one of compliance. We are inquiry driven, not compliance driven:

- What do my students need? How do I know?
- What will help students meet important targets? How do I know?
- How does my practice connect to student outcomes? How do I know?
- And what needs to change to obtain desired results? How do I know?

Turnaround work must allow teachers to modify pacing charts, augment adopted curriculum, and acquire new skills as they are needed—not just on the two days before school opens—and collaborate routinely to address the "how do I know" questions that guide their work throughout the year. The continuous improvement stance requires school administrators, staff, and bureaucratic structures in both schools and districts to become more flexible, service oriented, and collaborative. This disposition also requires schools and districts to invest in providing time for inquiry and technology to provide accurate and timely data.

Turnaround as a Recipe Versus the Turnaround Way of Doing Business

Although we have led you through a continuous improvement process in a step-by-step fashion, when working to improve student achievement, you may or may not follow the improvement cycle in the same linear manner as we have presented it. First, we are limited by our medium, print, which forces us to consider ideas in a linear sequence rather than simultaneously. Second, continuous improvement is a process, and processes consist of an ordered sequence of steps. However, these limitations should not lead you to believe that you must begin at the beginning and follow steps in the order described. You can enter the continuous improvement cycle at any point. Rarely do we get the luxury of beginning at the beginning, starting from scratch to identify learning needs, selecting a new program or intervention to address those needs, and then implementing the program and collecting data for program improvement. More commonly, we are told the ways in which our students are failing, we are required to implement programs not of our choosing to address those failures, and then we are given year-end data that evaluates our efforts.

So what is the value of knowing how to use data to create rapid-fire improvements focused on improving student outcomes? Again, it comes back to dispositions or the culture of your school. If you are "about" graduating or promoting students who have met grade-level standards as determined by a number of valid methods (not just one state test), and you are ready to deliver on your promise by any means necessary, then you can interrupt your regularly scheduled staff development to review student data and discuss learning needs. You can revise or amend prescribed curriculum by adapting changes that have shown promising results, and you can monitor both curriculum implementation and student progress frequently, so that you know well before the end of the year whether your theories about what helps students learn are validated. You can begin this process in August, December, March, or even May. Table 9.1

Table 9.1	Initiating Turnaround Activities at Different Stages of the Turnaround Cycle

Turnaround Formative Evaluation Activity	When You Can Use This Technique
Develop systems for distributed leadership.	You can do this prior to opening of school, at any regular meeting time during the year, at the end of the year in preparation for the next year's work.
Create program descriptions and prepare data.	You can have a committee do this work anytime during the year. Their efforts to describe what you are doing and prepare data will involve staff in thinking about their work and considering what information they find most useful in diagnosing student learning problems or judging their effectiveness as teachers.
Use data to identify the instructional focus.	Review data or student work to plan instruction at any point in the year: at the beginning of a unit, for a new lesson, for a semester, for groups of students needing special programs.
Create the Turnaround Plan.	You can do this at any point after you have reviewed student learning needs and decided upon some strategies or curriculum to address them. The plan can focus on an entire school, a grade level, a content area, a subgroup, or even teaching units within a course.
Design an evaluation of turnaround efforts.	You create the monitoring plan that provides feedback for improving your work at the same time you decide upon a course of action. It can be small, focused on one or two data-gathering activities such as a walk-through and a student assignment, or it can be formal, including surveys, standardized assessments, interviews, and corroborating structured classroom observations.
Manage evaluation: Select measures, administer, score, and summarize data.	For a large effort, you will want a formal plan created at a logical beginning point for your work: the beginning of the year or semester, or the end of the year. For smaller instructional foci, a teacher, a department, or a small committee could be in charge of selecting measures, collecting and summarizing data, and reporting to staff.
Implement a continuous improvement process focused on turnaround work.	This is the most important part of the process: doing it again! Once you decide to use data, focus on learning, revise instruction, monitor revisions, and discuss your results; unless you repeat the process, you do not have a continuous improvement cycle. You have what we call a one-shot case study. Your revised work can be expanded, can contract and focus on a smaller set of goals, can include different staff or students, or can revisit the original instructional focus with improvements. You will know you have adopted a turnaround way of doing business when you no longer talk about "continuous improvement" or a "Turnaround Plan" and you simply refer to your efforts as "planning for this year," or unit, or semester.

presents some examples of how you can begin turnaround for continuous improvement at any point in your school year.

LESSONS FROM LARGE-SCALE STUDIES ON SCHOOL TURNAROUND

To date, two large-scale studies of turnaround work have been released, and by the time this book has been published, we anticipate many more studies will be available. One study reviewed the turnaround efforts of 15 elementary schools associated with the University of Virginia Turnaround Specialist Program.[1] The second was a review of four institutional school improvement efforts, the state of California's accountability program, six school districts in southwestern Pennsylvania (Instructional Improvement Efforts by the Institute for Learning), and an evaluation of the Edison schools, conducted by the RAND Corporation.[2] The Virginia study was a set of 15 case studies of elementary school turnaround initiatives that produced and sustained school improvement for two years. The study identified 10 essential elements of the turnaround work in these schools (these are summarized in Table 9.2) but cautions that these elements do not constitute a recipe for turnaround success. Rather, they serve as indicators of each school's focus on instruction and its way of doing business.

Table 9.2 10 Essential Elements of Successful Turnarounds Identified in 15 Elementary Schools

Staff Dispositions	School Systems
An agreed-upon focus or mission	Distributed leadership
An agreed-upon set of core beliefs, including the belief that all children can learn; a commitment to teamwork and data-driven decisions; and a focus on shared responsibility and student success	The institutionalization of teams for planning, analysis of student progress, curriculum coordination, and instructional intervention
Instructional focus on frequent review of content and continuous assessment	Ubiquitous data sharing
School Context Variables	**Curriculum and Instruction**
Continuous staff development based on student needs	Programs that provide additional learning time and expert help for struggling students
Intensified efforts to inform and engage parents and community members	A focus on literacy

Source: Duke, 2006.

The RAND study was a survey of large-scale reform efforts to answer three questions about how data-driven decision making was being implemented in different settings across the United States: What types of data were schools using? How were they using data? What kinds of support were provided for the process?

The data-driven decision making (or D3M as it is sometimes called) review is only one aspect of turnaround work, but data use provides the impetus for turnaround work. What the researchers found validates the importance of professional judgment and staff understanding of learning, instruction, and content. The RAND study also reminds educators that their expertise and understanding of the unique variables operating in their local school are essential components of improving achievement. We particularly like the RAND Data-Driven Decision Making Model that provided the framework for conducting their study (Figure 9.1). The RAND model, used to organize study questions and findings, begins with the decisions that data will be used to inform. Thus, the starting point for data use in the RAND studies was not the "data" but was in fact the kinds of decisions study participants used their data to inform. The model makes clear and logical links from decisions to selecting relevant data, to transforming the data into useful information, and finally to using the information to act, which brings us back to the beginning of the data-driven decision-making cycle, with the actions creating a new set of decisions requiring information. The RAND framework reminds us that the match between the information (data) and the context (decisions to be made) in which data will be used is a fundamental aspect of data-driven decision making. We must be mindful that "data" don't drive turnaround work; our informed decisions drive our efforts.

Figure 9.1	Data-Driven Decision Making Model

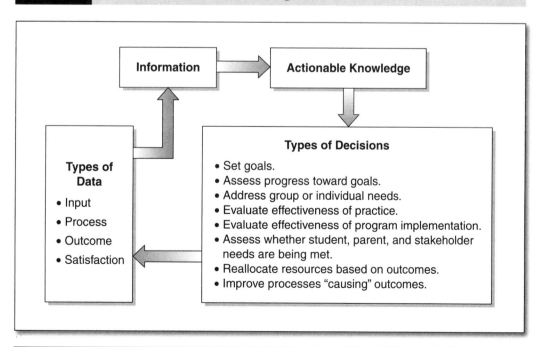

Source: Adapted from Marsh, Pane, & Hamilton, 2006.

Both the Virginia and RAND studies reinforce the conclusion that there is no recipe for turning around schools. The lessons from the RAND study serve as a warning to advocates of data-driven decision making as a panacea for struggling schools:

- Data-driven decision-making activities don't guarantee effective decision making.
- There is a need to include multiple data sources and human perspectives in analyzing data.
- It's important to spend time taking action and not get mired in analysis.
- High-stakes testing may be less useful for improving schools than locally administered, rapidly reported, diagnostic content assessments.

LESSONS FROM A MEASUREMENT EXPERT

The Virginia study was a direct assessment of school turnaround efforts. The RAND study examined only the data use aspects of school improvement. Our third set of lessons comes from Jim Popham, a measurement expert. Popham was an early proponent of behavioral objectives; his understanding of how to improve instruction shifted from writing clear objectives to providing clear instructional goals embodied in assessments. He is an advocate of criterion-referenced and formative classroom assessment as a necessary component of improving learning and instruction. Popham's textbooks and publications are distinguished by their clarity, use of humor, and emphasis on how to incorporate data into instructional decision making.

One of his smaller tracts, *Unlearned Lessons: Six Stumbling Blocks to Our Schools' Success*,[3] has particular relevance for turnaround work and data-driven decision making. The unlearned lessons are "mistakes" commonly made by educators when using measurement data. These mistakes or stumbling blocks are systemic and arise from unexamined assumptions that educators hold about standards, high-stakes standards-based assessments, teaching, and learning. Popham urges us to reveal unexamined assumptions and address them in the early stages of school turnaround, prior even to reviewing data and setting instructional priorities. Table 9.3 provides an overview of Popham's unlearned lessons. We recommend you read his well-written and crisp summary of some factors that can sabotage our efforts to turn around downward-trending achievement trajectories.

The Stumbling Blocks to School Success lurk in every aspect of the turnaround process, from how grade-level standards are understood by teachers to the quality and usefulness of high-stakes and local assessments, to selecting relevant instructional strategies, and finally in how teachers use data to improve instruction. Keep a copy of Popham's Stumbling Blocks as a checklist to ensure you aren't ambushed by unanticipated obstacles on your journey to reversing your school's achievement trajectory.

Table 9.3   Stumbling Blocks to School Success

Unexamined Assumptions—Caveat Emptor	Stumbling Blocks in the Standards and Accountability Movement Emerging From the Assumptions	Proposed Solutions for Improving Data Used to Turn Around Student Achievement
If teachers are provided with a set of important grade-level standards indicating what students should know or be able to do, students will learn what is important and catch up to grade level, and achievement gaps will disappear.	Current state and even national standards are not in a "teachable" format. There are too many curricular targets, many targets are broad and vague, and no one teacher could cover them all.	High-stakes assessments have a role in pointing out problem areas and in raising questions to be explored with local assessments and other data.
If states and districts create criterion-referenced tests based on state or national standards, teachers will have useful information for improving student achievement.	Assessments are purpose specific. Assessments designed to measure many broad goals and to summarize the percentage of students scoring Proficient are too short and too broad in scope to provide diagnostic information.	Teachers should rely more on formative, classroom assessments not constrained by the security issues needed for high-stakes accountability tests.
The focus of school-level improvement should be on having teachers implement best practices and follow the curriculum.	There is too much preoccupation with instructional process—what teachers do in a classroom, and not enough on learning—what we are asking students to do.	Teacher focus should shift from what they do to what they are having students do to acquire knowledge and skills. Student engagement and assessment activities will help teachers select appropriate instructional content and practices. Such activities are often called "backward planning," "task analysis," or "unpacking the standards."
Schools need to focus on enabling students to acquire the content and skills measured on high-stakes assessments.	There is an absence of affective assessment and other measures of valued outcomes that support learning and ensure students can be successful in life.	When the next phase of educational reform comes to pass, schools will be judged on their enduring outcomes: preparing students to participate and contribute to a democratic

(Continued)

Table 9.3   (Continued)

Unexamined Assumptions—Caveat Emptor	Stumbling Blocks in the Standards and Accountability Movement Emerging From the Assumptions	Proposed Solutions for Improving Data Used to Turn Around Student Achievement
		society; preparing students for careers or for vocational or higher education; developing students' individual interests, talents, and skills; and equipping students to become lifelong learners. We should be measuring these important outcomes along with those required by state and federal accountability laws.
State standards-based assessments will measure what has been taught.	Accountability tests are instructionally insensitive. Although a standards-based test is, by definition, criterion referenced, the requirements of test equating and reliability; the vagueness of standards, leading to a wide variety of item content across the years; and even the kinds of organizations developing standards-based tests have resulted in tests "acting" like norm-referenced tests. Teachers target what they think the test is measuring, but their efforts don't always result in improved test results.	Student progress should be measured in multiple ways that explain and augment high-stakes test results and provide diagnostic feedback for both teachers and students about what has been learned. Both accountability and classroom assessments should have multiple purposes, formats, targets, and ways of showing what students know.
When using assessment data, staff needs only to be able to interpret different kinds of score reports.	Assessment literacy is abysmal. Educators rarely challenge or assess the quality of tests they are asked to use or develop themselves. While the answers to these questions might be discouraging, if we know our tests have large shortcomings, we can gather supplemental information to improve the quality of our test-based decisions.	Teachers need tools for and skills in judging the quality of a test, its items, and the credibility of its results for measuring teaching and learning. They need to see the test development specifications, understand reliability and measurement error, and have subject-matter-based criteria for reviewing the quality and importance of its content.

LESSONS FROM A BROAD PRIZE–WINNING URBAN DISTRICT

Our final set of lessons for your consideration comes from our own experience working in a large urban school district, Long Beach Unified School District in Southern California. Long Beach has been nationally recognized by private foundations, the President of the United States, and the Department of Education as incorporating effective turnaround practices and using data effectively to reduce the achievement gap between historically low-performing subgroups of students and more advantaged groups. Long Beach received the Broad Prize for Urban Education in 2005 and was a finalist in 2002, 2007, 2008, and 2009, more times than any urban district in the nation.[4] Because we have been K–12 educators for much of our careers, we are well aware that generic procedures and advice are never effective for improving schools. Context always matters. Adaptation of procedures, measures, and intentions must precede action. Therefore we offer these lessons learned from a decade of work in Long Beach as considerations for your own work—points to review, debate, and use or modify as they fit the particular needs of your own school.

Closing the achievement gap in Long Beach began as a policy decision. The school board determined that its focus would be on improving standards of dress, behavior, and achievement. Notice that the board has outcomes broader than simply "becoming proficient in the grade-level standards." The mechanics of the work were handled by collaborative teams, curriculum leaders working with teachers to develop district content standards (the work preceded the NCLB). Area superintendents worked with principals to develop skills in monitoring instruction, involving teachers in walk-throughs, and establishing professional learning communities. District office staff, especially those involved in professional development and assessment, supported superintendents and principals in implementation of standards-based instruction and assessment.

The work was best characterized as inquiry driven, continually asking, "How are we doing?" and "What do we need to be better?" rather than data driven. The inquiry focus allowed us to review data from state and local tests more critically, to understand better what was useful and what was simply "indicative," and to assemble data to fill information gaps. We had a saying, "Data are like dead fish." Without an inquiry disposition driving data collection, interpretation, and use, the numbers didn't mean much. The work, which is now in its second decade, required outside funders acting as critical friends and supporting our principals in creating distributed leadership systems at their sites. Our work required expert support from both the central office and outside experts in curriculum and staff development. We had to invest in test development, scoring, reporting, and technology for making data available to teachers, all kinds of data, from classroom to state assessment to discipline to lesson plans. And what did we learn?

- The supervisors of principals were key actors in supporting change and monitoring programs.
- The culture needed to support taking risks and being wrong.
- Teaching had to focus on core competencies and strategic skills, because it was impossible to "teach all the standards."

- The federal and state accountability systems were almost impossible to understand and provided too little information for particular grade levels, subgroups, and classrooms.
- We needed to develop local monitoring assessments built upon clearly written test specifications using a variety of formats—essay, performance, project, multiple-choice—to assess important outcomes.
- Programs had to be evaluated annually, especially those provided by supplemental service providers or other outside organizations. Many simply did not work or needed important revisions to be effective in our district.

And how do lessons from a long-term effort that has political, fiscal, and professional support—from both inside and outside the system—relate to turnaround work focused initially upon making quick gains? How does this work establish systems for long-term continuous improvement? The takeaway for us is this: Always, always keep your eye on the sustainability of changes in the policy, programs, and systems that contribute to student success. Quick turnaround and rapid-fire experimentation are tactics for stopping a downward slide. However, turnaround work is simply a catalyst for changing the attitudes, skills, and culture of your school. The sustainability of these changes is the ultimate goal and the focus of our continuous improvement work in subsequent program revision cycles.

SUSTAINING TURNAROUND GAINS: THE ZHUAN JI STATE OF MIND

The term *turnaround* came to education from business, where it was used to describe efforts to halt downward trends and create a U-shaped growth curve. Similarly, the term *continuous improvement* is a Japanese management concept adapted from the philosophy of life called "kaizen." Kaizen assumes that every aspect of our lives deserves to be constantly and incrementally improved. The concept of kaizen was translated into Baldrige's Total Quality Management in the business world and into the concept of continuous improvement when it was adopted by educators. Not wanting to be left out of the "steal from business or an Asian culture" behavior that pervades our profession, we frantically searched for a piece of business or Asian wisdom that we could use as a last word of encouragement to those of you engaged in turning around low-performing schools.

Since turnaround work is often focused on schools in crisis, we thought that we could end this chapter with the oft-told story that the Chinese word for "crisis," *wei ji,* contains the morphemes for both *crisis* and *opportunity.* Therefore, we could exhort you to "carpe crisis" and create new opportunities for improving schools. Alas, we had greatly misunderstood the Chinese. We discovered that wei ji does contain the morpheme *ji,* but ji does not mean "opportunity" by itself. Ji assumes the meaning of "opportunity" only when used in conjunction with another morpheme that bestows that meaning. In the word for "crisis," ji means "at the crucial point." Or, on the brink of crisis!

Thus, it represents the oft-told "crisis = opportunity" fable, not an encouraging piece of Chinese wisdom at all!

Wei ji = Crisis ≠ Opportunity

Nevertheless, we knew ji did mean "opportunity" in some Chinese words, so all we needed to do was find an appropriate word. Sure enough, a review of the management literature uncovered just the word to encourage leaders to find the opportunity in difficult times, *zhuan ji*. Zhuan means to "turn into," and when ji combines with zhuan, it takes on the meaning of "opportunity." And the exhortation is just right for school turnaround participants. We are all engaged in turning schools into better places. We are all engaged in opportunities to turn for the better. So with a small character substitution, the Chinese still provide encouragement for those of us facing challenging circumstances or times. Instead of focusing on the crisis characters, wei ji, we can refer to our work as zhuan ji, the opportunity of turning what we have into something else, of transforming our schools for the better.

转机

Zhuan ji =Turn for the better

PART II

Leader's Guides for
The TurnAround ToolKit

Introduction to Leader's Guides

The leader's guide encapsulates the core content we've addressed in this book. We hope you will find the guide a helpful tool for organizing and leading the arduous, challenging, and ultimately very satisfying process of turnaround. Each chapter, as you know, reflects an important step in turnaround, and for each we summarize the central themes, tasks, decisions, and actions you'll need to navigate. Being forewarned is being forearmed: With your leadership team, you will want to consider how all the pieces fit together before involving others in the process.

Each section of this leadership guide starts with a Pocket Summary, also found at the beginning of each corresponding chapter, which provides both an advance organizer and a review of chapter material. The summaries present the major tasks, their primary purposes, and the steps needed to accomplish each. The "Task" column summarizes the central work to be accomplished. The "Major Activities" column lists the steps needed to complete each task as well as the tools that can support your work. These tools appear in the online Toolkit and are indicated in **bold** in the "Major Activities" column. The last column states the "Purpose" of each major task. The more you understand the purpose and function of what you are creating, the easier it will be to work with staff to put it in place.

A section on major management decisions follows the Pocket Summary. This section provides an overview of the personnel and resource access and allocation decisions you and your leadership team will want to consider as you get ready to engage your school in the chapter's tasks. Advance thinking about needed resources, such as staff time, expert help, data access, training, technology, and facilities, can help the process go more smoothly. You and your leadership team will want to review and get a general feel for these requirements so that you can optimally deploy your resources.

The Leadership Challenges section then attempts to give you a "heads-up" about obstacles you could encounter during the step and some tips for addressing them. Turnaround work by definition is done on a short timeline and focuses on some aspects of a school, but not necessarily all of them. The narrow focus and rapid implementation requirements can blind us to possibly fatal errors that we could inadvertently stumble into.

Our tips are suggestive, not exhaustive. You certainly will encounter your own version of unanticipated "opportunities" to rethink what you are doing and how you do it. Review the challenges before beginning your work, and assess whether you need to incorporate solutions for one or more of them in your plans.

Finally, in a section called Selected Resources to Support Your Work, we share references that we have found particularly relevant to the work of the chapter. These are books and websites you can use to expand your knowledge and explore specific aspects of school turnaround in greater depth.

Leader's Guide

1

Develop Systems for Managing Turnaround Activities

Distributed Leadership, Collaborative Teams, Expert Reviewers and Networks, Data Capacity

CHAPTER 1 POCKET SUMMARY

POCKET SUMMARY		
Task	**Major Activities**	**Purpose**
System 1. Establish a system of shared leadership.	• Create a new vision of school leadership. • Identify leaders for turnaround work. • Work with de facto leaders to establish collaborative groups or professional learning communities. • Conduct leadership development with collaborative group leaders. • Establish a system for school positional leaders to participate in, monitor, and support work.	• Build capacity to institutionalize the work. • Create staff and stakeholder support. • Develop skills and knowledge.
System 2. Develop a collaborative work process.	• Provide time for collaboration. • Develop guidelines for "safe" and productive participation of all members. **Tool 1.1 Collaborative Considerations Protocol** **Tool 1.2 Focused-Discussion Guidelines Protocol** • Spend time team building. **Tool 1.3 My Posse Protocol**	• Shift initiative from independent contractor to collaborative colleagues.
System 3. Create expert review groups or networks to leverage learning.	• Recruit an expert group. • Identify benchmark sites at which you can observe best practices. • Establish connections with stakeholder groups.	• Ensure your efforts will be informed by the best available information and expertise. • Support change by identifying benchmark schools.
System 4. Develop capacity for data collection, integration, and reporting.	**Tool 1.4 Guidelines for Selecting Software for Data-Guided Decision Making** • Train a data team to manage data collection, summarization, and reporting. • Develop accountability and assessment literacy. • Realign available systems. **Tool 1.5 Toolkit Tutorial: Key Accountability Concepts** **Tool 1.6 Toolkit Tutorial: Key Assessment Concepts** **Tool 1.7 Toolkit Tutorial: Test Score Interpretation and Reliability**	• Automate reporting for time-efficient meetings and data-informed decision making. • Develop local expertise in data use.

Thumbnails of Tools From This Chapter

The following tools can be found on the companion website for *The TurnAround ToolKit* at http://www.corwin.com/turnaroundtoolkit.

Tool 1.1

Collaborative Considerations Protocol

Purpose: People have different affinities for group work. Some feel they are more creative and energized when working on solutions as a member of a group. Others like to work through issues by themselves; they prefer quiet time prior to sharing ideas. The purpose of the protocol is to help group members identify their preferences for group work and to develop group respect for different styles. The protocol can lead a group to adopt strategies for accommodating different collaborative styles.

Time: 15 to 25 minutes

Resources: writing materials, chart paper and markers, handout with list of four questions about group work preferences, handout with evaluation questions

Steps

1. Introduction

We will be spending a lot of time together this year working on tough issues of learning and instruction. Our job will be to figure out ways to improve student achievement at our school both quickly and over the long term. We may not have much experience with some of the work we will be undertaking, for example, understanding data, diagnosing learning problems in an unfamiliar curricular area, or identifying strategies for effective parent involvement. Most of our work will be done in collaborative groups (professional learning communities). Not everyone likes group work. Some feel they work best alone to develop ideas before sharing them. Others feel group synergy helps them come up with better ideas. Nearly everyone can think of situations where he or she has felt one way about some group work and another way about other group tasks. Our meeting today is to help us learn more about our own and our colleagues' preferences and styles during group work. When we are finished, I hope all of us will know more about each other and be thinking of ways to make our work productive and fun.

2. Directions

Individual Responses (5 minutes): Take 5 minutes to write brief responses to each of the questions about your group working style and preferences. Jot the answers down below each question.

1. By nature, do you generally prefer to consider instructional issues and their solutions alone or with a group? Why might this be so for you?
2. Can you think of an occasion when you worked in your nonpreferred setting (alone or with a group) and the results pleasantly surprised you?

Tool 1.2

Focused-Discussion Guidelines Protocol

Purpose: The purpose of this protocol is to engage participants in developing behavioral guidelines for their group work. These are rules or norms that the group agrees to adhere to with the understanding that they can be modified should they not be useful. Group norms are designed to avoid off-topic rambling, venting, and personal attacks and to create a focus on solving problems and generating solutions or strategies, plans, and insights.

Time: 25–35 minutes

Resources: chart paper, handout with list of six norms areas, handout with evaluation questions

Steps

1. Introduction

We will be working together to identify and try out solutions to some of the biggest challenges our school is facing. Our discussions will be central to this work. Our staff encompasses a variety of working styles, preferences, experience, expertise, and temperaments. In order to make our group discussions productive while accommodating the diverse viewpoints of our staff, we need a set of operating principles. Today we will develop our first draft of guidelines for group work that we agree to follow. We can revise these guidelines at any time.

2. Directions

Small-Group Brainstorms and Recording (25 minutes): There are several aspects of group work that require agreement about what we expect. These are listed on your handouts. We will work in groups of five to seven (adjust numbers depending upon the size of the group) to develop guidelines for each of these six areas. If you can think of an area we did not include, your group may add it. After 15 minutes, your group should record its suggested guidelines on the six blank charts posted in the room.

Six Norms Areas

- Scheduling—Meeting time, place, frequency, duration, start and finish time
- Expectations—Attendance, tardiness, participation, sharing workload, respect (define)
- Consensus Process—How will we make decisions? Reach agreements? How will we show agreement?

Tool 1.3

My Posse Protocol

Purpose: The purpose of this protocol is to reveal similarities and differences in areas of teaching and learning and to discuss how this affects teachers' work. This activity helps participants better understand both what they have in common and the richness of their diverse experiences and values.

Time: 35 to 50 minutes

Resources: List of evaluation questions

Steps

1. Introduction

This activity will give us time to explore our similarities and differences on issues of student learning so that we work with self-awareness and respect for diversity.

2. Directions

You will be asked to join self-defined groups at least three times during this activity. I will give you a category; then you will group yourselves with others who share similar characteristics of the category. I will not define the categories; that is what you will do in your groups. Then we will discuss how belonging to a certain group with certain values, beliefs, experiences, and characteristics affects your professional decisions about how to define, implement, and evaluate instruction.

Round 1 (10 minutes): Group yourselves by the kinds of **educational outcomes** you most value, and discuss how this identification affects your work. During the last 5 minutes, each group summarizes what they discussed for the whole group.

Round 2 (10 minutes): Group yourself by how you define an **at-risk student,** and discuss how this identification affects your work. Again, use the last 5 minutes for summary reports.

Round 3 (10 minutes): Group yourself by the **subject matter** you teach or your favorite subject to teach, and discuss how this affects your work. Use the last 5 minutes for summary reports.

Debrief (15 minutes):

- Which of the three methods of identifying yourself has the biggest influence on your work?
- Which would you like to influence your work more?
- If you could hang with only one posse, which would it be and why?
- What did you learn about the diversity in this room? How might that be taken into account in our work?

Tool 1.4

Guidelines for Selecting Software for Data-Guided Decision Making

Steps

1. Assess District Readiness to Automate Data Reports

Instructional Technology Personnel: Does the instructional technology staff have the skills to install, implement, and maintain a data integration and reporting system and to train the users? If not, will we contract out these functions?

Assessment and Curriculum Expertise: Does the district have trained staff to work with teachers on test construction, interpretation, and data use? If not, does the district have access to services or contractors who can support the development and use of a variety of assessments?

District Policies and Culture: Does the district have a continuous improvement process in place for program review and improvement? Are staff comfortable with it, and do they rely on a variety of data to plan, monitor, and evaluate instruction? If not, is there leadership at the district and school sites for this work?

2. Consider the Costs Associated With Automation and Electronic Reporting

- What is the purchase cost? What is the installation cost? What is the cost of making our current systems compatible with the new software?
- What will it cost to train users and maintain the new software tools?
- What has the cost been in similar districts?
- What combination of in-house expertise and purchased support is most cost-effective?

3. Purchase Data Storage and Data Integration Software

- How well does the new data warehouse work with our current student information, personnel payroll, special education, discipline, attendance, and other distributed databases?
- Can the warehouse and data integration tools store data from multiple sources and in multiple formats?
- Who maintains the data and ensures its accuracy?

4. Select Data Reporting Software Tools

- Does the tool meet the Schools Interoperability Framework (SIF) standard? SIF specifications ensure that data systems work together. They are based on extensible markup language (XML),

Tool 1.5

Toolkit Tutorial: Key Accountability Concepts

Understanding Accountability Results

In addition to your school test results, you will be reviewing your school accountability results for information about the effectiveness of your programs. State and district accountability programs are generally based on one of three models:

1. The status model, which measures student status vis-à-vis accountability targets, such as whether students meet adequate yearly progress (AYP) goals,
2. The growth model, which measures the amount of growth students make from year to year and perhaps comparing growth to preset targets, or
3. The value-added model (a special case of a growth model), which measures whether the school improved the performance of individual students while adjusting for differences in prior achievement (or other variables).

Our colleagues at UCLA's National Center for Research on Evaluation, Standards, & Student Testing, Pete Goldschmidt and Kilchan Choi, together with the Council of Chief State School Officers (Goldschmidt et al., 2005) have prepared a clear, useful description of these three models that you can use to better understand the model your state has selected. Toolkit Table 1.5.1 summarizes the major differences among the three accountability approaches and lists the major limitations of each. When interpreting your accountability data, pay close attention to what information is *not* available—the limitations of your model—so that you can collect data to fill in those gaps during your formative evaluation.

Some of the major questions emerging from your accountability report will include the following:

- Is our progress or lack thereof unexpected? If so, where are the surprises?
- Do we see a consistent trend over time of meeting our targets or not meeting targets? If our progress is sputtering or erratic, what content, grade levels, or other school factors might be contributing to these performance patterns?
- What specific test data or other data do we need to gather to clarify our accountability results?
- What limitations must we keep in mind about our state's accountability model that might make results less valid for our school?

Accountability data are good for raising red flags and identifying major issues and big-picture trends. These data will not pinpoint where in the program problems may be occurring or why. However, accountability results, because they do provide a big picture, provide an excellent starting point for your data review and help you to identify content areas and sometimes grade levels for which you would like to look more closely at state and district assessment results.

Tool 1.6

Toolkit Tutorial: Key Assessment Concepts

High-Stakes Tests

Increasingly, classroom teachers and administrators are supervising or administering tests with high stakes for students and schools. "High stakes" refers to tests with serious, public consequences. The following list shows some consequences of success or failure on the related tests:

Promotion/Retention: Grade-level reading assessments, math facts tests, end-of-course math tests

Graduation: High school exit exam

Evaluation of School Quality (accountability): California Standards Test, Stanford 9

Course Placement: State end-of-course exams, grade-level writing tests

College Credit/Admission: Advanced Placement, Golden State, SAT1

> A "high-stakes test" is any test used as the only information to make decisions that have important consequences (positive or negative) for students.

Standardized Tests

When a single test score is used for high-stakes purposes, all students must have comparable testing conditions for the score to be valid. The comparable conditions have two purposes: to create a level playing field for all students and to be sure that the scores from the test have the same meaning when applied to different students.

Standardization means that the tests have common test directions, test items or prompts, test answer key or scoring guides, and rules for administering, handling, and scoring.

Examples of Standardized Tests (standardized testing conditions):

Benchmark Book Assessments

District writing prompts

California standards tests

Stanford 9

High School Exit

English Language Development test (or the IDEA)

Norm- and Criterion-Referenced Tests

All high-stakes tests are standardized (standard test administration conditions, times, directions); not all have the same *purposes* or kinds of scores. There are two major types of tests, norm-referenced and criterion-referenced.

> ### Tool 1.7
>
> **Toolkit Tutorial: Test Score
> Interpretation and Reliability**
>
> *(Or, you can count on me!)*
>
> **Norm-Referenced Interpretations: Percentiles,
> Stanines, Grade Equivalents, and Standard Scores**
>
> We began our discussion of data interpretation with the law of test purpose: The purpose of a test governs its interpretation. If a test is designed to rank and sort students to make placement decisions, the interpretation is norm-referenced, and test construction guidelines for creating norm-referenced tests need to be followed. Specifically, there must be a normal distribution of scores along which students can be sorted, the items must discriminate between students who do well on the test and students who do poorly, and the scores must report where each student's score ranks among those of his or her peers. The primary score interpretation is, "How much better did this student do than another?"
>
> As a side note, it could be that if a test is especially difficult, the highest-ranking student did not do particularly well on the test. That student would still get the highest percentile rank. Conversely, if the test is easy, students might in fact have answered quite a bit of the material correctly but ranked low among their peers, because more students answered more items correctly. There are some elementary grade reading tests (mostly at Grade 2) that students do very well on. Missing only one item can drop a student from the 99th to the 85th percentile.
>
> **Criterion-Referenced Interpretations:
> Proficiency Levels, Mastery Levels, Percentage Correct**
>
> If a test is designed to measure how well students have learned the content and skills defined by state standards, such as in a biology class, the interpretation is criterion-referenced. For these, the curricular content area is called a domain. Domain descriptions must be clear, and the domain sampling plan should represent what experts in the field, teachers, and the curricular materials identify as the important information to be learned. Scores describe student mastery or level of proficiency. You don't know where students rank or how many did better or worse, but you do know how much of the material was learned.
>
> **Dual Interpretations for Use on a Test Constructed Primarily
> as a Norm-Referenced Test or a Criterion-Referenced Test**
>
> Although Table 1.6.3 in Tool 1.6 summarizes testing purposes, interpretations, and common score types, when you interpret test scores, you should consult the technical manual to determine the original testing

Major Decisions for Developing Systems for Turnaround Work

The major leadership team management decisions involved in setting up the four systems described in the first chapter are listed in the box below.

> - Who will be involved in examining our programs and practices?
> - How can we schedule collaboration time?
> - How can staff prepare for school improvement work? What new skills and beliefs must they hold to participate effectively in the work?
> - What kind of relationships need to be created with the community, the district office, students, parents, and the media to understand, support, and assist in improvement work?
> - What will participants value in the process? How can we make it beneficial and prevent it from being burdensome?
> - What kinds of staff development—about program, about teaching and learning, about data—will be useful? How can we find the time and resources to support it?
> - How can we garner the external expert help we will need? What expert resources are available from the district, a local university, or other organizations?
> - What technology do we need for data collection, reporting, and analysis?
> - What kinds of technology support do we need to conduct our work?
> - Who would be interested in managing the data collection, analysis, and reporting for our work?

Leadership Challenges

Leadership challenges abound in the process of trying to realign systems. Beware the obstacles of changing roles, widening networks, and taking on new perspectives and data capacities:

- **Teacher time and roles.** Turnaround requires reorganizing teacher schedules for collaborative work and enhancing teacher responsibilities.

While these two challenges may appear unrelated, both are generally governed by the teacher's contract. Asking teachers to assume more responsibility (such as visiting other schools, monitoring programs) may require additional pay. Rearranging the school schedule impacts teachers and parents and may eat into state-required instructional time, which could affect funding. If your school is in a reconstitution or reorganization year according to your state or the federal accountability requirements, these negotiations are most likely accommodated in state laws or regulations. If your work is to fine-tune an already adequate or even exemplary school, you will need to work with union leaders, district leaders, and perhaps even community representatives prior to creating distributed leadership systems.

• **Creating a safe collaborative environment.** Collaboration requires trust and a safe environment in which all members can contribute and be heard. Schools, like all social groups, have informal leaders, cliques, and interest-based alliances. These informal "tribes" need to coalesce into the larger community dedicated to attaining the school's turnaround goals. The use of protocols in meetings is one step toward creating a safe collaborative environment. However, it will be important to work with the informal leaders, perhaps as an advisory council or leadership council, to get buy-in to the school's larger mission. Simultaneously, you can expect and should celebrate "resistance." The resistors often have points of view that raise issues the larger group may not have considered, and these can result in more creative solutions than would otherwise be developed.

• **Establishing expert review networks.** Experts abound. But experts who can work with practitioners and who are genuinely interested in adapting research findings, assessments, or other expertise to local situations are fewer in number. You will want to interview potential critical friends, network partners, or reviewers to ensure that your expert review team

1. is up to date in knowledge,

2. is creative and flexible in translating that knowledge into practice,

3. communicates collegially (does not patronize, does not proselytize, does not criticize),

4. is geographically or technologically available on short notice (Skype, e-mail, chat room, etc.), and

5. is affordable.

Many experts trade time for access to data, opportunities to do research, and opportunities to document the process in a book. For some (such as those at county education offices or universities, or nonteaching district staff), sharing their expertise is part of their regular work assignment.

• **Data access and compilation.** Beware the format in which various sources of data may exist and their compatibility. You may have electronic data on student scores on the state tests and student attendance, but if the data reside on different systems, the two may not "speak" to one another or to your data analysis program. You'll be in good shape if your district or state has a longitudinal student data system from which you can draw.

• **Data reporting.** The biggest challenge in this task is developing teacher expertise in accountability data, including understanding the structure and details of the state and federal accountability systems and understanding how test data are summarized and reported (descriptive statistics). All participants in the turnaround will need to increase their levels of understanding in all of these areas (hence the information guides in our Toolkit), but not everyone will need deep understanding. You may need to support interested staff members (perhaps those in pursuit of an advanced degree) so they can take special training to lead your school's data collection, analysis, and reporting efforts. While initially hiring a consultant is expedient, if continuous improvement becomes the way of doing business at your school, you will need in-house expertise.

SELECTED RESOURCES TO SUPPORT YOUR WORK

Deepening your understanding of shared leadership—*The Distributed Leadership Toolbox: Essential Practices for Successful Schools,* by M. E. McBeth (Corwin, 2008). This toolbox describes the differences between shared leadership (delegation) and distributed leadership and the kind of interactions that occur between and among school leaders and staff with the latter. It provides case studies to illustrate a distributed practice and links the dialogs that form the core of distributed leadership to improvement in teaching, learning, and student achievement.

Conducting group discussions, study groups, or professional development—*Corwin's Tips for Facilitators,* available from www.corwin.com under "Resources/Tips for Facilitators." The tips are actually a short course for leading effective professional development. They describe different purposes for professional development and provide strategies for each.

Ideas for addressing leadership challenges occurring in day-to-day operations, leading change, and leading learning groups—*Leading Every Day: 124 Actions for Effective Leadership,* by J. Kaser, S. Mundry, K. Stiles, and S. Loucks-Horsley (Corwin, 2002). This book lists bite-sized actions for leaders to use in dealing with all aspects of change. Especially relevant to your Realignment work are Book Two, "Leading Change," and Book Four, "Leading Effective Groups." We will cite this book again in later chapters as a source of guidance.

Developing assessment literacy—*Classroom Assessment: What Teachers Need to Know* (6th ed.), by W. J. Popham (Allyn & Bacon, 2011), and *Assessment for Educational Leaders,* also by Popham (Allyn & Bacon, 2006). These resources describe types, uses, and how to construct classroom assessments that improve teaching and learning. *Classroom Assessment* speaks to the assessment novice who is not convinced that testing isn't stealing valuable time from teaching. The *Educational Leaders* volume is a resource for test development and interpretation and for understanding tests scores and psychometric statistics. Jim Popham is witty, engaging, and irreverent, making his subject accessible and relevant. You could order any of his books and find them a hit with teachers.

Leader's Guide

2

Organize Information Needed to Redesign Programs

CHAPTER 2 POCKET SUMMARY

POCKET SUMMARY

Task	Major Activities	Purpose
Organize resources for needs assessment.	• Identify key sources of information about your instructional programs and available data on current quality.	• Analyze program-related data to identify areas needing improvement.
Create program descriptions to use in turnaround redesign.	• Catalog your programs. • Create brief program descriptions. **Tool 2.1 Program Catalog Template** **Tool 2.2 Brief Program Description Template**	• Understand the big picture to inform decision making. • Help teachers develop a shared understanding about the current instructional program.
Develop or select program quality measures.	• Create assignment review guidelines. **Tool 2.3 Program Quality: Assignment Rigor** • Gather protocols for looking at student work (LASW). **Tool 2.4 Program Quality: Protocols for Looking at Student Work** • Develop/select classroom walk-through guidelines. **Tool 2.5 Program Quality: Classroom Walk-Through Guidelines**	• Provide a small sampling of current practice. • Encourage discussion about what changes may be needed.
Align assessments with standards-based outcomes.	• Review school and district assessments against standards to check alignment with instructional goals. **Tool 2.6 Toolkit Tutorial: Aligning Assessment to Instruction**	• Clarify teaching targets. • Communicate what is expected to both teachers and students.
Organize data needed to develop a Turnaround Plan.	• Create a data inventory. **Tool 2.7 Data Inventory Template** • Review the quality of available data. **Tool 2.8 Data Quality Evaluation Guidelines: Assessment Reliability** **Tool 2.9 Data Quality Evaluation Guidelines: Archival and Self-Report Data** **Tool 2.10 Data Quality Evaluation Guidelines: A Rubric for Evaluating Data Quality**	• Explore multiple data sources. • Inventory available student data. • Determine areas where additional data are needed. • Capture judgments about potential usefulness of available data.

THUMBNAILS OF TOOLS FROM THIS CHAPTER

The following tools can be found on the companion website for *The TurnAround ToolKit* at http://www.corwin.com/turnaroundtoolkit.

Tool 2.1
Program Catalog Template

Program Name	Grade Levels	Target Population	Subject	Year in Use at Our School

Tool 2.2
Brief Program Description Template

Complete one for each separate program.

	Title, subject, grade levels, target population, years at school
Purpose/goals	
Required materials/resources	
Delivery method	
Required training	
Major activities	
Implementation issues	
Data supporting effectiveness	

Tool 2.3
Program Quality: Assignment Rigor

Review Procedure

Step 1: Review the assignment directions, stimulus materials, and academic content required for match to grade-level standards. Have a copy of grade-level standards for each participant in the review.

- Read through the assignment. Discuss the following:
  a. What is the reading level of the stimulus passes (if applicable)?
  b. What level of complexity is the content? Does it match the grade level?

Step 2: Determine the cognitive complexity and kind of knowledge students need to complete the assignment successfully. Have a copy of the assignment scoring guide, rubric, or grading criteria for each participant.

- Have participants complete the assignment or a portion of it to determine the kinds of skills and knowledge a student needs to receive an acceptable, that is, appropriate, score for their grade level.
- Discuss what prerequisite skills students need to complete the assignment. What prior knowledge or skills might they need that might not be part of the grade-level or course content? When would students have been taught the necessary skills (e.g., parsing a sonnet, complex mathematical operations, comparing points of view, etc.)?
- Find where the skills and knowledge necessary for the assignment are represented in the grade-level standards.
- Compare your results from Step 1 with this step.

Step 3: Debrief the assignment rigor, discussing the grade-level match, the importance of the assignment to the development of student skills and knowledge, and how the assignment could be improved. Focus on both the assignment and the scoring criteria in your revision suggestions.

- How might you select appropriate stimulus material to "bump up" the assignment?
- How would you rewrite the directions to require students to use more complex skills and to ask students to apply knowledge or demonstrate skill development?
- What would you revise in the scoring guide to provide clearer feedback to students about how to improve their performance? To provide better feedback to teachers about how to reteach groups of students failing to perform acceptably?

Tool 2.4
Program Quality: Protocols for Looking at Student Work

The National School Reform Faculty website functions as a clearinghouse for many useful Looking at Student Work (LASW) protocols and strategies, some of which are listed in Table 2.4.1. You can do one-stop shopping at their site, http://www.nsrfharmony.org/protocol/doc, which provides professionally produced protocols ready to download, print, and use. You will notice that the language of some of the protocols indicates they were written before the current focus on standards and reflects work of the early 1990s on multiple intelligences, constructivist learning, and the writing process. Nevertheless, these methods hold up well in a standards-based environment, because they focus on increasing the complexity and rigor of student assignments and producing thoughtful, creative, and competent learners.

Toolkit Table 2.4.1   Protocols for Looking at Student Work

Purpose	Protocol Name	Source
To help an individual teacher get professional perspectives about student learning needs and to provide suggestions for practice. Review is open-ended and unprompted.	Collaborative Assessment Conference	Harvard Project Zero http://www.nsrfharmony.org/protocol/doc/cac.pdf
To review assignments that allow students flexibility in how they approach the work and that require students to apply and/or create/evaluate/synthesize information.	ATLAS–Learning From Student Work	ATLAS Communities http://www.nsrfharmony.org/protocol/doc/atlas_lfsw.pdf
To help teachers get insights on issues of importance in their classrooms through collegial feedback on student work samples. Much like a medical team troubleshooting conference.	Consultancy	National School Reform Faculty http://www.nsrfharmony.org/protocol/doc/consult_stud_work.pdf

(Continued)

Tool 2.5
Program Quality: Classroom Walk-Through Guidelines

The following guidelines apply to any type of classroom walk-through. You may use the guidelines to develop your own procedures or to review and select an appropriate plan from one of the many published descriptions available.

Purpose: The purpose of a classroom walk-through for turnaround work is to assess whether a program is being implemented as intended or to review a very specific aspect of teaching to determine if more support needs to be provided.

Participants: Walk-through participants should include teachers of the same grade level and subject as those in the classroom being observed, a curriculum/instructional leader who knows what the practice should look like, and a group facilitator with no vested interest in the results or what is being observed. Optional participants may include the school's principal, administrators from a benchmark school (where the practice has been instituted successfully), or evaluation, curriculum, or supervisory staff from the central office. The optional staff need to be acceptable to the walk-through team and operate as nonevaluative personnel.

Training: We recommend that a staff development leader or a member of your expert group or group of critical friends introduce teachers to the walk-through concept, explain how it differs from formal classroom observations, explain the purpose and procedures, and then entertain questions and concerns. We also recommend the two following sources for walk-through training:

- A walk-through view on YouTube produced by UCLA–Anderson School of Management: UCLA SMP Classroom Walk-Throughs Introduction (November 18, 2007, http://www.youtube.com/watch?v=NLomeKu2Us)
- A classroom walk-through protocol developed by Perry and Associates and shared in "Seeing Through New Eyes" (Richardson, 2001).

Preparation: On the day of the walk-through, participants meet for a brief time (less than one hour) to establish the walk-through focus:

- The principal or walk-through facilitator explains the focus, lists the classrooms to be visited, and describes why those classrooms were chosen.
- Team members discuss what evidence will be gathered and assign evidence-gathering roles to individuals (e.g., reviewing posted student work, observing engagement, listening to lesson presentation).
- Members create or receive forms for recording evidence or determine how information is to be recorded in free-form evidentiary notes (again, to avoid an evaluative tone for the visit).

Tool 2.6
Toolkit Tutorial: Aligning Assessment to Instruction

TEST CONTENT ALIGNMENT TO CURRICULUM AND INSTRUCTION: DOMAIN DESCRIPTIONS AND BLUEPRINTS

A *domain description* provides clear definitions of the content and skills embedded in individual standards. It provides guidelines for selecting stimulus materials (reading passages, science drawings, social studies charts, mathematics problem types) for test items as well as rules for writing multiple-choice distractors or grading essays. Ideally, all tests are constructed from detailed domain descriptions. In reality, few states or testing companies work from domain descriptions. However, districts and schools can create descriptions to guide the development of local assessments. Toolkit Table 2.6.1 displays one page from a lengthy domain description created by a large urban district to guide development of district assessments. The full description is 27 pages. The far-left column restates the state standard. Notice how ambiguous the standard statement is when compared to the operational definitions of content and skills provided in the middle column. The far-right column displays sample item questions. The specification would be clearer to teachers if the sample questions included answer choices, which determine part of the item difficulty. Most states provide the standard and a set of sample items. However, standards are ambiguous and can be interpreted in a variety of ways. The explanation and content objectives are crucial for a clear domain definition and a clear standards definition.

Toolkit Table 2.6.1   Sample Domain Description for Grade 8 Reading Comprehension (Focus on Informational Materials)

Substrand: Structural Features of Informational Materials	Explanation	Example Items
Standard 2.1 Compare and contrast the features and elements of consumer materials to gain meaning from documents (e.g., warranties, contracts, product information, and instruction manuals).	**Literal Comprehension:** Students use explicit and implicit evidence to draw conclusions about the meaning of relationships, images, patterns, words, or symbols from at least two different informational documents. **Eligible Content and Assessment Objectives:** Informational passages are not necessarily familiar to students; however, they should be	1. Based on the information in the contract, which of these belongs in the empty box (of a graphic organizer)? 2. What type of bike lock appears to be the most expensive? (Students look at price chart and advertisements to answer the question.)

(Continued)

Tool 2.7

Data Inventory Template

Data Category	Data Source	Purpose	Subject(s)	Grade Level(s)	Respondents	Date Administered	Where Kept
Accountability							
State Tests							
District Tests (professional)							
Nonstandardized Local Tests							
Curriculum							

Tool 2.8

Data Quality Evaluation Guidelines: Assessment Reliability

DECODING RELIABILITY TERMINOLOGY

Should you be fortunate enough to read a technical manual for a published accountability test, you would find that several kinds of "reliability coefficients" are reported. The reliability coefficient terms appear in Toolkit Table 2.8.1, Data Quality Evaluation Guidelines: Assessment Reliability. Below we define the technical terms used in the table for your reference. Remember that reliability coefficients, with the exception of the standard error calculation, are correlation coefficients. They range from −1.0 through 0 to +1.0. High reliability is a positive coefficient, generally above .60 and most often .80 and above.

Standard Error: This is the amount of fluctuation in a test score contributed by sampling error if the test were to be readministered on several occasions. If your decision is about an individual student and it carries a high-stakes consequence, such as the need to pass a high school exit examination in order to graduate, the reliability of interest is the standard error associated with that student's score. Is a "fail" really a "fail" or a natural fluctuation in the score due to measurement error?

Test-Retest or Alternate Form: If you were to give the same test to the same group of students a second time, would their performance be somewhat the same on the two occasions? This is test-retest reliability, a simple correlation of the test scores of a group of students on Occasion A with those on Occasion B. If the correlation is high and positive (say, .80 or above), we say that the test is reliable. Similarly, if you are more interested in whether two versions of the test are measuring pretty much the same concepts and content, you give the same students both versions of the test (it could be at the same sitting) and correlate their scores on Version A with those on Version B to obtain alternate form reliability. Again, a positive and fairly high correlation suggests the two different versions are pretty much interchangeable.

Internal Consistency: This means that items written to measure the same construct behave similarly, or elicit similar responses. When you are administering a survey, you want the survey items measuring the same topic or construct, such as "satisfaction with this school," to act similarly. If parents answer one "satisfaction with the math program" item positively, their responses on other items designed to measure "satisfaction with the math program" should be positive as well. The reliability, or consistency, of responses on similar survey items are captured by the internal consistency reliability coefficient, often reported in a survey's technical manual.

Tool 2.9

Data Quality Evaluation Guidelines: Archival and Self-Report Data

DATA QUALITY ISSUES AND YOUR PROGRAM REVIEW

The credibility of any information you share with staff to identify program areas needing improvement rests upon the quality of data provided. The data available about programs, unless you have formal evaluation results to review, is often anecdotal, archival, or of unknown psychometric quality (no formal reliability or validity information). Nevertheless, data quality is as important a consideration for program and school context data as it is for student test data.

For example, archival (stored) data is usually quantitative, but just because it comes from a computer does not mean it is accurate. Think of the ways in which student demographic, enrollment, course completion, grade (less so), attendance, or dropout information could be inaccurate. Problems can occur in data entry, in updating, and in record duplication.

A second data quality issue concerns how the data were collected, when, from whom, and for what reason. Sound familiar? These are the same issues underlying the quality of assessment data as well. Like student achievement assessments, surveys should have a development plan that lists the major topics or concepts to be surveyed, such as satisfaction with grade placement, school communication, student behavior policies, and so on; that specifies how many items will be used to assess each topic; and that describes what the scoring scale will be. Surveys also need a sampling plan that records to whom the survey was given and how representative this group was of the entire school, grade level, or group of interest. If only high-achieving students and parents return surveys, you do not have an accurate picture of how well the school is serving all students. Surveys, which often have less than 100% return rates, can still be useful if we know something about the nonrespondents and consider this information when interpreting survey results.

The data quality of interviews and focus groups relies on many of the same factors as surveys and even test data: How were questions designed for interviews and focus groups? How were coding categories for the responses created? Are these categories meaningful to several raters and your staff? How were the respondents chosen, and who do they represent? If you purchase surveys, you should also ask for a technical manual; it should provide such data quality information as internal consistency reliability (do all items measuring the same topic behave similarly?), perhaps test-retest reliability, and a description of the topics surveyed, the number of items per topic, and the pilot test sampling plan. Toolkit Table 2.9.1 identifies major data quality concerns for the information you collect related to curriculum, instruction, and school context.

Tool 2.10

Data Quality Evaluation Guidelines: A Rubric for Evaluating Data Quality

An important part of your data inventory is your determination of the quality of the information a test provides. Below is a rubric for reviewing your assessments to determine how much confidence you will put in the results or whether you need additional information when using the scores.

Data Source	High Quality	Medium Quality	Poor Quality	Unknown Quality
Tests / State Accountability Test / District Standardized Tests / Publisher Tests (including tests constructed from item banks) / Local District or School Assessments	Technical manual / Content specifications with clear description of skills assessed / Validity studies with correlations provided for decisions you will be making / Standard errors for individual student scores (or groups) / Misclassification error rates for proficiency levels / Vertical scaling (if you are using growth models) / Norm group, if reported, is representative, and there are norms for your student population / Aligned to your curriculum / Teachers say scores are accurate for your students	Technical manual / General content specification / Some predictive, concurrent, validity correlations to important outcomes (other tests, GPA, etc.) / Internal consistency / Reliability correlations such as test-retest, internal consistency / Scale scores in addition to percentiles or percentage correct scores / Norm group, if reported, is representative but not of your population / Generally aligned with your curriculum, though a few mismatches / Teachers say scores are accurate for some groups of students	No technical manual / No content specifications but perhaps a general item development plan / No validity studies / Internal consistency reliability alone; no other forms reports / No measurement errors or misclassification errors reported / No standard or scale scores available / Percentile ranks (if reported) don't represent a normal distribution of students / No alignment to curriculum / Scores wildly inaccurate for your students	No information on test construction, validity, reliability, or comparative data / No information about how test aligns with your curriculum and how useful the scores are with your students

(Continued)

MAJOR DECISIONS FOR ORGANIZING INFORMATION

The major leadership team management decisions in documenting both your programs and available data involve finding the right people to do the job—those with the organizational skills and knowledge to pull things together.

- What are our major instructional programs, and who is most knowledgeable about them and able to succinctly describe them?
- Who is likely to have the best perspective on how various programs are supposed to work to "cause" student learning? (theory of action)
- What student data currently exist for our school, where are they stored, and how are they accessed? For example, are they available from the district or online?
- Who is most familiar with existing test data and other student data related to our school?

- Who understands the design and interpretation of accountability, district, school, and classroom assessments?
- Who can help us understand the alignment of our assessments to grade-level standards?
- What measures of program quality do we already use? Do we already review teacher assignments, student work, and program implementation?
- What resources do we have for creating and deploying new measures (classroom assessments, surveys, etc.)?
- Who can help us assess data quality?
- What checks exist to ensure data accuracy? How do we assess the accuracy of school-created data? Of data provided by the district or state?

LEADERSHIP CHALLENGES

The major leadership challenges in organizing the information you will need for your redesign revolve around building ownership and support for the effort, coming to grips with what may be innumerable programs and a massive amount of data, and understanding the kinds of data you really need. The development of program descriptions may reveal differing staff perspectives on what a program does and how it operates, and these must be addressed, as your school's programs are the key to turning around student achievement. Realignment includes not only new ways of doing business and new learning, but also new perspectives on "old" functions, such as curriculum delivery and instructional strategies, both of which constitute your educational program. Your staff may also be realigning their definition of "data" as you create the data inventory for your school. They may be surprised at how much information is potentially available to inform their work and how valuable it can be.

- **Creating teacher support for publicly sharing instructional practices.** Much of the work the turnaround team will do depends upon teacher comfort with and willingness to share their assignments and student work, their teaching practice during classroom walk-throughs, and their suggestions and experience about what works well and what they would like to change. The time it will take to create leadership teams for various turnaround tasks, data presentation, program implementation evaluation, and the tedious work of cataloging programs and information and keeping the school inventory up to date depends upon teacher leadership and collaboration. No time is wasted that is spent team building, making norms and expectations clear, creating consensus about the work, and, most of all, creating a safe environment for energetic discussions about practice. If structures for collaboration and consensus about sharing practice are not developed, you will find your efforts blocked by collective bargaining agreements, recalcitrant staff, and half-hearted or nongenuine participation in the redesign process.

- **Documenting programs.** Cataloging school programs is tedious work. How do you distill program goals and outcomes from mounds of teachers' guides, supplementary material, and required texts? How do you characterize complex materials and strategies without trivializing them? This might be a job for a graduate student or parent who has teaching experience. The task might begin with a list of programs and grow over time to complete program descriptions that evolve from your turnaround work.

- **Aligning assessments.** Most people don't have enough experience in writing operational statements about the skills and content implied by vaguely worded standards to create clear standards descriptions, or domain descriptions. Again, this task might best be completed by one of your expert reviewers, central office assessment staff, or teacher work groups over a period of a year. The most important aspect of the alignment process is to raise awareness that the score itself is not the most important thing to consider, and that score meaning is tied to test purpose and content. Once staff have developed sophistication about test scores, are able to raise the right questions, and know where to find information related to exactly how the tests assess their standards, they have enough expertise to forego more formal alignment procedures. Or you could assign your school's data team the responsibility of creating brief domain specifications and judging or raising questions about assessment alignment.

- **Drowning in data.** Water can kill you or sustain you. The same can be said for data. Your data inventory will help you determine whether the stacks of information available to your school are snuffing out the breath of reform or bringing fresh energy to your efforts. Do not be surprised if you find that despite having loads of data, you actually need more and different information. You most likely will find your accountability assessments useless for pinpointing specific instructional problems or assessing your curriculum. You may also discover that the district-developed or school-developed assessments are measures of convenience rather than reflecting clear definitions of important learning outcomes. None of these findings is a surprise. The data inventory can point out what you might ignore or find less useful as well as what you don't have and need to find (e.g., parent satisfaction surveys, Student Opportunity to Learn surveys, student focus group data, program quality data, and so on).

- **Too much testing and no time to teach.** Whenever teachers are asked to consider the assessments they are required to use, the inevitable response is, "All we do is test. I have no time to teach." Teachers involved in improving student learning need to understand that assessment, especially formative classroom assessment, is an instructional strategy and an important way to communicate expectations and provide feedback to students. This is a big shift and will take time. The shift also requires teachers to envision "teaching" and their responsibilities differently than they may have been taught in their education courses. Guest speakers, study groups, and visits to similar schools having much better student success can help teachers rethink the place of assessment in teaching and learning.

Selected Resources to Support Your Work

Analysis of teacher assignments to assessment instructional quality—*Classroom Assignment Scoring Manual*, by the National Center for Research on Evaluation, Standards, and Student Testing (CRESST, 2002), available online at www.cse.ucla.edu/products/teachers.html. Manuals are available for the elementary, middle school, and high school levels and provide detailed rubrics and anchor examples for analyzing language arts assignments.

Documenting programs and measuring program quality—*How to Assess Program Implementation*, by Jean A. King, Lynn Lyons Morris, and Carol T. Fitz-Gibbon (Sage, 1987). This guide, part of the *CSE Program Evaluation Kit*, provides practical guidelines for documenting program processes and implementation. It is an "oldie but goodie" that remains relevant today; we keep it in our libraries and refer to it often.

Understanding the walk-through process—*UCLA SMP Classroom Walk-Throughs Introduction*, available online at www.youtube.com. This YouTube video shows a walk-through in process. It captures the nonjudgmental and focused nature of these classroom observations.

Walk-through forms and description—*Snapshots of Learning: Classroom Walk-Throughs Offer Picture of Learning in Schools*, by Joan Richardson, available at www.perryandassociatesinc.com/8–06%20Tools%20-%20 Walk-Throughs.pdf. This document, available online in PDF format from Learning Forward, thoroughly explains the process and provides useful forms. It was written by two practitioners who have conducted many classroom visits all over the country for many different purposes.

Leader's Guide

3

Prepare Data Summaries and Displays

CHAPTER 3 POCKET SUMMARY

POCKET SUMMARY		
Task	**Major Activities**	**Purpose**
Identify data review questions.	• Questions drive interpretation. • Begin with questions about student outcomes. **Tool 3.1 Data Review Questions for Identifying Instructional Focus Areas** • Consider a range of program questions to create your Turnaround Plan. **Tool 3.2 Needs Assessment Questions for Identifying the Turnaround Focus**	• Identify questions to guide data selection and interpretation.
Use data inventory to identify data needed to answer program redesign questions.	• Find data sources in your data inventory to address each question. • Keep a list of important questions for which you lack data to use in the formative evaluation of your Turnaround Plan.	• Develop a reference to help you find data when needed.
Prepare tables and graphs from published reports.	• Keep in mind the questions each table or graph will address. • Begin with published reports. • Break up published information into bite-sized summaries. • Prepare explanations for complex data tables. • Keep displays simple. **Tool 3.3 Table and Graph Considerations: Student Performance** **Tool 3.4 Table and Graph Considerations: Achievement Gap Analysis** **Tool 3.5 Table and Graph Considerations: Important Comparisons**	• Develop model reports for your own data by reviewing state reports. • Develop tables and displays that tell a story and are easy to interpret.
Summarize local data.	• Select an appropriate score to summarize local test data. • Summarize survey data to best answer your needs assessment questions.	• Avoid data distortions that can lead to faulty interpretation.

THUMBNAILS OF TOOLS FROM THIS CHAPTER

The following tools can be found on the companion website for *The TurnAround ToolKit* at http://www.corwin.com/turnaroundtoolkit.

Tool 3.1

Data Review Questions for Identifying Instructional Focus Areas

Tool 3.2

Needs Assessment Questions for Identifying the Turnaround Focus

Tool 3.3

Table and Graph Considerations: Student Performance

Tool 3.4

Table and Graph Considerations: Achievement Gap Analysis

Tool 3.5

Table and Graph Considerations: Important Comparisons

MAJOR DECISIONS FOR PREPARING DATA SUMMARIES AND DISPLAYS

The major leadership team management decisions in preparing data summaries and displays involve creating a site-level team to be responsible for data collection, summarization, and reporting, if possible. You will also need to have experts available to help with the work of data preparation and to support your efforts in program redesign.

- What kind of advice do we need to help us limit our needs assessment questions to those that address the most important student outcomes?
- For what aspects of the school program do we have useful data to review?
- Who on campus can help with data summarization and display? What kind of support and training do we need to provide to our data team?
- Who can we find to review our work who has expertise in the data preparation and needs assessment processes?
- How do we keep our data presentations focused and manageable while still including all the relevant information we need for decision making?
- How shall we report data of shaky quality? What other information or insights can help us understand the data?
- What technical knowledge does staff outside of the data team need to know in order to correctly interpret tables and displays related to our needs assessment questions?
- What other information about the data sources—what they actually measure, their procedures, content, history, and so forth—do we need to add to help staff understand the data summaries and displays?

LEADERSHIP CHALLENGES

The leadership challenges in preparing data inventories and summaries revolve around (1) accessing the expertise you need to analyze and appropriately interpret your data and (2) understanding that the data can't answer all your questions:

- **Need for expertise in interpreting state and published test reports.** Most people have an underdeveloped understanding of what test scores mean, and certainly the majority cannot list the "threats to validity" of the scores when interpreting data. How much understanding is enough? When and how often do you bring in experts? When does technical information become distracting rather than illuminating?

- **Need to develop a tolerance for qualified answers to needs assessment questions.** Data are neither authoritative nor definitive. They suggest, raise issues, point to, and classify performance at one point in time. Data analysis does not yield unambiguous or "correct" answers. There is a need to help staff balance their need for "right" answers with the reality of the limitations on data interpretation. We have to help them avoid either/or thinking and to learn to live in the ambiguous space between "there is a probability that this is true" and "there is a probability that this conclusion is unsupported." Teachers can get discouraged or frustrated when data limitations and modifications are pointed out to them. We have to help them resist the temptation to say, "These results are useless; this test was a waste of time." The focus on data interpretation needs to be the jewels of information we find in the rubble of information we review.

• **Expertise in creating tables and displays.** Staff can develop data summarization expertise; however, some staff will find reducing large tables to smaller ones or creating graphs from tables more interesting and enjoyable than others. Find the data devotees, and provide them with training or mentoring to develop in-school data summarization capacity. Having your own data experts is a check on the outside reports you receive from the state or district. In our experience, neither the state nor the test publishers are immune from mistakes. We even know a third-grade teacher who discovered that the Stanford reports used the wrong norms for her year-round students! Those are the kinds of data sensibilities your data preparation activities should cultivate.

SELECTED RESOURCES TO SUPPORT YOUR WORK

Understanding growth models—*Policymakers' Guide to Growth Models for School Accountability: How Do Accountability Models Differ?* by Pete Goldschmidt et al. (Council of Chief State School Officers, 2005), available at www.ccsso.org/What_We_Do/Standards_Assessment_and_Accountability/Resources.html. Don't let the title put you off! This guide is a must-read for anyone wishing to understand growth models and their limitations. Unfortunately, once you read it, you might put a lot less faith in the growth model approach to measuring progress in an accountability system. Forewarned is forearmed!

Making accurate data displays—*Just Plain Data Analysis: Finding, Presenting, and Interpreting Social Science Data,* by Gary Klass (Rowman & Littlefield, 2008). We cite this source in many places in this book. We especially like the website that Gary Klass has developed to demonstrate the data analysis issues he raises in the book. It's not an unlisted address, but in case you don't know it already, visit Gary at http://lilt.ilstu.edu/jpda. You won't be sorry you did.

Understanding value added—In the rush to use value-added models, the constraints on their use and how they are interpreted are often forgotten. The *EPI Briefing Paper, Problems With the Use of Student Test Scores to Evaluate Teachers,* written by a who's who of educational statisticians, measurement specialists, and policymakers, is a must read prior to using value-added scores for school-level decisions. Find it at http://www.epi.org/publications/entry/bp278.

Leader's Guide

4

Identify the Turnaround Focus

CHAPTER 4 POCKET SUMMARY

POCKET SUMMARY

Task	Major Activities	Purpose
Select data for review, and set criteria for identifying strengths and weaknesses.	• Identify and sequence your prepared summaries and displays to address needs assessment questions. **Tool 3.2 (in Chapter 3 Toolkit), Needs Assessment Questions for Identifying the Turnaround Focus** • Set criteria for defining strengths and weaknesses. **Tool 4.1 Performance Criteria for Reviewing Student Outcome Data**	• Efficient data review. • Identify areas of weakness and strength.
Begin with the big picture: Analyze accountability data.	• Determine status relative to targets, and identify trends. **Tool 4.2 Understanding Your State Accountability System** • Examine important comparisons. **Tool 4.3 Data Discussion Summary Template**	• Enhance validity of decisions about areas of weakness.
Tighten your focus: Review state or local standards assessments.	• Examine achievement differences by grade level and content. • Start with mean score trends by content and grade level to identify patterns. • Examine differences in the proportion of high- and low-scoring students by grade level and content. • Examine trends for subgroups and compare with your benchmark school. • Summarize your review of state and local test data.	• Move from big picture to detail decisions. • Link inferences among different tests.
Clarify and corroborate instructional focus areas with local assessments.	**Tool 4.4 Discussion Protocol: Reviewing Sample Items or Released Tests** • Use local assessments for diagnosing specific learning needs.	• Fill in gaps in understanding of student needs.
Review other valued outcomes.	• Analyze dropout data. **Tool 4.5 Analyzing Dropout Rates to Determine Instructional Focus** • Examine progress on student preparation goals. **Tool 4.6 Suggestions for Reviewing Progress on Student Preparation Goals** • Consider English-learner reclassification rates.	• Include important outcomes other than test data, so you won't miss authentic and politically valued outcomes of schooling.
Choose the turnaround focus areas.	• Pinpoint the grade levels, content areas, and skills (if you have the data) that will serve as the focus for your Turnaround Plan.	• Specify the instructional focus to guide all turnaround work efforts.
Don't move on until you have identified your strengths.	• Use student achievement data to indicate skills and knowledge you can build upon to strengthen weak areas.	• Include areas of strength to leverage turnaround work.

THUMBNAILS OF TOOLS FROM THIS CHAPTER

The following tools can be found on the companion website for *The TurnAround ToolKit* at http://www.corwin.com/turnaroundtoolkit.

Tool 4.1

Performance Criteria for Reviewing Student Outcome Data

Data Source	Kind of Analysis	Performance Standards
Accountability or Published Tests Used Over Multiple Years	Status relative to established targets	• AYP percentage Proficient status • District-established yearly growth targets • State-established yearly growth targets
	Trends	• Change over time compared with benchmark school, state, or highest-performing schools • Change larger or smaller than standard error
	Benchmark comparisons	• Scores compared with those of demographically similar schools that are doing much better • Scores compared with those of schools we wish to emulate or compete with that are doing better
	Politically important comparisons	• District average • State average • Met accountability targets
	Content and grade-level patterns	• Improvement over time • Increase in students meeting targets, such as AYP or score of 3 or better on AP tests • Comparison of performance between content areas • Comparison of performance between grade levels
	Subgroup patterns	• Gap between percentage of subgroup scoring Proficient or better and percentage of all students scoring Proficient or better • Subgroup percentages scoring in lowest proficiency levels by various groups • Subgroup performance over time by grade and content
District- and School-Level Common Assessments	Skill diagnosis	• Skill areas with highest and lowest average percentage correct • Comparison of above with skills emphasized on state accountability tests
	Classroom comparisons	• Classrooms of similar students scoring highest and lowest • Classrooms doing well with struggling students
	Subgroup patterns	• Average percentage correct for different subgroups • Subgroup performance over time on district tests

Tool 4.2

Understanding Your State Accountability System

In order to interpret your state accountability reports and extract strategic and perhaps diagnostic information about student needs, you should consider the following questions:

1. Does your state use a status model (percentage reaching adequate yearly progress targets), a growth model (change in scores from Year 1 to Year 2 for the same group of students), or an improvement model (difference in scores between this year's grade-level cohort and last year's students in the same grade levels)?
2. Which assessments are used to calculate state accountability scores?
3. Are the same assessments used in every grade level, or do certain grades have different kinds of assessments? (For example, students in California have a writing test added to their multiple-choice state assessment in Grades 4 and 7.)
4. Which grade levels are included in the accountability scores? Are grades reported separately, or do accountability calculations aggregate across several grades?
5. How are tests combined or weighted if the accountability score is an index?
6. What number of students, or what percentage of the school population, constitutes a "significant" subgroup?
7. How are subgroups defined? Who is considered an English learner? Are English learners kept in a subgroup after having been reclassified? If so, for how long?
8. How are proficiency levels set? Are they the same for each grade and content?
9. Are classification errors (based on measurement error calculations) reported for each of the proficiency levels reported?
10. How is "safe harbor" calculated in your state? How do you qualify for safe harbor? No Child Left Behind has a safe harbor provision to provide flexibility and fairness in the calculation of adequate yearly progress (AYP) results. A school can be forgiven low test scores from one or more subgroups if the subgroup is improving and the school as a whole has met AYP. Alternatively, some states calculate AYP using confidence intervals to certify that school growth or decline wasn't simply a function of measurement error. The confidence intervals at the 75% confidence level are also considered a safe harbor. This method of meeting AYP targets eliminates chance as a factor in reaching or failing to reach a yearly target. States such as California, Delaware, Indiana, Montana, Oklahoma, South Dakota, and Wisconsin use the confidence interval approach to double-check that AYP results to be sure that real improvement accounts for school results.

Tool 4.3

Data Discussion Summary Template

Template: Data Discussion Summary

Area	Data Used	Findings	Questions Raised	Other Data to Examine
Progress Toward Targets				
Trends				
Grade Level by Content				
Subgroup Trends by Grade Level and Content				

(Continued)

Tool 4.4

Discussion Protocol: Reviewing Sample Items or Released Tests

Materials Needed: Release tests by subject and grade level or sets of sample items (at least 10 release or sample items per standard or skill area), test administration directions that teachers will follow.

Goals for Sample Item Review Sessions

At the end of the review session, teachers will know the following:

• How item formats on the high-stakes assessment differ from those on district, department, or curriculum tests
• How the overall difficulty level of a test under consideration differs from that of other common assessments and class work
• What kinds of knowledge and skills are assessed and the relative emphasis of each
• How the test matches their current curriculum
• What test preparation activities will provide ethical and appropriate preparation

Assessment of Item Format and Test Difficulty Levels

1. How many items are attached to a reading passage? To a topical math or language arts section (e.g., measurement, sentence variety, etc.)?
2. How are reading and language skills "integrated" into the test? By what means? Are questions about language arts (e.g., grammar, style, spelling, and rhetorical strategies) intermingled with items about reading comprehension and attached to reading passages, or are the language arts questions in a separate section of the test and labeled as such? Do students have advance notice about the type of question in reading or language arts the test section contains?
3. How many distractors are there per multiple-choice item?
4. How are distractors written? Do they represent common student mistakes? Correct answers but not the "best" answer given the stimulus material?
5. Are there novel item formats that students need to know how to navigate?
6. What test-specific language, syntax, or directions need to be taught to students so that they understand what is being tested (e.g., use of double negatives, choices like "all of the above" or "none of the above," etc.)?
7. How many different genres of reading passages are there, and how many examples per genre (e.g., functional, nonfiction, fiction)?

Tool 4.5

Analyzing Dropout Rates to Determine Instructional Focus

Analyzing Dropout Rates to Determine Instructional Focus

Question	Review Data Needed	Possible Instructional Focus
At what grade are we losing students? Where are they going?	• Student information system enrollment numbers by grade level • Exit surveys for students who withdraw from school	• If students are dropping out to work, innovative instructional delivery systems • If students are moving but enrolling elsewhere, systems for tracking and validating student information • If students are dropping out due to discouragement or disengagement, course revisions to ensure that content is accessible and instruction is differentiated
Is the high school exit exam responsible for dropouts?	• Correlation of high school exit exam results with dropout rates	• Ensure students are learning content needed to pass exit exam. • Provide appropriate practice for the exam • Provide support for students who fail the exam
Are course requirements responsible for dropouts?	• Identification of required courses that cause students to repeat (usually Algebra), and the grades and test scores of repeaters • Identification of where students are getting behind in credits	• Revision of course content for repeated courses • Revision of placement and curriculum for courses where students fail time after time • Consider alternate course delivery systems, such as online courses, a Copernican schedule, and so forth
Are personal goals and community expectations affecting student completion?	• Kinds of parent involvement, mentoring, counseling, or community support that would change student expectations	• Adopting Advancement With Individual Determination (AVID) to build skills • Creating a college-going culture and embedding this into required courses

Tool 4.6

Suggestions for Reviewing Progress on Student Preparation Goals

Preparation Goal for Your Level of Schooling	Intermediate Targets	Data to Identify Instructional Strengths and Weaknesses
Middle School Readiness	• Ability to comprehend information text • Fluency in math facts • Prealgebra skills	• Reading test scores • Passage-based writing assessments and assignments • Yearly math facts assessments • End-of-course math exams
High School Readiness	• Study skills • Basic concepts in social studies, science, math, and literature	• Assignment completion, grades • State assessments • Preliminary Scholastic Achievement Test (PSAT) • ACT PLAN—College Readiness Test for 10th Graders and Pathfinder curriculum assessments • Advancement With Individual Determination (AVID) assessments
College Readiness	• Course completion: math, science, history, literature • Community service • Selection of a preferred area of study	• Course credit accumulation and grades • PSAT and SAT scores • AP enrollment and scores • Community service project completion • Patterns of courses taken
Vocational Readiness	• High school skill acquisition • Specialized skill acquisition	• High school exit exam • Course credit accumulation • Number of students in extracurricular or elective program

MAJOR DECISIONS FOR USING DATA TO IDENTIFY THE TURNAROUND FOCUS

The major leadership team management decisions in conducting a data review to identify student learning needs to involve the who, how, and what of the work that needs to get done. The central management tasks are to create a climate of inquiry; to help team members suspend judgment, explore possibilities, and raise important questions about the information before them; and to entertain multiple hypotheses about what learning problems might lurk in student outcome data.

- How many people should be involved in this step, and who should they be? How should they be selected and trained?
- Do we need outside facilitators or any expert help for the data review?
- How do we present data from different sources—accountability, state, district, and local tests—without overwhelming staff?
- What protocols do we have for reviewing student outcome data to diagnose learning needs?
- How do we handle data discrepancies and issues of data credibility?
- How will we resolve conflicting perspectives and reach consensus on priority needs?
- What is the best level of specificity for our focus statement?

LEADERSHIP CHALLENGES

The leadership challenges in identifying your instructional focus involve helping your teams understand, value, and reach agreement on what the data and their professional judgment reveal about current and needed pathways to higher learning:

- **Clarifying the meaning of data.** Data analysis rests upon understanding the measures and accountability rules underlying numerical summaries and scores used in reports. It is very difficult to know the level of detail necessary to interpret accountability data and to understand the limits of interpretation for systems that can change their decision rules, sometimes as often as yearly. It is also frustrating for groups viewing data to keep in mind what the data do and do not allow them to say with any confidence. However, data review does help develop habits of asking good questions about what appear to be "facts," digging deeper into what is tested (and not tested), and examining standards emphases (not all standards are equal). Data review also helps staff to consider how much of a student's score could be the result of factors such as item format familiarity, test-taking skills, and reading comprehension versus how much is a result of what a student knows. These are important discussions.

- **Keeping the focus on student learning rather than on what teachers do.** Discussions about instructional focus naturally transform themselves into discussions about curriculum and instruction: what teachers could be doing rather than what students are struggling with as learners. You will notice that learning focus statements might start out as prescriptions for practice rather than descriptions of student needs. You will need to take time to help teachers refocus on what the learning issues appear to be rather than what teaching issues are associated with student outcomes.

- **Managing data discussions to avoid tedium and frustration.** There are many, many data sources available to identify your instructional focus. Too many!! Keeping staff interested and on task is an art, as is helping them handle frustration with contradictory and incomplete information. You may wish to hire a facilitator for this task (or borrow one from the district office) who is experienced in moving groups along while processing complex or off-putting information.

- **Resolving differing perspectives.** Don't be surprised if on occasion, different people see different patterns in the data or interpret the patterns differently. Be prepared for some defensiveness as well—none of us would want to easily accept that a course that we teach is the source of the problem. Keep the discussion on track with collaborative problem solving, and avoid personal attributions. Where there are major disagreements on what the data mean, ask the groups to consider analyses that could be conducted or additional data that could be collected to resolve the disagreement. Here again, you may need to seek outside expertise.

SELECTED RESOURCES TO SUPPORT YOUR WORK

Assessment literacy—*Assessment for Educational Leaders*, by W. James Popham (Allyn & Bacon, 2006). This reference also appears in the Chapter 2 Leader's Guide. The explanations of test uses, accountability systems, and statistics used in testing are especially relevant to the data review work of this chapter.

Accountability system literacy—*Educational Accountability Systems*, CSE Technical Report 687, by Robert L. Linn (CRESST/University of Colorado at Boulder, 2006). This report was written for the scholar and is not for the faint of heart, but it was written by one of the most important educational measurement experts in the country. Worth reading for the last two paragraphs alone, which declare that (1) current accountability systems cannot be used to conclude that differences in school results are solely due to differences in school quality, and (2) the best use of accountability data is to describe what is happening and raise hypotheses about your school that can be checked using additional information.

Using data to redesign programs—*Show Me the Proof: Tools and Strategies to Make Data Work for You* (Advanced Learning Press, 2005b) and *Beyond the Numbers: Making Data Work for Teachers and School Leaders*, by Stephen White (Advanced Learning Press, 2005a). Written for teachers serving on data teams, these two books provide accessible strategies for linking insights gleaned from data analysis to concrete instructional changes. They include helpful strategies for organizing and analyzing data, using multiple data sources (triangulation), and getting to the deeper implications of data. The books provide useable tools for teacher collaboration in a school setting.

Leader's Guide

5

Redesign Programs to Address the Turnaround Focus

CHAPTER 5 POCKET SUMMARY

POCKET SUMMARY		
Task	**Major Activities**	**Purpose**
Redesign programs to address instructional focus.	• Introduce the concept of *theory of action* early in the redesign process. **Tool 5.1 Toolkit Tutorial: Basing Our Turnaround Plan on a Theory of Action or Change** • Adopt an attitude of rapid-fire experimentation.	• Make cause-and-effect relationships explicit.
Clarify the turnaround focus.	• Specify how you will know you have met your long-term goals. • Identify short-term outcomes needed to accomplish long-term goals.	• Define expected outcomes.
Redesign the program.	• Begin redesign with curriculum, instruction, and staff development. • Build continuous improvement into teaching practice. • Select needs assessment questions for program redesign. **Tool 5.2 Needs Assessment Questions for Curriculum, Instruction, and Staff Development** • Review data to address needs assessment questions. • Consult experts to help address redesign questions. **Tool 5.3 Resources for Program Redesign**	• Identify instructional redesign. • Build in monitoring strategies.
Build program support into the redesign.	• Review school context variables that support instruction. **Tool 5.4 Needs Assessment Questions for School Context Variables** • Embed program support into the Turnaround Plan.	• Identify support needed for instructional program changes.

THUMBNAILS OF TOOLS FROM THIS CHAPTER

The following tools can be found on the companion website for *The TurnAround ToolKit* at http://www.corwin.com/turnaroundtoolkit.

Tool 5.1

Toolkit Tutorial: Basing Our Turnaround Plan on a Theory of Action or Change

All rational (i.e., recognizably sane during working hours) beings operate on implicit "theories of action." We base our decisions on subconscious and powerful cognitive hypotheses about cause and effect. A teacher who has students memorize math facts believes that memorization is the appropriate avenue for learning certain kinds of knowledge (and research supports this). The teacher then uses drill techniques to produce fluency and accuracy in her students' ability to do mental arithmetic. She is operating from a theory of action, a model for her decisions based upon her understanding of what will cause her students to learn.

A Turnaround Plan makes explicit the theories of action of the group of professionals charged with improving student outcomes. Because there are some bugs in their current theories, the evidence being that students are not as academically successful as the teachers think they should be, the first step in creating a Turnaround Plan is to capture new theories of action, or "theories of change," that will revise some of the less successful theories of action and lead to better student achievement. For example, one of my theories of action about how to prepare students for algebra could be to assess student readiness and then separate students into groups based on their mastery of prealgebra concepts and skills, thinking that homogeneous grouping will lead to more efficient and focused instruction. If, in fact, I have followed this practice over a long period of time, and my students are not mastering prealgebra skills despite homogeneous grouping and targeted instruction, then I need to come up with a new theory of action. The theory of change must identify clearly what I will be doing differently and what outcomes I am expecting from this change. More formally, the theory of change connects program activities to program outcomes.

Where do these theories of change come from? If we all have certain theories of action, and if what we are doing based on these theories isn't successful, how do we introduce new information to revise our guiding heuristics? Many sources of information can be introduced into discussions of what activities we need to change in order to improve student outcomes:

• Practices observed in schools like ours that are doing much better: our benchmark schools
• Research on learning and instruction to identify new practices and curriculum
• Data from our own formative evaluation efforts that can inform us about what is working well
• Professional experience: teacher wisdom about what has worked over the years

The discussions we engage in to generate our Turnaround Plan essentially engage our current theories of action and ask us to create theories of change. Our theory of change becomes the platform upon which we build our turnaround work.

Tool 5.2

Needs Assessment Questions for Curriculum, Instruction, and Staff Development

Curriculum		
Area	Needs Assessment Questions	Data Suggestions
Organization and Pacing	• What is the order of content and skill introduction? • What is the relative emphasis of content versus skills in the course? • How much time is suggested to spend on major units/topics/skills? • Are the skills new to this grade, do they build upon prior learning, or it is assumed that they are foundational and are not taught this year? • When are the skills introduced or required for learning this year's content? • How much time is allocated to their instruction, or how frequently are they used? • Which materials introduce or employ the skills and knowledge? What is their quality (accuracy, clarity, effectiveness with students)?	• District pacing charts • District or state text blueprints with content-skill emphases • Curriculum guides
Alignment	• Is our curriculum aligned with state standards?	• State standards documents • Curriculum pacing guides • State testing blueprints • Assignments and assessments
Rigor	• What grade-level skills are reflected in assignments? • What is the complexity of reading material and content?	• Grade level of materials—complexity of language, choice of reading material or topics • Program quality data: rigor
Operationalized Standards	• Do we have clear goal statements (knowledge, skills, core competencies) for each curriculum area? • Do teachers have a shared understanding of these goals linked to standards?	• Classroom assessments • Assignments keyed to standards • Lesson plans

(Continued)

Tool 5.3

Resources for Program Redesign

RESOURCES FOR THE REALIGN AND REDESIGN PHASES

The What Works Clearinghouse (WWC, http://ies.ed.gov/ncee/wwc) was created by the Institute of Education Sciences (U.S. Department of Education) to provide educators with a central source of scientific evidence about what works in education. Mathematics Policy Research administers the WWC under contract to the department. The WWC has reviewed research on eight topics—adolescent literacy, beginning reading, character education, dropout prevention, early childhood education, elementary school math, English language learners, and middle school math—and has published practice guides synthesizing research and providing recommendations for practitioners. Here are some of their guides for the turnaround process:

Realign

Turning Around Chronically Low-Performing Schools

Using Student Achievement Data to Support Instructional Decision Making

Redesign

Curriculum and Instruction

Organizing Instruction and Study to Improve Student Learning

Effective Literacy and English Language Instruction for English Learners in the Elementary Grades

Assisting Students Struggling with Reading: Response to Intervention and Multi-Tier Intervention in the Primary Grades

Improving Adolescent Literacy: Effective Classroom Intervention Practices

Encouraging Girls in Math and Science

Assisting Students Struggling with Mathematics: Response to Intervention for Elementary and Middle Schools

Long-Term Outcomes

Helping Students Navigate the Path to College: What High Schools Can Do

Dropout Prevention

Tool 5.4

Needs Assessment Questions for School Context Variables

School Climate Questions and Data Suggestions			
Area	Needs Assessment Questions	Archival Data	Self-Report Data (Surveys, Interviews, Focus Groups)
Safety	Do students, parents, and community perceive the school as safe, orderly, and prepared for emergencies (civil and natural disasters, police action in the neighborhood, etc.)?	• Safety plan • Records of suspensions, expulsions • Discipline policies • Attendance and truancy records	• Do students feel safe at school? • Are students safe in transit to and from school? • Do students attend all classes? • Are students safe in restrooms?
Student Behavior	Does the school have policies and programs to deal with important behavioral issues such as bullying, drug use, alcohol and tobacco use, and sexual harassment?	• Availability of clinics, screening, behavioral counseling on site • Attendance policy • Discipline policy • Attendance records • Tardiness records • Records about fights/incidents • Records of suspensions and expulsions	• Do students feel class time is interruption free? • Are halls and gathering places free of students during class?
Integrated Student Support Services	Does the school have mental health referral services for students, staff, and parents?	• Mental health referrals • Onsite mental health support (counseling groups, school psychologist or social worker appointments)	• Do students report they have friends at school? • Do they generally like others at school and in classes?
Positive Relationships	Do teachers, students, parents, and administrators report they have positive working relationships and methods for dealing with disagreements?	• Records of campus fights, conflict • Student, parent complaints	• Does each student have at least one friend at school? • Do students feel comfortable asking teachers for help?
Pride	Are students proud of their school? Do they attend regularly, participate in activities, athletics?	• Newspaper coverage • Percentage of students participating in athletics	• Do students feel proud of their school? • Do they attend school functions?

MAJOR DECISIONS FOR REDESIGNING PROGRAMS TO ADDRESS THE TURNAROUND FOCUS

The major leadership team management decisions for redesigning your program involve facilitating collegial data reviews and solution-oriented discussions, helping staff to make their theories of action explicit and reach consensus on them, and wrangling the expert help and research knowledge you may need to move forward productively.

> • How do we help staff develop the dispositions needed for turnaround work and program redesign: ready to experiment, explicit about their mental models of what should cause improvements in student achievement, using assessment as an instructional improvement strategy, and willing to review data and change course on a short timeline?
>
> *(Continued)*

(Continued)

- How do we clarify our instructional focus so that we can identify the most important content and skills in it? That is, what are the skills that affect many aspects of student learning?
- What questions do we need to ask about our current curriculum to help us address how to improve it?
- What questions do we need to ask about instruction? Staff development?
- What data do we have to address program (curriculum, instruction, staff development) redesign? What data can we collect quickly that would inform our decisions?
- What questions about school context, climate, staff quality, and parent/community involvement can we ask to create support for our proposed program changes?
- What school context data do we have? What useful data could be collected quickly?
- How can we best draw on available data and our professional knowledge to reach consensus on the theory of action that will drive our redesign effort?
- When do we bring in experts to help with Redesign? Where do we find them? How will we use them effectively?
- How will we communicate and build wider support for our theory of action? How can we create a graphical representation of our theory of action to communicate our work to others and to develop and implement our Turnaround Plan?

LEADERSHIP CHALLENGES

The leadership challenges of the redesign work revolve around the limitations of existing data and the role of professional judgment in the process. These include the following:

- **Lack of program quality data.** Unless your school has been actively engaged in a collaborative review of program implementation or standards alignment, you have not yet developed the structures or collegial trust needed to collect data about the quality of your instructional program. Grade-level or subject-matter working groups need to be created and to begin feeling comfortable with reviewing shared assignments for rigor and alignment to standards, with reviewing student work samples to identify both learning problems and grade-level match, and with visiting each other's classrooms or having their classes visited by small teams focused not on judging teaching but on specific aspects of program implementation. This is where you begin. Should you have collaborative structures and professional trust already developed, but no data, you could collect these data for program redesign on a fairly short timeline and use them in your review.

- **Lack of data about student, parent, and teacher perceptions of teaching and learning needs.** Again, unless your school routinely collects data about parent satisfaction, involvement, and knowledge of their student's progress; about student opportunities to learn, safety, and classroom climate; and about teacher perceptions of student opportunities to learn and student needs, you will lack data for determining how to improve school context to support your program revisions. These data can be gathered quickly and easily on short, focused telephone surveys, on classroom surveys, or even on Internet surveys. Since you will need these data for program monitoring, you will want to develop strategies for gathering school context information as soon as possible.

- **Need to respect teacher professionalism while deepening understanding of content and pedagogy.** Most program revision requires staff development to help teachers practice and get feedback on any new instructional strategies they might decide are needed. Teachers are pretty open to learning about new strategies. However, strategies always are embedded in knowledge or subject-matter expertise. A new understanding of the subject matter leads to a new understanding of how to present it to students. Helping teachers acquire a better understanding of their subject without implying that what they currently know is "wrong" or "not smart enough" is a balancing act that must be navigated with tact and in a very safe (nonevaluative) environment. Experts, master teachers, coaches, and even publishers' representatives who are engaging and deeply understand the challenges of teaching a particular subject can be essential for this task.

- **Resolving differences of perspective.** Yes, yes, we've mentioned it at every step, and here it is again. Staff differences in educational philosophy and pedagogical preferences can lead to different theories of action. Try to reach common ground; alternatively, go forward with two alternatives and let the data collected subsequently decide.

SELECTED RESOURCES TO SUPPORT YOUR WORK

Overview of the curriculum redesign process and elements of curriculum—*Deciding What to Teach and Test: Developing, Aligning, and Leading the Curriculum* (3rd ed.), by Fenwick W. English (Corwin, 2010). This classic, reissued in 2010, is a primer on curriculum development and review and on gathering data to improve curriculum. It provides a great background for redesign work and is accompanied by supplemental videos.

Research-based instructional strategies linked to improved student learning—*Organizing Instruction and Study to Improve Student Learning: A Practice Guide* (U.S. Department of Education's Institute of Education Sciences, 2007), available from http://ies.ed.gov/ncee/wwc/publications/practiceguides. It covers seven research-based instructional strategies: spacing learning over time, integrating examples into problem-solving practice, combining graphics with verbal descriptions, connecting and integrating abstract and concrete conceptual representation, using assessments to promote learning, helping students allocate study time well, and helping students build explanations by focusing on deep questions. The guide provides strategies that can be integrated into any subject at any grade.

School context: parent involvement strategies—*What Successful Schools Do to Involve Families: 55 Partnership Strategies,* by Neal Glasgow and Paula Jameson Whitney (Corwin and National Association of Secondary School Principals, 2009). Although the book focuses on strategies for reaching out to parents of diverse student groups, the methods for including families in discussions about homework, literacy, mathematics, and students with special needs provide tips for creating support for program redesign. We especially liked the chapter on how school leaders can use parent involvement to increase student achievement.

Leader's Guide

6

Develop and Implement the Turnaround Plan

CHAPTER 6 POCKET SUMMARY

<table>
<tr><th colspan="3" style="text-align:center">POCKET SUMMARY</th></tr>
<tr><th>Task</th><th>Major Activities</th><th>Purpose</th></tr>
<tr>
<td>Develop the Turnaround Plan.</td>
<td>

- Translate your theory of action into a plan.
- Avoid overly elaborate plans.
- Include program redesign, management, and monitoring activities in your plan.

Tool 6.1 Turnaround Plan Template
</td>
<td>

- Develop an action-focused, list-style plan.
</td>
</tr>
<tr>
<td>Implement the Turnaround Plan.</td>
<td>

- Carry out activities listed in your plan.
- Collect monitoring data during implementation.
- Monitor the quality of teaching and learning.

Tool 2.3 Program Quality: Assignment Rigor

Tool 2.4 Program Quality: Protocols for Looking at Student Work

Tool 2.5 Program Quality: Classroom Walk-Through Guidelines

- Monitor staff development needs.

Tool 6.2 Staff Development Survey Template

Tool 6.3 Survey Development Cheat Sheet

- Monitor student learning frequently and informally.

Tool 6.4 Teacher Test Analysis Procedures

Tool 6.5 Student Test Analysis Procedures

- Consider implementation challenges.
- Document your successful efforts.
</td>
<td>

- Focus on doing, monitoring, and revising.
</td>
</tr>
</table>

THUMBNAILS OF TOOLS FROM THIS CHAPTER

The following tools can be found on the companion website for *The TurnAround ToolKit* at http://www.corwin.com/turnaroundtoolkit.

Tool 6.1

Turnaround Plan Template

Plan Focus	Short-Term Course Outcomes		
Plan Activity (code for sorting)	Activity	Persons Responsible	When
Staff Development			
Resource Acquisition			
Instructional Strategy Implementation			

Tool 6.2

Staff Development Survey Template

Check the response that best captures your opinion.

	Doesn't Apply or No Opinion	Strongly Disagree	Disagree	Somewhat Agree	Agree	Strongly Agree
The session increased my awareness of [insert topic of staff development].						
The session changed the way I think about [insert change expected in staff development].						
The session helped me identify new information and tools for [state student outcome staff development is linked to].						
The session increased my understanding of effective strategies and practices in working with [state student or parent group].						
The session helped me develop new skills to apply to [state student learning problem].						
The meeting connected me with other teachers who share the same concerns and might be able to help me implement the strategies discussed today.						
I would like more meetings like this one.						

Suggestions and Comments

1. Give an example of an action you will take with your students based on what you heard today.
2. What did you like best about the day?
3. What ideas, strategies, or practices need more clarification?
4. What topics would you like to cover in future sessions?

Tool 6.3

Survey Development Cheat Sheet

Step 1. Determine the survey purpose.

- To evaluate quality or overall satisfaction.
- To identify how an activity is being implemented (how often or with what modifications)
- To determine satisfaction with a specific activity or rate it's quality
- To identify student opportunity to learn: What kind of and how much practice they are given

Step 2. Determine the topics or program components you wish to assess.

- Program Redesign
  o Curriculum—Content covered, skills taught, materials for differentiation, quality and accuracy of materials
  o Instruction—Specific strategies, specific direct instruction lessons, assignments, feedback, assessments
  o Staff Development—Quality of instruction, relevance, how adapted, when used and to what effect, challenges of implementing
- School Context
  o Classroom Climate—Student-teacher relations, positive support for student learning, respect, order
  o Safety
  o Student Behavior—Tardiness, absences, motivation, respect for other students and adults out of class
  o Staff level of preparedness, knowledge of content
  o Parent Involvement—Awareness of student grades, homework, learning challenges and successes, availability to volunteer, comfort in contacting school, feeling welcome and an integral part of the school community
  o Community Support—Resources available, interest in helping school, opinion of quality
- Question Sources—Your needs assessment questions for program redesign

Step 3. Determine the survey audience: teachers, parents, students, community, other.

Identification of the survey audience(s) will influence

- topics selected (audience needs to be familiar enough to respond);
- tone and language (avoid jargon with parents, students, and community);
- length (teachers and other professionals can probably tolerate longer surveys); and
- administration method.

Tool 6.4

Teacher Test Analysis Procedures

METHODS

Method 1: Class Profile of Skill Needs

- Prepare a "map" for each common assessment listing the skills assessed and the item numbers testing that skill.
- After you score all students' tests, organize them from high to low by total raw score (number correct).
- Go through the entire stack, one skill at a time, to identify the number of students missing a majority of items for that skill.
- Prepare a tally sheet by listing skills, and then put a tally mark in a summary box next to each skill for every student who misses the correct answer on a majority of the items testing that skill (e.g., three out of four). Once you have tallied all of the tests for Skill 1, repeat until all identified skills have been tallied.

Method 2. List of Students Needing Help

- Follow the same procedure of organizing tests from high to low score and examining data for one skill at a time.
- Instead of making a tally mark, write the names of the students struggling in a particular skill area.

Method 3. Summarize Student Test Analysis Forms

- Collect student test analysis forms after each test.
- Record students' self-reported weakest areas on your summary sheet.

This Common Assessments Skill Summary can be used for any of the three types of methods:

Section and Skill	Question Numbers Assessing This Skill	Summary of Students Doing Poorly on This Skill

---

Tool 6.5

Student Test Analysis Procedures

MY ITEM ANALYSIS: WHICH SKILLS DO I NEED TO IMPROVE?

At the end of this assignment, you will know exactly which kinds of questions proved difficult for you. Once you have completed your analysis, you will create a personal plan for improving your skills.

Step 1. Get your corrected answer sheet and circle all questions you missed.

Step 2. Use the chart below to record the number of questions you missed for each skill tested.

The skills the test assessed are listed in the left column of the chart. The numbers of the questions that test each skill are listed in the middle column. Refer to your answer sheet, and count the number of items you got **incorrect or didn't answer** for each skill. Remember that you may have to skip around to find all of the questions related to a skill.

Example: You missed questions 1, 3, 5, 6, 7, and 9 in Section 1. Your chart will look like this:

Section and Skill	Question Numbers	Number Missed
Section 1. Vocabulary Development		5
Identify and understand synonyms.	1, 2, 3, 4	2
Use general context clues.	5, 6, 7, 8	2
Use knowledge of Greek, Latin, and Anglo-Saxon word parts.	9, 10, 11, 12	1

Step 3. Identify the skills where you missed the most questions.

- Circle the **one skill** in each section where you had the most mistakes. If a skill is measured by only one item and you missed that question, you should circle the skill. If you had an equal number of mistakes on more than one skill, circle all skills with the highest number missed.
- Circle the **section** where you missed the most items.

You can use this Test Analysis form to tally your skills and error numbers.

MAJOR DECISIONS FOR DEVELOPING AND IMPLEMENTING THE TURNAROUND PLAN

The major leadership team management decisions for developing and implementing your plan involve what you will do to help your teams understand what a Turnaround Plan is and how to use it to push your work ahead.

- How is a Turnaround Plan different from previous school improvement or strategic plans?
- How do we best make explicit our theory of action?
- How does the theory of action help us develop our Turnaround Plan?
- What do we need to monitor our turnaround activities?
- Who will administer the management plan and keep us moving?
- Have we considered a range of challenges that might arise and strategies for handling them?
- How will we document our successful efforts for replication?

HELPFUL INFORMATION FROM PREVIOUS CHAPTERS

As we build in activities to monitor our work, we are entering data collection and evaluation territory. In Chapters 2 and 3, we spent a good amount of time covering the collection and review of data for plan development. In this chapter, we covered how some of these strategies will be used again in plan implementation. Three monitoring strategies you will want to build into your Turnaround Plan appear in Chapter 2 and in the Chapter 2 Toolkit. Use of these tools helps to monitor the quality of program implementation and to provide data for midcourse corrections in curriculum, instruction, and staff development.

Tool 2.3 Program Quality: Assignment Rigor

Tool 2.4 Program Quality: Protocols for Looking at Student Work

Tool 2.5 Program Quality: Classroom Walk-Through Guidelines

LEADERSHIP CHALLENGES

The major leadership challenges of developing and implementing your Turnaround Plan lie in building ownership and understanding of the theory of action and its implications for action. These are as follows:

- **Basing your design on a theory of action.** A theory of action diagram showing your hypothesized cause-and-effect relationships for turnaround activities is simple and intuitive. However, it is not a planning strategy much used in schools, and it may seem contrived to staff. We find it easiest to identify end-of-course, semester, or grade-level outcomes as the first step in our diagram, and then have staff propose the connection to long-term outcomes. We enter those short- and long-term outcomes into a diagram, connect them with an arrow, and then move on to the "causes." Soon it's clear that the theory of action diagram is a quick distillation of the work we plan to do; it shows links to expected results and becomes less an academic exercise than a heuristic model for our turnaround work.

- **Lack of data for making redesign decisions.** Most schools do not have comprehensive data collection systems to inform them about student attitudes, opportunities to learn, school climate, parent attitudes, or even staff expertise levels. When confronted with the need for information, make a note that you will want to build data collection for these needs into your turnaround work. Meanwhile, you can convene focus groups, ask them a few open-ended questions, and note results. Or you can sample a group of parents with a telephone survey, create a brief and easily tallied student survey, and/or rely on teacher experience to fill in gaps.

- **Understanding that implementation of a shared vision is not a scripted curriculum.** Implementation is not "following the scripted curriculum." It does require, however, that all participants commit to the same goals and incorporate and adapt some of the same teaching strategies, student engagement techniques, assignment types, and assessments. These are subtle distinctions, and without some experience in implementing the shared vision and experience in how that vision can be maintained while it is adapted by individuals to fit their styles and students needs, you could find resistance or grumbling about the "scripted curriculum." Administrators, coaches, and staff development specialists need to help teachers understand the difference between buy-in and consistency, on the one hand, and loss of professional autonomy on the other.

SELECTED RESOURCES TO SUPPORT YOUR WORK

Coaching to implement program change—*Results Coaching: The New Essential for School Leaders,* by Kathryn Kee, Karen Anderson, Vicky Dearing, Frances Shuster, and Edna Harris (Corwin, 2010). We are strong believers that the best administrative support for teacher change is coaching (not necessarily by the administrator!). This new publication provides an overview of the coaching process as it unfolds at schools. Topics include building trust, confidence, and competence; thinking processes that move people to action; considering multiple options; and clarifying goals.

Documenting teaching practice—*The Teaching Performance Record,* by CaseNEX LLC and the University of Virginia (2009). The TPR is a research-based observation checklist and classroom observation system that can be used to document teaching practices and teacher reflection on practice. Important variables include lesson planning, student engagement, feedback, assessment, and monitoring. The TPR can record data digitally for instantaneous data analysis and longitudinal comparisons. You can see the Teaching Performance Record in action at http://tpr.casenex.com/case/#sec1, where there is a demonstration of how the observation and checklist are used.

Monitoring program implementation—*How to Assess Program Implementation, by* Jean A. King et al. (Sage, 1987). This handbook is for the do-it-yourself evaluation team wishing to develop monitoring measures to assess program quality. It's old enough to be a classic and relevant enough to be a must-have. We like the sections linking the monitoring strategies to evaluation questions and data analysis methods.

Strategies for monitoring student progress—*Scoring Rubrics in the Classroom,* by Judith Arter and Jay McTighe; *Implementing Student Led Conferences,* by Jane M. Bailey and Thomas Guskey; *Developing Grading and Reporting Systems for Student Learning,* by Thomas S. Guskey and Jane M. Bailey; *Natural Classroom Assessment,* by Jeffrey K. Smith, Lisa F. Smith, and Richard De Lisi. All four are part of the *Experts in Assessment Series,* edited by Thomas Guskey and Robert J. Marzano (Corwin, 2001). These four volumes in a series designed to make assessment understandable to practitioners provide another do-it-yourself resource for groups focusing on specific strategies to monitor student progress.

Leader's Guide

7

Design an Evaluation of the Turnaround Plan

CHAPTER 7 POCKET SUMMARY

POCKET SUMMARY

Task	Major Activities	Purpose
Understand the role of evaluation in turnaround work.	• Evaluation distinguishes turnaround work from less-urgent reform. • The turnaround evaluation is formative. • The elements of evaluation design.	• Understand multiple uses of formative evaluation.
Identify evaluation questions.	• Start with the theory of action or Turnaround Plan. **Tool 7.1 Formative Evaluation Questions for a Turnaround Plan** • Make questions specific to your work. • Consider a range of questions; then prioritize. **Tool 7.2 Template for Prioritizing Evaluation Questions**	• Use your theory of action and/or your Turnaround Plan to develop evaluation questions.
Create a sampling plan.	• Decide whether you need a comparison group. • Consider sampling versus census data collection.	• Consider how generalizable you need your evaluation results to be. • Determine from whom you need to collect data.
Select or develop measures to address evaluation questions.	• Identify the data needed. • Consider a range of measures or data sources. **Tool 7.3 Advantages and Limitations of Common Data Collection Techniques** • Create blueprints or specifications for instrument development or selection. **Tool 7.4 Blueprint Components for Common Measures** **Tool 7.5 Test Evaluation Criteria for Published Achievement Tests** • Employ multipurpose measures. • Use multiple measures when feasible. • Consider trade-offs between feasibility and credibility in selecting instruments. • Convert measures into monitoring activities.	• Select or develop measures and data collection strategies.
Specify data analysis strategies and decision rules.	• Plan data analysis strategies for summarizing and interpreting data. • Establish decision rules for judging implementation quality and student progress.	• Choose data summary strategies that answer questions. • Know in advance what success means.

Task	Major Activities	Purpose
Flesh out the management plan.	• Review and revise the Turnaround Plan management activities. **Tool 7.6 Template for a Data Collection Management Plan** • Distribute responsibility for data collection. • Avoid preventable data collection disasters. **Tool 7.7 A Catalog of Data Collection Disasters**	• Identify management activities to support data collection and analysis, and embed them in Turnaround Plan.
Document your evaluation design.	**Tool 7.8 Template for a Formative Evaluation Design**	• Document plans, and establish checklist of evaluation tasks that need to be completed.

THUMBNAILS OF TOOLS FROM THIS CHAPTER

The following tools can be found on the companion website for *The TurnAround ToolKit* at http://www.corwin.com/turnaroundtoolkit.

Tool 7.1
Formative Evaluation Questions for a Turnaround Plan

Program Implementation Quality
- How do the activities "look" when implemented?
- What is the range of implementation quality? What does minimal or poor implementation look like? What does high quality look like, or even implementation adapted to work better than originally planned?
- What factors contribute to well-implemented activities? What barriers to implementation occur?
- How do teachers view staff development activities? What has affected their teaching practice? What has not? What changes would need to occur before staff development affected teaching practice?
- What changes in teaching do you observe? In student engagement? In assignments? Assessments? Class or school climate? Student skill acquisition?
- What activities improved parent understanding of the program or involvement?

Student Progress
- How well are students acquiring the skills transmitted in the redesigned program? What learning problems continue to occur? Why might this be so?

Linkages With Theory of Action
- What is the relationship between specific redesign activities and student short-term outcomes?
- What is the relationship between specific changes in staff expertise, parent involvement, student behavior, and so on and student short-term outcomes?

Tool 7.2
Template for Prioritizing Evaluation Questions

Program Component and Question	Rank 1 Required	Rank 2 Essential and Immediate	Rank 3 Essential but Not Time Sensitive	Rank 4 Nice to Know

Tool 7.3
Advantages and Limitations of Common Data Collection Techniques

Surveys or Questionnaires	
Advantages	**Limitations**
Can probe several aspects of a program on one measure	Depth of information sometimes sacrificed for breadth
Comments can be anonymous; therefore more candid	Respondents may provide responses they think are socially desirable rather than their true opinions
Questions are standardized for all respondents	Questions may mean different things to different respondents
Opportunity to add comments can provide specific suggestions for improvement	Respondents often provide more information orally than in writing
Can be administered electronically	Require literacy and/or access to computer
If respondents are limited to a choice from a selected set of responses, measures are easily scored	
Interviews	
Advantages	**Limitations**
Can be done by phone at times convenient to respondents	Costly and time-consuming
Allow people who can't read or don't use a computer to participate	May need to find bilingual interviewers
Provide flexibility and depth if probing questions are asked	Interviewer could influence responses
Observations	
Advantages	**Limitations**
Observers themselves learn (such as teachers observing other teachers' lessons)	Must be done in an atmosphere of trust
Reveal what is actually happening, not what is reported to happen	Presence of observers may influence classroom practice
Help develop a shared understanding of the program	Costly: scheduling, release time, training

Tool 7.4
Blueprint Components for Common Measures

Data Type	Blueprint Information
Student selected or brief response assessment	• Content to be sampled • Concepts and skills to be assessed • Item format • Rules for writing distractors • Number of items per skill • Total number of items
Student essay or performance assessment	• Content to be sampled • Concepts and skills to be assessed • Rubric scale • Type of rubric: holistic versus analytic • Rubric dimensions
Student, teacher, parent self-report survey	• Concepts and topics to be assessed • Response scale • Number of items per topic/concept • Number of items per survey
Archival data: student information system (attendance, grades)	• Kind of data • Rules for data collection • Data calculation (if applies) • Data verification method
Archival data: documents (teaching guides, lesson plans, etc.)	• Kind of data • Topics and themes to review • How data will be summarized
Archival data: records from online learning modules	• Content, skills • Time allocated for module • Number practice items • How items are scored or feedback is provided

Tool 7.5

Test Evaluation Criteria for Published Achievement Tests

Criterion	Review Questions
Instructional Contribution	Is there a teacher-friendly assessment description providing unambiguous descriptions of the skills and knowledge tested?
	Can the assessment description and score reports be used for planning, monitoring, or evaluating instruction?
Validity	What evidence is there that the *content* reflects the grade-level standards or domain being assessed? Look at the content sampling plan, test blueprints/specifications, and item development rules, and compare these with your curriculum emphases.
	What evidence is there that the skill or *construct* underlying the test is assessed? Look for a series of experiments using the test or criterion-group correlational studies that show the presence or absence of the construct either before or after treatment or in the criterion groups.
	What evidence is there that the test predicts other valued outcomes? Look for evidence of correlational studies (correlation coefficients) between test scores and other assessments, similar assessments, grades, and other indicators.
	What evidence is there that instructional decisions based on the scores have led to accurate inferences? For example, have students been placed correctly using the test?
Reliability	What evidence exists, in the form of an internal consistency correlation coefficient (for example, the Kuder Richardson or KR-20 reliability score), that the items are all measuring a similar construct or quality?
	What evidence is there that students classified into different categories—for example, pass/fail, Proficient/Basic—are accurately placed? What is the ratio of false positives to false negatives at important cut points?
	What evidence, in the form of a correlation coefficient and equal means and standard deviations, exists that this form of the test is equivalent in difficulty to an "alternate form" (if you are indeed using an alternate form)?
	How much do student scores fluctuate over time when taking this test on repeated occasions (without intervening instruction)?

(Continued)

Tool 7.6

Template for a Data Collection Management Plan

Measure	Measure Name _____		Measure Name _____		Measure Name _____		Measure Name _____		Measure Name _____	
Sampling Plan (circle plan for each measure)	Sampling method • All • Random • Stratified random • Purposive • Group		Sampling method • All • Random • Stratified random • Purposive • Group		Sampling method • All • Random • Stratified random • Purposive • Group		Sampling method • All • Random • Stratified random • Purposive • Group		Sampling method • All • Random • Stratified random • Purposive • Group	
	Person	Timeline	Person	Timeline	Person	Timeline	Person	Timeline	Person	Timeline
Select/Purchase										
Create Blueprints/ Write Items										
Produce										
Schedule Administration										
Precode										

(Continued)

Tool 7.7

A Catalog of Data Collection Disasters

DISASTER #1. MEASUREMENT MAYHEM

Useful test or survey results are grounded in well-written, unambiguous questionnaire, interview, or test items aligned to detailed blueprints that describe exactly what is being assessed. Before you are mugged by your measures, be sure to review them for clarity, relevance, and bias. Although you alone can find something lacking in nearly every test or survey item you review, do try to get others with different educational levels (parent surveys), cultural perspectives, or reading ability to review your measures as well. The purpose of the review is to be sure you are presenting respondents with tasks they will interpret similarly to the way you interpret them. Educators tend to use jargon terms such as *restructuring, literacy, at risk* (or even *turnaround*) that might have different meanings to different audiences. It is much better to discover that some questions are ambiguous before data collection than after. Building in a review process for your instruments not only minimizes chances that you will have to throw out some questions but also helps you find potentially biased or offensive questions.

A biased question is one to which students of identical ability who have had similar instructional experiences respond to differently. Biased questions are difficult to identify until you are wildly different responses to an item for different groups, such as males versus females. Truly biased items are rare, and all subject-matter test items are biased against students who have had no instruction in that particular topic. However, item reviews can be quite effective in finding offensive items. Items that present racial or gender stereotypes or that delve into potentially embarrassing issues should be revised. Good examples of potentially offensive yet commonly occurring survey items are those about parent education levels. If parents have had little education, students or parents may find it embarrassing to answer that parents have not completed elementary school, much less high school, and may give inaccurate responses.

DISASTER #2. LANGUAGE LANDMINES

The instructions for tests, phone surveys, and online surveys need to be clear and unambiguous. Words such as *indicate* are not as effective as phrases such as *circle the response* or *write your answer in the space below*. While you might use directions for assessment and survey tasks as being quite clear, respondents are certain to find ambiguities and loopholes you never anticipated. Whenever possible, have a staff member, hopefully your most contentious, read data collection directions to identify potential ambiguities.

DISASTER #3. DILETTANTE DATA COLLECTORS

Too many of us skim test or survey instructions and say to ourselves, "yeah, yeah, this is just like last year." Others of us don't read administration guidelines in advance and are literally one paragraph

Tool 7.8

Template for a Formative Evaluation Design

Formative Evaluation Design (Your Focus Here):

Evaluation Questions	Data Needed	Data Source	Sample	Data Collection Strategy	Criteria for Judging Progress

MAJOR DECISIONS FOR DESIGNING AN EVALUATION OF THE TURNAROUND PLAN

The major leadership team management decisions for designing your evaluation involve determining what the formative evaluation process will look like and who will design and implement it.

- Who should be included in the evaluation design process? All staff? The data team? An outside expert?
- Who should manage the evaluation work and coordinate it with the turnaround program implementation activities?
- How do we best use our theory of action diagram and Turnaround Plan activities to identify important and specific formative evaluation questions?
- Should we assess all teachers, parents, and students with our program quality and student progress monitoring measures, or should we sample some groups, all groups?

- What exactly are the best measures to answer our evaluation questions, which should reflect our program quality and student progress monitoring needs?
- How do we get multiple uses from a single survey, classroom walk-through, review of student work, or even review of student assessment data so as to reduce the testing burden?
- Who should be responsible for finding, selecting, and/or developing measures?
- Who should be responsible for setting up administration procedures, distributing measures, collecting the measures, scoring the tests, and storing the data?
- When in the design process do we need expert help? Where can we get the help?
- How do we use our expert reviewers, critical friends, and benchmark school partners to help collect or review monitoring data?
- Who should be responsible for integrating the measures identified for the evaluation design into the Turnaround Plan? For updating the management plan?

LEADERSHIP CHALLENGES

The major leadership challenges in designing your formative evaluation involve issues of capacity and resources. These include the following:

- **Balancing the need for evaluation and measurement expertise with the need for staff to understand how evaluation fits with turnaround work.** The evaluation design is a framework for understanding how to continuously improve practice and allow students to continuously improve their skills. Evaluation also requires some understanding of research methods, threats to the validity of research findings, what constitutes useful formative evaluation questions, how to find or develop measures with an acceptable level of reliability and validity, and how data from the measures can be summarized and used. The obvious personnel for the evaluation task are experts from the district, a university, or the school's data team. However, many of the evaluator's habits of mind need to be incorporated into teaching practice. Thus, striking a balance between getting the evaluation created correctly and bringing staff along so they buy into the monitoring strategies and willingly support data-collection activities is a major challenge. One approach is to use some of the activities in *Building Evaluation Capacity* (Preskill & Russ-Eft, 2005) with your expert as a facilitator to bring teachers along and reduce resistance to evaluation work.

- **Finding surveys, monitoring tests, and other important measures— make or buy?** While you should avoid the "if it moves, measure it" approach to turnaround monitoring, you will find that you are collecting data more systematically on a wider variety of topics more frequently than your staff is used to. Again, a balancing act. And where do you get all those neat tests? We like the sources listed in the Chapter 6 Leader's Guide: the *CSE Evaluation Kit* and the *Experts in Assessment Series* for creating your own measures, and the *Teaching Performance Record* for published and available-for-purchase surveys. The Internet has sources, as does your local federally subsidized regional educational laboratory (http://ies.ed.gov/ncee/edlabs/). When teachers participate in creating student assessment blueprints and tests, or when they use blueprints to create tests, they learn a lot about what the standards mean, about the kinds of learning problems students have when they don't answer correctly (because these are revealed by selection of distractors on multiple-choice items), and about how high-quality work is defined in various subjects (through the development of scoring rubrics).

• **Managing the evaluation and the turnaround work.** There is much to like about having the same person or team responsible for managing the turnaround implementation, including monitoring activities, and the evaluation work of data collection, storage, summarization, and analysis. However, you may not have the budget to release one or more staff members for the job or to hire experts. Err on the side of developing capacity and using available resources (the district, the county, the state) in new and clever ways.

SELECTED RESOURCES TO SUPPORT YOUR WORK

Helping staff understand evaluation—*Building Evaluation Capacity: 72 Activities for Teaching and Training,* by Hallie Preskill and Darlene Russ-Eft (Sage, 2005). Use 1 or use all 72 of the activities to help teachers understand what evaluation is and how it can help them improve teaching and learning. It's all in this book, ready to use right out of the box. Some of the intriguing topics include evaluation politics and ethics; multicultural and cross-cultural aspects of evaluation; evaluation models, approaches, and design; building and sustaining support for evaluation; and reflections on learning. The bread-and-butter aspects of evaluation are all there as well: focusing the evaluation, issues of validity and sampling, collecting evaluation data, analyzing data, reporting, and managing the evaluation.

Identifying suitable tests for monitoring student progress—*Benchmark Assessment for Improved Learning,* by Joan Herman, Ellen Osmundson, and Ron Dietel (CRESST, 2010), available at www.cse .ucla.edu/products/policy/R2_benchmark_report_Herman.pdf. Use this resource to understand the purposes of benchmark assessments and how to select and use them to improve students' learning. The report also presents recommendations for building districts' and schools' capacity to use the data.

Designing surveys and survey software—QuestionPro (www.question pro.com), StatPac (www.statpac.com), and Survey Monkey (www.survey monkey.com) are in the business of selling statistical software. Their products and statistical analysis software are most likely more complex than you need for your formative evaluation work. However, their websites have free advice on how to word survey questions and responses and how to plan a survey project (they call it a questionnaire project) as well as free survey analysis software. Survey Monkey is widely used in K–12 settings, QuestionPro in higher education. The price is right, and the free advice is accurate and consistent among the three sites.

Designing a formative evaluation—*Evaluator's Handbook,* by Joan L. Herman, Lynn Lyons-Morris, and Carol Taylor Fitz-Gibbon (Sage, 1987). The handbook consists of brief descriptions of all evaluation activities in the order they occur for formative and summative evaluations. Chapter 3, "Conducting a Formative Evaluation," is a hip-pocket guide to turnaround monitoring and management activities. All steps are included: focusing the evaluation, selecting methods, collecting and analyzing information, and reporting findings.

Leader's Guide

8

Analyze Evaluation Data and Revise the Program

CHAPTER 8 POCKET SUMMARY

<table>
<tr><td colspan="3" align="center">**POCKET SUMMARY**</td></tr>
<tr><td>**Task**</td><td>**Major Activities**</td><td>**Purpose**</td></tr>
<tr>
<td>Analyze evaluation data.</td>
<td>

- Know the score (meaning).
  Tool 8.1 Score Summary Methods for Common Measures
- Summarize results for each measure using descriptive statistics.
  Tool 8.2 Descriptive Statistics for Common Measures
</td>
<td>

- Transform raw data so that it is more useful in addressing evaluation questions.
</td>
</tr>
<tr>
<td>Create data tables and displays.</td>
<td>

- Consolidate data related to the same evaluation question.
  Tool 8.3 Mapping Measures to Evaluation Questions for Data Analysis
- Summarize data in multiple ways.
- Summarize evidence of practical significance.
</td>
<td>

- Simplify the presentation of multiple measures related to the same question.
</td>
</tr>
<tr>
<td>Refine the program: Make midcourse corrections.</td>
<td>

- Check to be sure you are implementing the program.
- Identify indicators sensitive to short-term redesign activities.
- Check the relationships in your theory of action.
- Use data to make midcourse corrections.
</td>
<td>

- Achieve the rapid-fire experimentation cycle.
</td>
</tr>
<tr>
<td>Revise the program.</td>
<td>

- Annually examine long-term impact.
- Begin your yearly review by judging findings in terms of prespecified criteria.
- Look at trends over time.
- Corroborate findings with multiple indicators.
- Examine subgroup performance.
- Test relationships in your theory of action.
- Revise to address weaknesses.
- Revise to build upon strengths.
- Consider a new plan.
</td>
<td>

- Revise and redesign annually.
</td>
</tr>
<tr>
<td>Communicate the results of your turnaround efforts to stakeholders.</td>
<td>

Tool 8.4 Communication Considerations

- Base communication on audience needs.
- Plan to provide data for formal reports.
- Incorporate reporting activities into your Turnaround Plan.

Tool 8.5 Communications Calendar Template
</td>
<td>

- Build support for your work.
</td>
</tr>
</table>

THUMBNAILS OF TOOLS FROM THIS CHAPTER

The following tools can be found on the companion website for *The TurnAround ToolKit* at http://www.corwin.com/turnaroundtoolkit.

Tool 8.1

Score Summary Methods for Common Measures

Evaluation Question	Measure	Type of Score	Summary Method
Did our students increase in proficiency this year?	Standards-based state or commercial test	Scale score; Percentage scoring in each proficiency category	Graph or table providing two-year comparison of percentage scoring Proficient or higher
How do our students compare to national norms?	Published norm-referenced test	Percentile rank, stanine, NCE score	Graph or table comparing scale or NCE scores for your students and comparison group
What do teachers, students, parents report is occurring? What are student, teacher, parent attitudes toward program?	Survey	Percentages responding at positive end of scale or negative end of scale; Average ratings	Graph or table showing percentage choosing each survey rating for each question; Graph or table with mean score for each question; List of comments arranged from most to least frequent
What challenges do we face implementing the program?	Walk-throughs with structure observation; Case study notes; Notes from teacher meetings	Tally of issues observed	Table with list of issues and frequency; Chart of topics raised in discussion or notes or in observations, which is then organized by recorder
What learning issues do students face?	Classroom common assessments (selected response)	Item difficulty analysis: percentage answering each item correctly	List of items with percentage answering correctly and percentage choosing each distractor

Tool 8.2

Descriptive Statistics for Common Measures

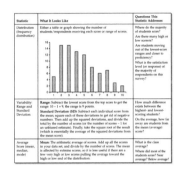

Statistic	What It Looks Like	Questions This Statistic Addresses
Distribution (frequency distribution)	Either a table or graph showing the number of students/respondents receiving each score or range of scores.	Where do the majority of students score? Are there many high or low scorers? Are students moving out of the lowest-score ranges and closer to proficiency? What is the satisfaction level (or response) of the majority of respondents on this survey?
Variability: Range and Standard Deviation	**Range:** Subtract the lowest score from the top score to get the range: $10 - 1 = 9$; the range is 9 points. **Standard Deviation (SD):** Subtract each individual score from the mean, square each of these deviations to get rid of negative numbers. Then add up the squared deviations, and divide the total by the number of scores (or the number of scores − 1 for an unbiased estimate). Finally, take the square root of the result (which is essentially the average of the squared deviations from the mean score).	How much difference exists between the highest- and lowest-scoring students? On the average, how far away are students from the mean (average) score?
Average Score (mean, median, mode)	**Mean:** The arithmetic average of scores. Add up all the scores in your data set, and divide by the number of scores. The mean is affected by extreme scores, so it is less useful if there are a few very high or very low scores pulling the average toward the high or low end of the distribution.	What is the class average? Where did most of the students score? Near average? Below average?

Tool 8.3

Mapping Measures to Evaluation Questions for Data Analysis

Evaluation Question	Measure	Analysis: Data Summary or Display Method	Contextual Information to Use in Data Interpretation
Generic: Replace with local questions.	• Data source or data collection strategy	• Which score (raw, percentage, or transformed) will you use? • Which score results will be reported: averages, distributions, parts of distributions, such as highest and lowest "scores"? • How will results be summarized: table or graph contents?	• Unusual circumstances in test administration • Low survey response rates • Measure not well aligned with outcomes • Lack of expertise of classroom observers
Are turnaround activities being implemented as planned? List specific program redesign turnaround activities.	• Classroom assignment rigor • Student work samples • Classroom walk-through data • Sample lesson plans • Revised pacing charts • Student Opportunity to Learn surveys • Teacher Opportunity to Learn surveys		
Are students progressing toward meeting grade-level or course-specific outcomes? Insert additional rows of this chart for each separate outcome reported.	• Student work samples • District- or school-level common assessments • Classroom formative assessments		

Tool 8.4

Communication Considerations

Audience	Key Concerns	Reporting Considerations
Teachers	• Are we implementing the turnaround changes as intended? • Are our efforts working? • Are students improving? • Is my practice changing in ways I think it is?	• Present descriptive information • Provide context linked with data • Present multiple data sources
Students	• How did I do on the test? • What did other students say on the survey?	• Provide brief, student-centered information
Parents	• How is my student doing? • How does this school compare to others? • Are students from this school successful at the next level? • What resources exist to help my struggling student? • What enrichment are you providing my talented student? • Is my student happy at school?	• Present data clearly and simply • Avoid jargon • Provide anecdotes and examples • Provide balanced picture, no spin
Principal Supervisors	• Will the school make its accountability targets? • Is the school safe, are classes well managed, and are students respectful? • Do parents want to send students to the school? • Is the principal effective at supervising teachers and instruction? • Are teachers competent and effective? • How can the school improve?	• Explain the why and how of outcomes • Provide information on how to replicate success • Present multiple data sources, descriptive information
School Board	• Does the community think the school is effective? • Do parents want to send students to the school? • Is the school meeting accountability goals? • Are we hearing good things on the street about the school? • How can the school improve?	• Provide politically important comparisons • Describe progress and its causes • Present only robust findings (can't handle all of the qualifications of formal research studies) • Present balanced picture, no spin • Avoid too much information (gather questions ahead of report)

Tool 8.5

Communications Calendar Template

Audience	Report Purpose and Audience Key Concerns	Formal Report Annual Progress Report Technical or Research Report Newsletter or Press Release	Date	Informal Report Oral Presentation One-Page Summaries or Data Sheets	Date
Outside authority: grant officer, state oversight officer, and so forth					
Board of Education					
District Administration					
School-Level Administration					
Students					

MAJOR DECISIONS FOR ANALYZING EVALUATION DATA AND REVISING THE PROGRAM

The major leadership team management decisions related to data analysis and program revision are shown in the box below.

- How do we improve data credibility if we have informal measures or assessments with unknown psychometric properties?
- What are the best strategies for presenting data so that they will be clear and informative?
- What are the variations and adaptations in program implementation we observe?
- How do implementation variations relate to differences in student achievement?
- What is working well? How do we know?
- Where are students struggling? How do we know?
- How has our experience altered our theory of action?
- What program redesign is needed for the next cycle?
- With whom do we share our struggles, progress, and results to engage support or improve credibility? How? When?

LEADERSHIP CHALLENGES

Leadership challenges associated with data analysis and program revision again focus on issues of capacity, ownership, and consensus on moving forward to greater improvement:

- **Finding data summarization expertise.** Summarizing data, selecting a scoring or score transformation method, creating distributions and averages, and calculating correlations is anathema (cursed, detested, loathed) to many people. However, it's one of those skills that is really straightforward and becomes comfortable with practice. Nevertheless, you may wish to have an expert help with data summarization and creation of tables and displays. We would urge you to transfer that expertise to your school data team or an eager staff member or two, because knowledge of data summarization is crucial to the discussions you will have about midcourse corrections and program revisions.

- **Being overwhelmed with tasks: data collection, meetings, communication.** Because a book is linear, it doesn't capture the number of simultaneous events that occur during turnaround work: changing practice; trying new materials; meeting to review assignments, student work, and classroom observation notes; summarizing data; talking about what the results suggest; revising your work along the way; communicating with important audiences; and all while doing the jobs each of you were hired to do, most likely with fewer staff, less time, and maybe less money. If you are getting well funded for your turnaround activities, spend time charting the simultaneous tasks, the need for expertise, and the need for extra hands to summarize data, make tables, and write meeting summaries; and consider how you can get additional personnel. Management never became so important!

• **Facilitating program refinement and program revision discussions.** There is an art to helping people use data to guide changes. Data discussions are greatly enhanced when you select a fitting protocol to guide your work. You might consult *The Power of Protocols,* by Joseph P. McDonald and others (Teachers College Press, 2007), the website of the National School Reform Faculty (www.nsrfharmony.org/resources.html), or one of the many educational consulting groups offering training in group facilitation.

• **Building consensus, ownership, and support.** Yes, here we are again: It can be difficult to reach consensus on what the data mean and their implications for action. No new strategies here—draw on the ones that have been successful in your setting thus far.

SELECTED RESOURCES TO SUPPORT YOUR WORK

Understanding practical significance—*Practical Significance: A Concept Whose Time Has Come,* by Roger E. Kirk (1996). Don't let the seemingly technical title scare you. For those of us with a statistical (mis)education, Dr. Kirk's explanation of the difference between statistical and practical significance will set you free of rules that need to be broken. A seminal article.

Education and the media—*Reports for Journalists,* Hechinger Institute on Education and the Media, available from http://hechinger .squarespace.com/guides-for-journalist. Led by Richard Lee Colvin, journalist and former education reporter for the *Los Angeles Times,* the Hechinger Institute provides training to reporters in educational journalism. If you don't know about the Hechinger Institute at Columbia University, get to know them. This institute provides training and guides for media personnel covering education. They are school friendly and they write well, and you would do well to read what reporters are being told about how to understand leadership, research, classrooms, teaching, and other topics that constitute our work. A good insight into public concerns and how to build bridges with your local press and community.

Student outcomes—*The Data Guidebook for Teachers and Leaders: Tools for Continuous Improvement,* by Eileen Depka (Sage, 2006). Chapters 3 through 9 provide both tools for discussing data and explanations of how to develop, summarize, and use a variety of measures for improving your program. Specific measures discussed include standardized and state assessments, district assessments, and holistic and analytic rubrics. The focus is on using student outcome measures, but the discussion guidelines can be used for any assessment.

Data collection and analysis—*Just Plain Data Analysis: Finding, Presenting, and Interpreting Social Science Data,* by Gary M. Klass (Rowman & Littlefield, 2008) and its companion website: http://lilt.ilstu.edu/jpda.

We like Dr. Klass's work and his website. Even though his background is in social science, the principles presented apply. The book includes chapters on indicators, tables and charts, measuring educational achievement, and finding the data. The chapters on voting and measuring inequality, although not strictly on topic for us, have lessons for data collection and analysis at schools.

Using school data—*Schools and Data: The Educator's Guide for Using Data to Improve Decision Making* (2nd ed.), by Theodore B. Creighton (Corwin, 2007). Buy it. Read it along with this chapter. It provides a more traditional statistics guide with analyses beyond what you will need to analyze school-level data. Comprehensive but accessible, it is a step-by-step, easy-to-follow, easy-to-understand guide to using existing school data. We find Chapters 1 through 4 most relevant to our work with statistics in schools, collecting and organizing data and using correlation. (Testing the theory of action requires some correlation or regression analysis.) There is a chapter explaining regression that is important to understand, as value-added models are regression models. The chapters on inferential statistics, *t*-test, ANOVA, and so forth are for experimental research, but still good to know when reading and critiquing research articles.

Endnotes

Foreword

1. The forthcoming report is an update of *How the World's Best-Performing School Systems Come Out on Top,* available at http://www.mckinsey.com/client service/Social_Sector/our_practices/Education/Knowledge_Highlights/Best_performing_school.aspx.

Introduction

1. Calkins, Guenther, Belfiore, & Lash, 2007, p. 8.

2. Schmoker, 1999.

Chapter 1

1. Hord & Sommers, 2007.

2. Harris, 2002.

3. Harris, 2002; Portin, Schneider, De Armond, & Gundlach, 2003.

4. Kaser, Mundry, Stiles, & Loucks-Horsley, 2002.

5. McDonald, Mohr, Dichter, & McDonald, 2007, p. 24.

6. Center for Collaborative Education, n.d.

7. McDonald, Mohr, Dichter, & McDonald, 2007, p. 25.

8. Hite-Mills, 2007.

9. Preskill & Russ-Eft, 2005, pp. 150–153.

Chapter 3

1. We use the term *address* because sometimes data don't answer questions, but instead raise new questions (full employment for data collectors!).

2. The term "rapid-fire experimentation" is taken from an article in *Education Next* titled "The Big U Turn," by Emily A. Hassel and Bryan C. Hassel. It captures the pace, attitude, and content of turnaround work.

3. Klass, 2008.

Chapter 5

1. The terms *theory of action* and *theory of change* are often used interchangeably to refer to an underlying cause-and-effect explanation of how what we are doing is expected to cause our intended outcomes. When theories of action or change are formalized and used to guide program development or evaluation design, they are called *logic models.*

2. Pedagogical content knowledge identifies the distinctive bodies of knowledge for teaching. It represents the blending of content and pedagogy into an understanding of how particular topics, problems, or issues are organized, represented, and adapted to the diverse interests and abilities of learners, and presented for instruction. Pedagogical content knowledge is the category most likely to distinguish the understanding of the content specialist from that of the pedagogue (Shulman, 1987, p. 4).

Chapter 6

1. Schmoker, 2003.

Chapter 7

1. With respect to turnaround, the terms *work, activities,* and *plan* are used interchangeably in this book. We are trying to avoid making the plan a focus of our efforts and want to redirect attention to the turnaround actions, which are listed in the plan but certainly are not guaranteed to occur just because we have a plan.

2. We use the term *theory of action* throughout this book, as it is an older and more commonly used term in educational reform than *logic model.* In fact, the term *logic model* is preferred in all large-scale federal evaluations. Logic models are required by most federal grants as part of the evaluation design, and creating them is a thriving industry for the professoriate. We suggest you use the term *logic model* to describe your theory of action diagram whenever a potential funder visits with an intention to fund your efforts. It's guaranteed to impress!

Chapter 9

1. Duke, 2006.

2. Marsh, Pane, & Hamilton, 2006.

3. Popham, 2009.

4. The Broad Prize for Urban Education was established in 2002 by Los Angeles philanthropists Eli and Edythe Broad with four goals: (1) Reward districts that improve achievement levels of disadvantaged students. (2) Restore the public's confidence in our nation's public schools by highlighting successful urban districts. (3) Create competition and provide incentives for districts to improve. (4) Showcase the best practices of successful districts. The prize is the largest education award in the country given to school districts. It is awarded each year to honor urban school districts that demonstrate the greatest overall performance and improvement in student achievement while reducing achievement gaps among low-income and minority students.

Resources and References

American Educational Research Association (AERA), American Psychological Association (APA), and National Council on Measurement in Education (NCME). (1999). *The standards for educational and psychological testing.* Washington, DC: American Educational Research Association.

Arter, J., & McTighe, J. (2001). *Scoring rubrics in the classroom.* In T. Guskey & R. Marzano (Series Eds.), *Experts in Assessment Series.* Thousand Oaks, CA: Corwin.

Bailey, J. M., & Guskey, T. (2001). *Implementing student led conferences.* In T. Guskey & R. Marzano (Series Eds.), *Experts in Assessment Series.* Thousand Oaks, CA: Corwin.

Baker, E. L. (2003, Summer). Multiple measures: Toward tiered systems. *Educational Measurement: Issues & Practice, 22*(2), 13–17.

Baker, E. L. (2005). Aligning curriculum, standards, and assessments: Fulfilling the promise of school reform. In C. A. Dwyer (Ed.), *Measurement and research in the accountability era* (pp. 315–335). Mahwah, NJ: Erlbaum.

Baker, E. L., & Linn, R. L. (2004). Validity issues for accountability systems. In S. Fuhrman & R. Elmore (Eds.), *Redesigning accountability systems for education* (pp. 47–72). New York: Teachers College Press.

Ball, D. L. (1992). *Implementing the NCTM standards.* Retrieved from ncrtl.msu.edu/http/ipapers/html/pdf/ip922.pdf

Ball, D. L. (1996). Teacher learning and the mathematics reforms: What we think we know and what we need to learn. *Phi Delta Kappan, 77,* 500–508.

Bloom, B. S., Hastings, J. T., & Madaus, G. F. (1971). *Handbook of formative and summative evaluation.* New York: McGraw-Hill.

Boudett, K. P., City, E. A., & Murnane, R. J. (Eds.). (2006). *Data wise: A step by step guide to using assessment results to improve teaching and learning.* Cambridge, MA: Harvard Education Press.

California Department of Education. (2009, June 9). *English language arts content standards for California public schools, kindergarten through grade twelve.* Retrieved from http://www.cde.ca.gov/be/st/ss/documents/elacontentstnds.pdf

Calkins, A., Guenther, W., Belfiore, G., & Lash, D. (2007). *The turnaround challenge: Why America's best opportunity to dramatically improve student achievement lies in our worst-performing schools.* Boston: Mass Insight Education and Research Institute.

CaseNEX LLC and University of Virginia. (2009). *Teaching performance record.* Retrieved from http://tpr.casenex.com/content/index.php

Center for Collaborative Education. (n.d.). *Setting norms for collaborative work.* Retrieved from http://www.turningpts.org/pdf/SettingNorms.pdf

Cohen, D. (1990). A revolution in one classroom: The case of Mrs. Oublier. *Educational Evaluation and Policy Analysis, 12*(3), 327–345.

Cohen, D., & Ball, D. (1990). Policy and practice: An overview. *Educational Evaluation and Policy Analysis, 12*(3), 347–353.

Creighton, T. B. (2007). *Schools and data: The educator's guide for using data to improve decision making* (2nd ed.). Thousand Oaks, CA: Corwin.

Darling-Hammond, L. (1995). Practices that support teacher development. *Phi Delta Kappan, 76*(8), 591–596.

Data Use for Improving Learning. A part of Assessment and Accountability Comprehensive Center. http://datause.cse.ucla.edu

Depka, E. (2006). *The data guidebook for teachers and leaders: Tools for continuous improvement.* Thousand Oaks, CA: Sage.

Dufour, R., & Eaker, R. (1998). *Professional learning communities at work: Best practices for enhancing student achievement.* Bloomington, IN: National Educational Service.

Duke, D. (Ed.). (2006). *Keys to sustaining successful school turnarounds.* Charlottesville, VA: Darden Curry Partnership for Leaders in Education. Retrieved from http://www.darden.virginia.edu/uploadedFiles/Centers_of_Excellence/PLE/KeysToSuccess.pdf

Eckerson, W. W. (2006). *Performance dashboards: Measuring, monitoring, and managing your business.* Hoboken, NJ: John Wiley and Sons.

Elmore, R. (2000). *Building a new structure for school leadership.* Washington, DC: The Albert Shanker Institute.

Elmore, R. (2003). A plea for strong practice. *Educational Leadership, 6*(3), 6–10.

English, F. W. (2010). *Deciding what to teach and test: Developing, aligning and leading the curriculum* (3rd ed.). Thousand Oaks, CA: Corwin.

Fullan, M. (1993). *Change forces: Probing the depths of educational reform.* Oxford, UK: Taylor and Francis.

Glasgow, N., & Whitney, P. J. (2009). *What successful schools do to involve families: 55 partnership strategies.* Thousand Oaks, CA: Corwin and National Association of Secondary School Principals.

Goldschmidt, P., Roschewski, P., Choi, K. C., Hibeeler, S., Blank, R., & Williams, A. (2005). *Policymakers' guide to growth models for school accountability: How do accountability models differ?* A paper commissioned by the CCSSO Accountability Systems and Reporting State Collaborative on Assessment and Student Standards. Washington, DC: Council of Chief State School Officers.

Gronn, P. (2000). Distributed properties: A new architecture for leadership. *Educational Management and Administration, 28*(3), 317–338.

Grossman, P., Wineburg, S., & Woolworth, S. (2000). *What makes teacher community different from a gathering of teachers?* Seattle, WA: Center for the Study of Teaching and Policy.

Guskey, T. S., & Bailey, J. M. (2001). *Developing grading and reporting systems for student learning.* In T. Guskey & R. Marzano (Series Eds.), *Experts in Assessment Series.* Thousand Oaks, CA: Corwin.

Harris, A. (2002). *Distributed leadership in schools: Leading or misleading?* International Confederation of Principals. Retrieved from http://www.icponline.org/index.php?option=com_content&task=view&id=130&Itemid=50

Hassel, E. A., & Hassel, B. C. (2009, Winter). The big U turn. *Education Next, 9*(1), 20–27.

Hechinger Guides for Journalists. Hechinger Institute on Education and the Media. http://hechinger.squarespace.com/guides-for-journalist

Henerson, M. E., Morris, L. L., & Fitz-Gibbon, C. T. (1987). *How to measure attitudes.* Newbury Park, CA: Sage.

Herman, J., Aschbacher, P. R., & Winters, L. (1992). *A practical guide to alternative assessment.* Alexandria, VA: Association for Supervision and Curriculum Development. Retrieved from http://www.cse.ucla.edu/products/guidebooks/APractical.pdf

Herman, J., Morris, L. L., & Fitz-Gibbon, C. T. (1987). *Evaluator's handbook.* Newbury Park, CA: Sage.

Herman, J., Osmundson, E., & Dietel, R. (2010). *Benchmark assessments for improved learning.* Los Angeles: CRESST. Retrieved from http://www.cse.ucla.edu/products/policy/R2_benchmark_report_Herman.pdf

Herman, J., & Winters, L. (1992). *Tracking your school's success: A guide to sensible evaluation.* Newbury Park, CA: Corwin.

Hess, F. M., & Gift, T. (2008). How to turn schools around. *American School Board Journal, 195*(11). Retrieved from http://www.aei.org/article/28827

Hite-Mills, L. K. (2007). *The art and science of problem solving: An introduction to programming skills.* Bloomington, IN: AuthorHouse.

Hord, S. M., & Sommers, W. A. (2008). *Leading professional learning communities: Voices from research and practice.* Thousand Oaks, CA: Corwin.

Innovation Network. (n.d.). *Logic model workbook.* Retrieved from http://www.innonet.org/client_docs/File/logic_model_workbook.pdf

Institute of Education Sciences. (2007). *Organizing instruction and study to improve student learning: A practice guide.* Washington, DC: U.S. Department of Education. Retrieved from http://ies.ed.gov/ncee/wwc/pdf/practiceguides/20072004.pdf

Institute of Education Sciences. (2008). *IES practice guide: Turning around low performing schools.* Washington, DC: U.S. Department of Education. Retrieved from http://ies.ed.gov/ncee/wwc/pdf/practiceguides/Turnaround_pg_04181.pdf

Institute of Education Sciences. (2009). *IES practice guide: Using student achievement data to support instructional decision making.* Washington, DC: U.S. Department of Education. Retrieved from http://ies.ed.gov/ncee/wwc/pdf/practiceguides/dddm_pg_092909.pdf

Johnstone, C. J., Moen, R. E., Thurlow, M. L., Matchett, D., Hausmann, K. E., & Scullin, S. (2007). *What do state reading test specifications specify?* Minneapolis, MN: University of Minnesota, Partnership for Accessible Reading Assessment.

Just for the Kids. National Center for Educational Achievement. http://www.nc4ea.org/index.cfm/e/initiatives.just_for_the_kids

Kaser, J., Mundry, S., Stiles, K., & Loucks-Horsley, S. (2002). *Leading every day: 124 actions for effective leadership.* Thousand Oaks, CA: Corwin.

Kee, K., Anderson, K., Dearing, V., Shuster, F., & Harris, E. (2010). *Results coaching: The new essential for school leaders.* Thousand Oaks, CA: Corwin.

King, J. A., Morris, L. L., & Fitz-Gibbon, C. T. (1987). *How to assess program implementation.* Newbury Park, CA: Sage.

Kirk, R. E. (1996). Practical significance: A concept whose time has come. *Educational and Psychological Measurement, 56*(5), 746–759.

Klass, G. (2008). *Just plain data analysis: Finding, presenting and interpreting social science data.* New York: Rowman & Littlefield. Companion website: http://lilt.ilstu.edu/jpda/

Linn, R. L. (2006). *Educational accountability systems.* CSE Technical Report 687. Boulder: CRESST/University of Colorado at Boulder.

Marsh, J. A., Pane, J. F., & Hamilton, L. S. (2006). *Making sense of data-driven decision making in education: Evidence from recent RAND research.* Rand Education Occasional Paper. Retrieved from http://www.rand.org/pubs/occasional_papers/2006/RAND_OP170.pdf

Mayeske, G. W., & Lambur, M. T. (2001). *How to design better programs: A staff centered stakeholder approach to program logic modeling.* Crofton, MD: The Program Design Institute.

McBeth, M. E. (2008). *The distributed leadership toolbox: Essential practices for successful schools.* Thousand Oaks, CA: Corwin.

McDonald, J., Mohr, N., Dichter, A., & McDonald, E. (2007). *The power of protocols: An educator's guide to better practice* (2nd ed.). New York: Teachers College Press.

Perry, G. (2006). *What is a walk-through?* Retrieved from http://www.perryand associatesinc.com/walkthrough_05a.pdf

Popham, W. J. (2000). *Modern educational measurement* (3rd ed.), Boston: Allyn & Bacon.

Popham, W. J. (2003). *Teach better, test better: The instructional role of assessment.* Alexandria, VA: Association for Supervision and Curriculum Development.

Popham, W. J. (2006). *Assessment for educational leaders.* Boston: Allyn & Bacon.

Popham, W. J. (2008). *Classroom assessment: What teachers need to know* (5th ed.). Boston: Pearson/Allyn & Bacon.

Popham, W. J. (2009). *Unlearned lessons: Six stumbling blocks to our schools' success.* Cambridge, MA: Harvard Education Press.

Popham, W. J. (2011). *Classroom assessment: What teachers need to know* (6th ed.). Boston: Allyn & Bacon..

Portin, B., Schneider, P., De Armond, M., & Gundlach, L. (2003). *Making sense of leading schools: A study of the school principalship.* Seattle: University of Washington, Center on Reinventing Public Education.

Preskill, H., & Russ-Eft, D. (2005). *Building evaluation capacity: 72 activities for teaching and training.* Thousand Oaks, CA: Sage.

QuestionPro. http://www.questionpro.com

Richardson, J. (2001, October/November). Seeing through new eyes: Walk throughs offer news ways to view schools. *Tools for Schools, 5*(2). Retrieved from http://www.learningforward.org/news/articleDetails.cfm?articleID=1097

Richardson, J. (2006, August/September). Snapshots of learning: Classroom walk-throughs offer picture of learning in schools. *Tools for Schools, 10*(1). Retrieved from http://www.learningforward.org/news/issueDetails.cfm?issueID=104

Sanders, J. R. (1994). *The program evaluation standards: How to assess evaluations of educational programs* (2nd ed.). Thousand Oaks, CA: Sage.

Schmoker, M. (1999). *Results: The key to continuous school improvement* (2nd ed.). Alexandria, VA: Association for Supervision and Curriculum Development.

Schmoker, M. (2003, February 12). Planning for failure? Or for school success? *Education Week,* Retrieved from http://mikeschmoker.com/planning-for-failure.html

Shulman, L. (1987). Knowledge and teaching: Foundations of the new reform. *Harvard Educational Review, 57*(1), 1–22.

Smith, J. K., Smith, L. F., & De Lisi, R. (2001). *Natural classroom assessments.* In T. Guskey & R. Marzano (Series Eds.), *Experts in Assessment Series.* Thousand Oaks, CA: Corwin.

Spillane, J. (2004). *Distributed leadership: What's all the hoopla?* Chicago: Institute for Policy Research, School of Education and Social Policy, Northwestern University.

Spillane, J., & Diamond, J. (2007). *Distributed leadership in practice.* New York: Teachers College Press.

StatPac. http://www.statpac.com

Strunk, W., & White, E. B. (1999). *The elements of style* (4th ed.). New York: Longman.

Survey Monkey. http://www.surveymonkey.com

Tips for facilitators. Retrieved from http://www.corwin.com/repository/binaries/TipsforFacilitators.pdf

UCLA School Management Program. (2007). *UCLA SMP Classroom Walk-Throughs Introduction* [video]. Retrieved from http://www.youtube.com

White, S. (2005a). *Beyond the numbers: Making data work for teachers and school leaders.* Englewood, CO: Advanced Learning Press.

White, S. (2005b). *Show me the proof.* Englewood, CO: Advanced Learning Press.

W. K. Kellogg Foundation. (2004). *Logic model development guide.* Battle Creek, MI: Author. Retrieved from http://ww2.wkkf.org/DesktopModules/WKF.00_DmaSupport/ViewDoc.aspx?fld=PDFFile&CID=281&ListID=28&ItemID=2813669&LanguageID=0

Index

Note: In page references, f indicates figures and t indicates tables.

CORWIN
A SAGE Company

The Corwin logo—a raven striding across an open book—represents the union of courage and learning. Corwin is committed to improving education for all learners by publishing books and other professional development resources for those serving the field of PreK–12 education. By providing practical, hands-on materials, Corwin continues to carry out the promise of its motto: **"Helping Educators Do Their Work Better."**